LINCOLN LEGENDS

LINCOLN LEGENDS

Myths, **HOAXES**,
and Confabulations
Associated with
Our Greatest President

Edward Steers Jr.

With an Introduction by
Harold Holzer

THE UNIVERSITY PRESS OF KENTUCKY

Publication of this volume was made possible in part by
a grant from the National Endowment for the Humanities.

Editorial and Sales Offices: The University Press of Kentucky
663 South Limestone Street, Lexington, Kentucky 40508-4008
www.kentuckypress.com

13 12 11 19 09   5 4 3 2 1

The Library of Congress has cataloged the hardcover edition as follows:

Steers, Edward.
    Lincoln legends : myths, hoaxes, and confabulations associated with our
greatest president / Edward Steers Jr. ; with an introduction by Harold Holzer.
        p.   cm.
    Includes bibliographical references and index.
    ISBN 978-0-8131-2466-7 (hardcover : alk. paper)
    1. Lincoln, Abraham, 1809–1865—Legends. 2. Presidents—United
States—Folklore. 3. Legends—United States. 4. Folklore—United States.
I. Title.
E457.2.S795 2007
973.7092—dc22
2007019871
ISBN 978-0-8131-9241-3 (pbk: acid-free paper)

This book is printed on acid-free recycled paper meeting
the requirements of the American National Standard
for Permanence in Paper for Printed Library Materials.

∞ ❀

Manufactured in the United States of America.

Member of the Association of
American University Presses

Respectfully dedicated to
John R. Preer Jr.
Christian B. Anfinsen
Jesse Roth
Allen M. Spiegel

Funny how life just falls in place somehow.

CONTENTS

ACKNOWLEDGMENTS

I am indebted to a great many people without whose generosity and help this book would not be possible. First and foremost, I am indebted to Harold Holzer, author of the introduction. Harold has been a good friend, a coauthor, and an invaluable source of knowledge on nearly every aspect of Abraham Lincoln's life. I am also indebted to James O. Hall, the dean of assassination scholars, for making his research files readily available and sharing his vast knowledge on Lincoln's assassination with me over the years. I wish to thank Michael Musick of the National Archives and Records Administration, who was an invaluable aid when searching through the vast repository of military and civilian documents within his domain. Many projects have been enriched as a result of his help. Similarly, David Vancil, head of the Special Collections Department of the Cunningham Memorial Library at Indiana State University, guided me through the extensive Neff-Guttridge Collection and provided me with numerous copies of documents and photographs so necessary to parts of this study. I wish to thank Ray A. Neff, who spent several hours with me explaining his views on Lincoln's assassination. A special thanks goes to William C. "Jack" Davis of Virginia Tech, who sent me his entire files on Lincoln's assassination from the time when he was editor of *Civil War Times Illustrated*. They proved invaluable to my own research. I thank Frank J. Williams, another outstanding Lincoln scholar and friend, for generously providing me with materials from his extensive library of Lincolniana. Richard Sloan, Thomas R. Turner, Terry Alford, and Joseph H. Nichols generously took time to examine various parts of the manuscript, correcting errors and making numerous suggestions to improve the text. I am indebted to each of them. I thank Steven L. Carson, past president of the Lincoln Group of the District of Columbia and editor of the *Manuscript Society News*, for generously sharing his files and writings with me. My good friends Joan L. Chaconas and Laurie Verge of the Surratt House Museum have always been available to answer questions and provide material from the great collection under their care. I am also indebted to the late Lloyd Ostendorf, Lincoln scholar and friend of many years, for providing me with copies of his Gettysburg Address document and freely discussing his own research and conclusions as to the document's authenticity. I am indebted to Dwight Pitcaithley, Michael Burlingame, Thomas Schwartz, William Hanchett, and Wayne C. Temple, Lincoln scholars of the first order, for providing me with their insight into several of the topics appearing in this book. I am also indebted to my good friend Joseph E. Garrera, executive director of the Lehigh Valley Heritage Museum, for his encouragement and generosity in support of this project. Catherine Quillman of the *Philadelphia Inquirer* kindly provided me with her research on Nathan Simms and the photograph of his tombstone that appears in this book. I also thank Kenneth Trimble of West Chester, Pennsylvania, for providing me copies from his files on Nathan Simms. Chuck Hand shared his collection of materials on Adah Sutton and Mariah Vance. Last but not least, I am indebted to two longtime colleagues, Kieran McAuliffe and James Hoyt. Kieran's artistic skills and innovative mind have been an invaluable aid to my own work. Without Jim Hoyt's technical expertise and willingness to respond to the continuous glitches that plague my computer world, I would still be stranded somewhere in cyberspace.

INTRODUCTION

Harold Holzer

I t is probably true that no other American life has been as exhaustively chronicled and, concurrently, as recklessly mythologized as that of Abraham Lincoln. As if the true story of his rise from obscurity to immortality were not inspiring enough, fabulists began early in Lincoln's national political career to add the patina of exaggeration to burnish his emerging legend. A two-mile walk to and from school became four; an acre of self-made rail fencing became a hectare; an occasional bout with melancholy became suicidal depression; a reputation for honesty became a mania; an abundance of strength became Herculean. His impoverished, illiterate birth mother, who died young, and about whom little was ever learned, emerged as his inspirational patron saint—wise, "remarkable," and "godly."[1]

Lincoln claimed none of these virtues for himself or his ancestors when writing about himself. (His parents were "of undistinguished families—second families, perhaps I should say," he confessed.) "There is not much of it," he self-effacingly asserted of his first attempt at an autobiographical sketch, "for the reason, I suppose, that there is not much of me." And then he cautioned: "If any thing be made out of it, I wish it to be modest, and not to go beyond the material."[2] Mythmakers ignored his request. They felt compelled to fill in the gaps with hyperbole—as if he needed it.

The mythmaking began early, and before Lincoln's very own eyes, at the Republican State Convention at Decatur in May 1860. To wild applause from the assembled delegates, Lincoln's cousin John Hanks—ironically a Democrat in politics—marched down the aisle toting two of the walnut rails his famous relative had allegedly split as a youth on the frontier. Attached to the old fencing or flooring was a banner that read: "Abraham Lincoln. The Rail Candidate for President in 1860. Two rails from a lot of 3,000 made in 1830 by Thos. Hanks and Abe Lincoln, whose father was the first pioneer of Macon County."[3]

To those who wondered if he had truly hewn the log rails himself, Lincoln disarmingly admitted that it was hard to know for certain whether they were the very same rails he had split "down on the Sangamon River." But "whether they were or were not," he quickly added, "he had mauled many better ones since he had grown to manhood."[4] That was good enough for the legend-makers. By the time the party's presidential nominating convention met at Chicago shortly thereafter, the dark horse hopeful had been magically transformed into Abe Lincoln "The Railsplitter," candidate for the White House. The nickname stuck.

So, for generations, did Hanks's far more serious—and historically problematic—assertion that upon witnessing a slave auction at New Orleans, the young Lincoln had righteously vowed: "By God . . . If ever I get a chance to hit that thing, I'll hit it hard."[5] The only problem was that Hanks never accompanied Lincoln to the Crescent City and could never have observed his cousin's reassuringly noble reaction to the horrors of human bondage. Nevertheless, mythmakers found it appealingly convenient to portray Lincoln as a lifelong slavery opponent destined from an early age to bring freedom to millions. It was not just, as historian Don Fehrenbacher wisely notes (and as the author of this volume repeats in these pages), that "the legendary Lincoln, created in part out of dubious recollected material, may have been, in the long run, as powerful an influence in American life as the historical Lincoln."[6] It was also because, as Fehrenbacher observed earlier, Lincoln the man was not only personally mythologized—he became "the central figure of a national mythology" as well.[7] It was as if a white society that for so long had ignored the hypocrisy of slavery in a country founded on the principles of liberty and the pursuit of happiness could console itself only by believing that a Great Emancipator was preordained to cleanse the republic of its poisonous incongruity.

Though he never himself chose, John Ford–like, between fact and fiction—"print the legend," orders the character in Ford's film *The*

Man Who Shot Liberty Valance—Lincoln was not averse to the idea of embracing American myth when it was politically useful. En route to his inauguration in 1861, he told a special session of the New Jersey state senate at Trenton that he still harbored deeply ingrained memories of "a small book" he had "got hold of . . . away back in my childhood": Mason Locke Weems's *Life of Washington.* Parson Weems's best-seller had all but invented the myths of Washington cutting down the cherry tree and lobbing a coin across the wide Potomac, but its strained credulity did not bother the president-elect trying to earn respect as he faced down a nation-threatening secession crisis.

"I remember all the accounts there given of the battle fields and struggles for the liberties of the country," Lincoln ruminated that day about the book, "and none fixed themselves upon my imagination so deeply as the struggle" of the Continental Army to cross the river, fight the Hessians, and endure the "hardships" of the New Jersey winter. Such stories "fixed themselves upon my memory more than any single revolutionary event," he told the legislators, "and you all know, for you have all been boys, how these early impressions last longer than any others."

Indeed, to Lincoln, such inflated stories had years earlier convinced him—and continued to convince him—that America offered "a great promise to all the people of the world for all time to come." In other words, the legend affirmed that the Union was worth fighting to preserve. Parson Weems's myth-laden hagiography was inspiring enough to make Lincoln believe, moreover, that like Washington himself, he could become a "humble instrument in the hands of the Almighty . . . for perpetuating the object of that great struggle."[8] And so the mythologizing of one American hero fueled the emergence of another. In a sense, one American legend begat a second.

And yet it should be remembered that "Honest Abe" was also a passionate advocate for the truth, especially when it concerned secondhand reports about his own life. "[L]et me go down linked to the truth," he was heard to tell his law partner, William H. Herndon, in 1858, "—let me die in the advocacy of what is just and right."[9]

"He was utterly incapable of insincerity," according to a friend of thirty years' standing, Jesse Fell. Echoed Jason Duncan, an old acquaintance from his New Salem days: "He had less prevarication than almost any man with whom I was ever acquainted." And yet another New Salem friend, Mentor Graham, agreed: "Honesty and impartiality were his great virtues." As his stepmother fondly recalled: "He never told me a lie in his life—never Evaded—never Equivocated[,] never dodged."[10] Even in the final months of Lincoln's life, his wife attested, he remained "almost a monomaniac on the subject of honesty."[11]

During the 1860 presidential campaign, although he secluded himself in his Springfield hometown and did no electioneering of his own, Lincoln lived up to this reputation. Though silent, he never dodged. He was quick to dash off adamant letters whenever he was misrepresented or libeled by opponents. He seemed almost to take pleasure in recalling and setting the record straight on the minutest details of his speeches, appearances, and personal behavior. He even meticulously hand-corrected a proof copy of William Dean Howells's campaign biography. "Wholly wrong," the candidate scrawled in response to one of its misrepresentations.[12] He liked writers whose "word is good to the utmost hair's breadth."[13]

In that spirit, Abraham Lincoln would have certainly liked Edward Steers Jr. For twenty productive years, Steers has labored to correct the legend and tell the truth and nothing but the truth— whether about the nature of the conspiracy that ended Lincoln's life, or the complicity of the physician who treated his murderer after the assassination ("His name is still Mudd," Steers famously concluded). Steers is a relentless researcher, a wise analyst, a reliable resource for his fellow scholars and countless readers, and a no-nonsense talker and writer. No detail is too obscure to earn his attention, no claim too ingrained or improbable to escape his close scrutiny. His precision and capacity for obtaining and retaining information have become the stuff of legends of their own.

In a way, it was inevitable that Ed Steers and the Lincoln legend should meet—and that the legend would never again be quite the same. On the following pages, Steers tackles some of the most stubborn and persistent of all the Lincoln myths, providing both historical proof and historiographical understanding to coolly analyze and, in most cases, dismiss them.

All the old myths are served up to be re-analyzed: Lincoln's supposed once-in-a-lifetime romance with Ann Rutledge; the lingering rumors about his illegitimacy; his supposed born-again Christian conversion and baptism; and his long-disputed "appearance" before a congressional committee, while president, to defend his controversial wife. Here, too, are the modern-age legends and canards. The recent portrayals of the allegedly gay Lincoln, the "discovery" of the "reading copy" of his Gettysburg Address, and the hoax surrounding the supposedly "lost" pages of John Wilkes Booth's diary are all painstakingly reconsidered here and convincingly deflated anew.

Steers also usefully—and one hopes, definitively—lays to rest any lingering doubt that Lincoln was the author of one of the most famous condolence letters in the English language, his note to the Boston widow Lydia Bixby in 1864. Even though Mrs. Bixby's claims of particular suffering and loss subsequently turned out to be wildly exaggerated, the letter itself has lost none of its poignancy. Yet perhaps because the object of Lincoln's sympathy proved to be less than sympathetic herself, claims that the president's assistant private secretary, John Hay, wrote the letter designed to console her have received increased currency in recent years. Ed Steers's meticulous analysis will be much read—and much appreciated—by those who have followed this historical debate and remained convinced that the masterful words long attributed to Lincoln are indeed his own.

Many of the legends and near-legends exhumed and subjected to fresh scrutiny in this book concern the Lincoln assassination, and on this subject no author's word is taken more seriously than that of Ed Steers, for his 2001 book *Blood on the Moon* remains the gold standard among the many studies of the cathartic event. Readers will understandably be eager to know how Steers has culminated his lifelong study of the subject to reach definitive conclusions on such still-mystifying stories as the identity of "Peanut" John Burroughs, the man who held John Wilkes Booth's horse; the case for and against Dr. Samuel Mudd, the physician who treated the assassin's broken leg; and the breadth of the conspiracy that led to the president's tragic death. To say that the author offers what may reliably be called the last word on these subjects would be a vast understatement.

Still, however persuasive my friend Ed Steers's work remains, it is probably too much to expect that there will be no more "hoaxes" or "confabulations" in circulation to exaggerate or mythologize the Lincoln story, and no more gullible audiences eager to embrace the next round of wild "discoveries" about the sixteenth president's life and death. Legends die hard—and Lincoln's have proven more resilient than most.

After all, how can one do battle against myths born of myths? Consider the fact that Lincoln not only loved a book about George Washington that enshrined an iconic Washingtonian fable, but that his affection for the book also created a legend of its own. When he told the New Jersey state senate his tale of reading the book "away back in my childhood," Lincoln left out the part about how he acquired the book, perhaps wary of gilding the lily.

In fact, he had borrowed the volume from Josiah Crawford, a neighboring farmer. In those hardscrabble days, young Abe slept under the eaves of a leaky log cabin roof. One night, as he cradled the book near to him, rain dripped into the crawl space and damaged the volume. Lincoln penitently confessed the damage to the neighbor who had lent it to him, and then offered to work off his debt in manual labor. In this way, Lincoln paid for the book through the sweat of his brow—but as a result, he got to keep the book and read and re-read it many times.[14] Studiousness, honesty, confession, hard work—these virtues attached themselves to Lincoln as inseparably as Parson Weems's saga had stuck to him. It hardly seemed to matter that, as another old neighbor later testified, "Lincoln felt that Crawford had treated him unkindly in regard to this Book & wrote some rude verses on the subject in which he ridiculed Crawford in a Most unmerciful Manner."[15] When in doubt, print the legend.

But the yearning for the truth can be as strong as the craving for heroic virtue—especially among dedicated scholars. "There is a vast difference between pure fiction and folklore, though it is often hard to detect," the historian Roy P. Basler wrote in 1969, some fifteen years after he had edited the monumental edition of the Lincoln canon *The Collected Works of Abraham Lincoln*. "It has been part of my study to attempt, at least, to keep Lincoln the man continually before the reader as he studies the legend, for nowhere is it easier to hang oneself upon the horns of historical dilemma than in the study of the man and this myth."[16]

Now Ed Steers, too, joins the ranks of Lincoln historians who have worked assiduously and successfully to separate fact from both fiction and folklore. Thanks to his fine work, those historical dilemmas will be easier than ever to avoid, and the temptation to hang oneself by embracing them much easier to resist.

The traditional birthplace cabin preserved in the beautiful marble building located at the Abraham Lincoln Birthplace National Historic Site in Hodgenville, Kentucky. (Courtesy of the National Park Service)

CHAPTER ONE

THE BIRTHPLACE CABIN
Fact or Fiction?

The structure now enshrined in the great marble building in Kentucky is a fraud when represented as the actual house.
—Robert Todd Lincoln

There has always been an acknowledgment on the part of Lincoln authors as well as the government agencies in charge of the memorial that positive identification of the cabin at this late date could not be established. However, this admission does not imply that it can be proven the cabin is spurious, and until such positive evidence is available it is unjust and almost sacrilegious to discredit this relic which has brought impressive sensations to thousands of children, women and grown men as well.
—Louis A. Warren

SITTING ATOP A GRASSY KNOLL overlooking the rolling Kentucky countryside is a magnificent marble building whose outward appearance looks like a Greek temple erected in honor of some ancient god. Inside the temple, however, there are no altars or statues to mythical gods or goddesses. Instead, one finds a simple log cabin not unlike any of the thousands of log cabins that dotted the countryside of rural America. The honor chosen for this log cabin over all the others is due to the place its occupant holds in the hearts of his countrymen. It was in this simple cabin that life came to Abraham Lincoln, America's greatest president.

While several presidents have attempted to exploit their log cabin origins, none is more cherished by the American people than Abraham Lincoln. It is safe to say that every schoolchild can make the connection between these two icons of our heritage. From his humble beginning in a dirt-floor cabin to the grandeur of the White House,

Abraham Lincoln symbolizes the American dream. That a simple log cabin should come to be housed in a magnificent Greek temple affirms the special place Lincoln holds in our collective memory. It is in his honor that we hold this cabin in special, almost reverent regard.

It is only in recent years that the authenticity of the Lincoln birthplace cabin has come under question. In the forefront of the skeptics is none other than the National Park Service, the government agency charged with the stewardship of the memorial cabin and surrounding site. The cabin, once described as the birthplace of Abraham Lincoln, is now described as his "traditional" birthplace, which means that whatever its true heritage, the cabin has been accepted as the symbol of Lincoln's birthplace.[1]

While the Park Service and historians are concerned over the question of the cabin's authenticity, it is of little concern to the American people. The cabin has become a symbol representing the pride and affection the people hold for Lincoln. As is so often the case in human experience, it is perception rather than reality that matters, and the perception is that the birthplace cabin is an authentic shrine. Where, then, did the memorial cabin come from, and what is the path it followed that eventually landed it inside the memorial building located on the birthplace farm?[2]

THE GOVERNMENT'S OWNERSHIP began on April 16, 1916, when the House of Representatives passed bill H.R. 8351, accepting a deed of gift from the Lincoln Farm Association for the farmland and log cabin in which Abraham Lincoln was born. Authenticating the farm presented no problem because the line of ownership left a paper trail that could be verified through deeds and similar legal transactions. The cabin, however, was a different story. From the very beginning of its stewardship of the birthplace cabin, the National Park Service was faced with proving that the logs now enshrined in the cabin memorial are the very logs that made up the cabin when Abraham Lincoln was born.

For the first fifty years after his death, as many as fifteen sites challenged one another for the distinction of being the birthplace of Abraham Lincoln. But the Park Service accepted only one as the true site. Lincoln himself answered the question in a letter to Samuel

Haycraft dated May 28, 1860, when he wrote: "I was born Feb. 12, 1809, near where Hoginsville now is, then in Hardin County."[3] Two weeks later he wrote a second letter in which he pinned down the location more precisely: "As my parents have told me, I was born on Nolin [Creek], very much nearer Hodgin's-Mill than the Knob Creek place is."[4] The birthplace site exists approximately a mile and a half from Hodgen's Mill on Nolin Creek. With the location of the birthplace established, the only question left hanging is whether the current cabin housed in the memorial building is the actual birth cabin.

In 1895, Alfred W. Dennett, a New York restaurant owner and would-be entrepreneur, purchased the Lincoln farm with the idea of turning it into a tourist attraction. Missing, however, was a log cabin that could serve as the birthplace cabin. A year later, Dennett purchased a log cabin from his neighbor, John Davenport. Davenport claimed that the cabin he sold to Dennett was the actual birthplace cabin that once sat on the Lincoln farm. Dennett didn't ask Davenport for proof that the cabin was authentic. Truth be told, he didn't care. He needed a cabin, and Davenport's would do just fine. Twenty years later, the National Park Service accepted the farm and cabin, and although it had doubts as to the cabin's authenticity, it never made its doubts public.[5]

No one challenged the cabin's authenticity until 1948, when Lincoln scholar Roy Hays published an article in the *Abraham Lincoln Quarterly* entitled "Is the Lincoln Birthplace Cabin Authentic?"[6] Hays's article gave rise to a renewed interest in the cabin and generated a debate between those who believed the cabin was authentic[7] and those who believed it was nothing more than "the connivings of a couple of scamps."[8]

Shortly after Lincoln was elected president in November 1860, Dr. George Rodman, whose farm bordered the old Lincoln property, bought a log cabin then standing on the birthplace farm and moved it to his property approximately one mile to the north. Rodman believed the old cabin to be the birthplace cabin. Years later Rodman sold his farm and the old cabin to John Davenport. Davenport and his wife lived in the cabin from 1875 until he sold it to Alfred

The birthplace cabin rested on a special concrete base while the memorial building underwent construction. The cabin proved too large for the building and was altered by shortening the length and width by three feet and two feet, respectively, to fit the memorial. (From a stereographic image by the Underwood and Underwood Company, ca. 1909; author's collection)

Dennett in 1895. Dennett moved the cabin back to the Lincoln farm near where the original Lincoln cabin stood.[9]

The cabin was not on its new site long before the 143 logs were disassembled and shipped to Nashville, Tennessee, for that state's centennial celebration in 1897. Dennett had hooked up with an agent and publicist, the Reverend James W. Bigham, and the two men took their "Lincoln logs" around the country, setting up the cabin wherever a fair was being held. What is missing from the story up to this point is that Dennett and Bigham had also taken on tour a log cabin they claimed was the birthplace of Jefferson Davis. The two showmen proudly pitched their exhibit as the birthplaces of the Civil War's two presidents, Abraham Lincoln and Jefferson Davis.[10]

As the two cabins moved from show to show, being disassembled and reassembled, it was inevitable that the logs would become mixed. It soon became impossible to tell any of the logs apart. Davenport and Bigham were losing money, and after suffering losses through several exhibitions, they placed the disassembled logs in storage in a warehouse on Long Island, New York.[11]

Dennett, suffering from financial difficulties and failing to pay his taxes, conveyed the Kentucky farm along with the logs (still in storage in Long Island) to David Crear in February 1899, in lieu of a debt he owed to Crear. Despite Dennett's transferring the land and logs to Crear, Dennett tried to convince the U.S. government to buy the cabin. Dennett was hoping to make enough money off of the sale to bail him out of debt. After the government turned him down, Dennett filed for bankruptcy in 1901, claiming his only asset was his clothing valued at $20.[12] Dennett then filed suit against Crear to regain title to the farm. The LaRue County Circuit Court ruled that the original conveyance from Dennett to Crear was fraudulent (on Crear's part) and ordered that the farm be sold by a commissioner of the court at public sale.[13] On August 28, 1905, Robert J. Collier, the publisher of *Collier's Weekly* magazine, purchased the birthplace farm for $3,600.[14] While Collier now owned the farm, Crear still retained possession of the logs, which remained in storage on Long Island. In 1906, Collier agreed to pay Crear $1,000 for the logs and turned the entire package, farm and logs, over to the privately owned Lincoln Farm Association.[15]

The Lincoln Farm Association, concerned over the cabin's authenticity, set out to authenticate the logs now in its possession. The organization obtained three affidavits attesting to the origin of the logs. John Davenport swore to having moved in 1875 with his wife into the cabin on his property. He further stated that he sold the cabin to Alfred Dennett in 1895, who then moved it back to the Lincoln site that same year.[16] A second affidavit, by Mrs. Zerelda Jane Goff, who lived near the Lincoln farm, stated that a family named Skaggs lived in the old Lincoln cabin before the war and that a man by the name of Lafayette Wilson had hauled the logs to George Rodman's farm in 1860. Rodman, as stated earlier, had purchased a log cabin from the Lincoln farm in 1860 and moved it to his property before selling it to John Davenport in 1875.[17] The third affidavit was ascribed to by Lafayette Wilson, the man mentioned in the Goff affidavit. Wilson claimed that a man named Daniel Dyer (not George Rodman) hired him to move the logs and that he moved

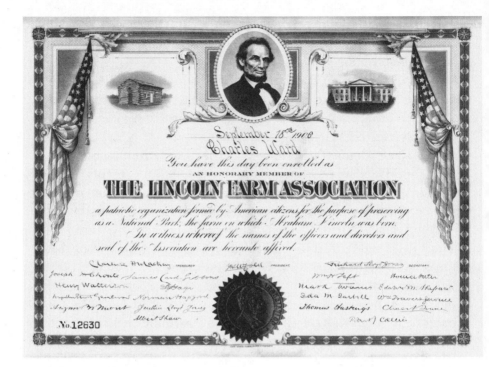

A contribution of twenty-five cents entitled the donor to membership in the Lincoln Farm Association and this certificate. (Author's collection)

them in March 1860 to the farm later occupied by John Davenport, not George Rodman.[18] Clearly there was a discrepancy between the affidavits. Did Wilson move the logs to Rodman's farm or to John Davenport's farm? Apparently the Lincoln Farm Association didn't care which farm the logs were hauled to. It was enough that the logs were moved from the Lincoln farm and eventually wound up on John Davenport's farm in 1875.

These affidavits were submitted to a commission of four historians, who, after reviewing the evidence, declared the logs authentic. In submitting their findings, the panel of historians wrote: "Many more witnesses could be had testifying substantially to the facts, but this would be merely cumulative and we close the testimony with the submission of the facts to the public, believing that *the American people will not be so unreasonable or critical* as to demand more conclusive evidence of the birthplace of this great American."[19] The Lincoln

Transferring the logs from their storage place on Long Island to Hodgenville, Kentucky, where they were eventually assembled inside the memorial building. (Courtesy of the Library of Congress)

Farm Association was satisfied, and construction was started on the memorial building that would house the famous logs.

The cornerstone of the memorial building was laid, with the blessing of President Theodore Roosevelt, on February 12, 1909, the one hundredth anniversary of Lincoln's birth. In 1911 the memorial building, complete with the Rodman-Davenport-Dennett log cabin, was dedicated and marched into history and the hearts of the American people. But not all of the American people made a place for the cabin in their hearts. Chief among the dissenters was Robert Todd Lincoln, the president's only surviving son. Robert Lincoln, in a 1919 letter to Otto Wiecker of New York, wrote, "The structure enshrined in a great marble building in Kentucky is a fraud when represented as the actual house."[20] Despite Robert Lincoln's harsh criticism, the memorial remained a treasured place, and visitors continued to flock to the site. The controversy, what little there was, faded away over the next thirty years.

Then, in 1948, Roy Hays, an insurance investigator from Grosse Pointe Park, Michigan, with a passion for research and Abraham

The memorial building was erected in 1911 to house the birthplace cabin. The Lincoln Farm Association donated the cabin logs, along with the farm, to the U.S. government. (Author's collection)

Lincoln, wrote an article for the *Abraham Lincoln Quarterly* in which he presented his research findings on the cabin's authenticity.[21] Hays attempted to trace the cabin's provenance prior to 1860, when George Rodman moved a log cabin from the Lincoln farm to his own. Hays concluded that the cabin was not authentic and merely represented a "traditional cabin" cleverly promoted by two would-be entrepreneurs, Alfred Dennett and James Bigham. Balancing Hays's position is that of Louis A. Warren, who wrote a series of articles on the cabin that he published in *Lincoln Lore,* a newsletter Warren published. Warren believed the cabin might contain authentic logs, while Hays believed none of the logs were authentic.

Hays's conclusion was based on the interviews of two individuals intimately associated with the birthplace site during contemporary times, Jacob S. Brothers (born 1819) and John B. Rowbotham. In an interview Brothers gave in 1903, he stated: "In the year 1827 when I was eight years old, my father purchased the old farm on which Abraham Lincoln was born. We lived in the house in which Lincoln was born. After some years, my father built another house almost like the first house. The old house was torn down, and to my knowledge, the logs were burned for firewood. Later he built a hewed log house. The pictures we often see of the house in which Lincoln was born are the pictures of the first house built by my father."[22]

Brothers's statement seems clear enough. The Lincoln birthplace cabin was turned into firewood sometime in the 1830s, and a new log cabin was constructed that later was thought by others to be the Lincoln cabin. Brothers's statement became the basis for those who claimed the current cabin is not authentic but rather a replacement cabin purchased by Alfred Dennett in 1895 and eventually acquired by the Lincoln Farm Association (through Robert Collier) in 1906.

However, there are several troublesome aspects to Brothers's statement. First, his father did not own the Lincoln farm in 1827; he purchased it in 1835, eight years later. He lived on the farm for only five years, from 1835 until 1840. In 1840 he was evicted for failure to pay the purchase price. Brothers failed to defend the suit against him and simply moved on. Jacob Brothers, the son, would have been twenty-one years old at the time, not eight. Wherever Jacob Brothers lived in 1827 at the age of eight, it was not in the Lincoln cabin, leaving us to conclude that he must have been talking about another cabin.

According to Brothers, his father built two cabins in the five-year span, the second one "hewed." This story implies that the first of the two cabins was not "hewed," but made of round logs, which represents an unusual amount of cabin building within a short period of five years—especially for a family that was evicted for failure to pay its mortgage. And finally, Brothers's statement about the "pictures we often see of the house in which Lincoln was born are the pictures of the first house built by my father" doesn't match his statement. The picture Brothers refers to is a photograph of the John Davenport cabin purchased by Dennett and Bigham and taken on tour along with the alleged cabin of Jefferson Davis. It is the logs from these two cabins that became the memorial cabin of today.

The hewed cabin in the photograph Brothers referred to is inconsistent with his affidavit, where he indicates the first house built by his father was made of round logs, not hewed ones.[23] Brothers was eighty-four years old at the time of his affidavit and was recalling events that occurred seventy-six years before. The inconsistencies in his statements cast serious doubt on their reliability as to the Lincoln cabin and its authenticity. Brothers seemed as confused as everyone else about which cabin and which logs became the birthplace cabin.

The second point developed by Hays concerning the cabin's authenticity is in a statement by John B. Rowbotham. Rowbotham was an artist working for the firm of Moore, Wilstach and Baldwin, publishers of Joseph Barrett's *Life of Lincoln*.[24] In 1865 Rowbotham traveled to the site of the birthplace specifically to sketch the cabin for Barrett's book. While he located the farm, he could not find the cabin. In a letter to William H. Herndon on June 24, 1865, Rowbotham wrote: "The site of Mr. L's birthplace is on this farm [Richard Creal farm] about five hundred yards from Mr. Creal's house.—Some rocks indicating the site of the chimney are still there."[25] The cabin was gone; only a few rocks from the chimney remained.

In his own studies in support of the cabin (or several of its logs) being authentic, Louis A. Warren, director of the Lincoln National Life Insurance Museum and Library and editor of *Lincoln Lore*, discovered several statements that bear on the question. Warren discovered a letter written by a soldier in the 19th Illinois Infantry describing his visit to the farm in the fall of 1861:

> I was then acting as a scout and was sent to where he (Lincoln) was born. I hunted up the owner of the place; he was living on the place but not in the same cabin. I asked him if he was shure (sic) this was the cabin where the President was born. He said he was. . . . There had been no window in the house and he had put a half sash window and had put flat rocks under some posts when there (sic) bottoms had rotted. Looking from the door to the left end was the fireplace which took up ½ of the end. It was made of rocks and clay about 7 feet and split sticks and clay the rest of the way up. On the right at the far side of the room was the bedstead. . . . The stairway was a pole with 1½ inch auger holes and wooden pins drove through about a foot on each side of the pole. Some flat stones were sunk level with the ground in front of the fireplace was all—the door was made of split boards with wooden hinges and a wooden latch.[26]

Warren tells of two other accounts that add to the oral tradition. A LaRue County correspondent wrote in the *Missouri Telegraph* on November 23, 1860: "The Lincoln farm is old and well worn. In

The "Davenport" cabin reconstructed on the Lincoln birthplace farm in 1895. The Reverend James W. Bigham, acting as Alfred Dennett's agent, had Russell T. Evans photograph the cabin in September 1895. (Courtesy of the Library of Congress)

an old field near a running brook the ruins of a pioneer cabin are pointed out as the birthplace of the President-elect." The second account is from another soldier, Robert Harvey, who wrote in the *Nebraska State Journal* on February 11, 1909:

I saw the rude log cabin, in which Lincoln was born, in October, 1862. It was a few days after the battle of Perryville, Kentucky, when in the early afternoon we approached a low one story cabin on our left. A rail fence ran along in front and on one corner was stuck a cracker box lid on which was chalked, "Birthplace of President Lincoln." The chimney was at the end of the building we were approaching, and was built of splints or sticks and daubed with mud. The roof was of clapboards and held in place by poles laid lengthwise. . . . There was a door and a square window on the side facing the road and some of the logs had the appearance of being much decayed. A pear tree stood at the farther end of the building, but its uninviting fruit remained unmolested.[27]

The "Abraham Lincoln–Jefferson Davis" cabin during its erection in Central Park in Louisville, Kentucky. Following the displaying of the alleged Lincoln and Davis birthplace cabins at the Nashville Centennial Exposition in 1897, the logs from the two cabins became mixed. Purchased by the Lincoln Farm Association in 1906, they were moved to Louisville, Kentucky, where they were assembled into a single cabin in Central Park. The logs were then stored in the Louisville Public Warehouse awaiting completion of the memorial building. (*Louisville Courier-Journal*, June 15, 1906)

If we are to believe the above, it seems there was a cabin on the site as late as 1862 and that it was gone by 1865. Where it had gone is not clear, although the proponents of the cabin's authenticity would say that it had gone to the John Davenport farm and from there to the Lincoln Farm Association, ending up in the memorial building.

Oral tradition by its very nature is hearsay. The oral traditions presented by Hays and Warren fall short of answering the question of the traditional cabin's authenticity. What is clear from Hays's research is that the logs that make up the cabin housed in the memorial are mixed, coming from two cabins (and as many as three). Whether any of these logs are original to the cabin in which Lincoln was born is not clear, but it seems well established that there was no cabin at the farm site in 1865, if not earlier. Perhaps the most telling clue to the cabin's authenticity is attributed to Reverend Bigham, Dennett's publicist who tried to convince fairgoers that the cabin touring the country was the real McCoy. Many years after the cabin logs had been installed in the memorial building, a reporter asked Reverend Bigham if the cabin was really Lincoln's birthplace. The Reverend answered, "Lincoln was born in a log cabin, weren't he? Well, one cabin is as good as another."[28]

The cabin that now sits in the memorial building is the cabin that Dennett and Bigham took on tour. It is the same cabin that was photographed by Russell T. Evans and published in *McClure's* magazine in 1895. Dennett and Bigham created the appearance of the cabin, not Thomas Lincoln, Lincoln's father. The only hope for those who want the cabin to be authentic is that some of the logs may have come from the Lincoln birthplace cabin, but that is highly doubtful since Dennett and Bigham foisted a hoax on the American people, telling them that their cabin was the authentic cabin when it was actually a cabin they had built from local logs taken from another cabin.

Although Dennett and Bigham perpetrated a hoax on the thousands of people who paid to see Lincoln's birthplace cabin, and later conned the Lincoln Farm Association into believing the cabin was authentic, the National Park Service has never represented the cabin as authentic. It continues to refer to the cabin as "traditional."

Despite its shady past, the Lincoln cabin represents a shrine that accurately reflects the origin of our greatest president and a place where people can come and pay homage to his great life and the heritage of our nation. Dwight Pitcaithley, former chief historian of the National Park Service and the person once responsible for the factual representation of our national historic sites, summarized it best when he wrote, "The public's perception of the Lincoln cabin is important to the nation's image and an indispensable part of the nation's ritualistic public tribute to its own humble origins. It is symbolic of a need for an accessible past and a willingness to embrace myths that are too popular, too powerful, to be diminished by the truth."[29] To which we can add, Amen.

CHAPTER TWO

LINCOLN'S FATHER

The Paternity of Abraham Lincoln

> There is a tradition come down through the family that Nancy Hanks,
> the mother of President Lincoln, once lived at my grandfather's, and
> while there became the mother of a child said to be my grandfather's,
> Abraham Enloe.
>
> —William A. Enloe

IN 1997, A LEGISLATIVE ASSISTANT to a North Carolina congressman wrote me inquiring about a local tradition in western North
Carolina that Abraham Lincoln was born in Rutherford County, the
bastard son of a man named Abraham Enloe and a servant girl working in the Enloe household named Nancy Hanks. The writer wanted
to know if there was any truth to the story. The letter sent me to an
old file I had built up over the years with the title "Myths." In it were
dozens of stories having to do with Lincoln's paternity.

Accusations that Abraham Lincoln was "low flung," a nineteenth-
century euphemism for bastard, began shortly after his nomination
as the Republican candidate for president and persist to this day.[1] Of
all the myths associated with Lincoln, the paternity myth ranks near
the top. A survey of the Internet reveals dozens of sites dealing with
Lincoln's parentage, showing that the question still generates interest
and debate.

In the early world of politics, negative campaigning was the
rule—much as it is today. Charges of illegitimacy were often hinted
at because of the negative effect on the accused. Illegitimate persons were thought to be "defective" when conceived out of wedlock.
Bastard children were "stained" with the sins of their birth parents.
Lincoln's detractors often pointed to his own reluctance to comment
on his father and mother as evidence of his knowledge, and shame,

The traditional photograph of Thomas Lincoln,
Abraham Lincoln's father. (Courtesy of the Lincoln
Memorial University, Harrogate, Tennessee)

of his illegitimate birth. His physical appearance differed strikingly
from Thomas Lincoln's, adding credibility to his enemies' claim that
Thomas Lincoln was not his real father.

Ten days after Lincoln received the Republican Party's nomination as its candidate for president, he received a letter from a man
near his birthplace in Kentucky inquiring about his parents and
birth.[2] The letter was from Samuel Haycraft, who served as clerk of
the Circuit Court of Hardin County, Kentucky, from 1816 to 1857.[3]
Haycraft remembered a family named Lincoln from fifty years earlier that lived in the area and wrote to Lincoln inquiring if he was
a member of the same family. Haycraft mistakenly believed that
Lincoln's stepmother, Sarah Bush Lincoln, was his birth mother.

Lincoln replied to Haycraft in a letter dated May 28, 1860: "In the main you are right about my history. My father was Thomas Lincoln, and Mrs. Sally Johnston, was his second wife. You are mistaken about my mother—her maiden name was Nancy Hanks. I was not born at Elizabethtown; but my mother's first child, a daughter [Sarah], two years older than myself, and now long since deceased, was."[4]

Around the same time that Lincoln received Haycraft's letter, he received a second letter from journalist John Locke Scripps. Scripps needed biographical material for a campaign biography he wanted to write.[5] Lincoln sent Scripps a lengthy autobiography that began: "Abraham Lincoln was born Feb. 12, 1809, then in Hardin, now in the more recently formed county of Larue, Kentucky. His father, Thomas, & grand-father, Abraham were born in Rockingham county Virginia, whither their ancestors had come from Berks county Pennsylvania."[6]

Because there were no records of his birth, Lincoln relied on his parents for the details of when and where he was born and who his natural parents were. Lincoln's maternity has never been in doubt, but his paternity has been challenged on numerous occasions. Louis A. Warren, the chronicler of Lincoln's ancestry and early life in Kentucky, has explained some of the early confusion surrounding Lincoln's parentage. When Samuel Haycraft and others learned that Lincoln's birth mother was a woman named Nancy Hanks, not Sarah Bush Lincoln, they remembered a woman by that name who had lived in their community, and that she had an illegitimate child. All of this was true, but the Nancy Hanks they remembered was not Lincoln's mother but his great aunt, and her illegitimate child was Dennis Friend Hanks, Lincoln's cousin once-removed.[7] Dennis moved into the Lincoln cabin in 1818 shortly after his aunt and uncle, who had been raising him, died during a milk sickness epidemic that also killed Lincoln's mother. The confusion was natural, given that the aunt and niece had the same name and lived in the same community.[8] Several people mistakenly tarred Lincoln's mother with her aunt's indiscretions.

Coupled with this mistaken identity was the fact that no record could be found in the Hardin County courthouse of Thomas and Nancy's marriage.[9] It wasn't until 1878 that a marriage bond and minister's record for Thomas Lincoln and Nancy Hanks was discovered among the records of Washington County in Springfield, Kentucky.[10] It turned out that the couple were married in Washington County before moving to Hardin County. While the records put to rest the myth that Thomas and Nancy lived a common law marriage, they did little to quell the rumors of Lincoln's illegitimate birth.

Lincoln's close friend and law partner, William Herndon, fueled the story when he set out to document Lincoln's life following his death in 1865. Herndon undertook interviewing and writing to nearly everyone who had touched Lincoln's life in one way or another. He came to the conclusion that Lincoln's father was sterile as a result of a severe case of mumps when he was an adult.[11] He relied on statements like the ones gathered from Erastus R. Burba and Charles Friend. Burba, clerk of LaRue County, wrote:

> It is a settled belief here that Abram's [Abraham's] true name is not Lincoln—Some have thought it to be Enlows—this I doubt for I have conversed with the old man Enlows in a manner that satisfied me to Contrary—Others give it to Cessa, the old man is still living and had some reputation in Earlier days of living rather inclined to the company of women—In fact I have heard him say that he knew Nancy as well as he ever Knew any woman. And he further says that Thomas Lincoln was not considered all right in Consequence of having the Mumps or something else, that he has been with him often in baithing together in the water.[12]

Twenty-three years later Herndon was still collecting anecdotal information about Lincoln's legitimacy. In a letter dated July 31, 1889, Charles Friend, the grandson of Dennis Hanks's father, Charles Friend, wrote Herndon the following passage: "You ask me a question was he Thomas Lincoln Castrated. I heard a cousin of my fathers Judge Jonathan Friend Cessna say that his father Wm Cessna says that Thomas Lincoln could not have been Abe's father for one of Thomas' testacles was not larger than a pea or perhaps both of them wer no larger than peas, and 'Uncle Billie' Cessna sayed he believed that Abe was my uncle and based this reason on the fact that Nancy Hanks first child Denis was Charles Friends boy. Be that as it may, let it go."[13]

As happened with other interviewees, Friend confused Lincoln's aunt Nancy Hanks with Lincoln's mother. And so the rumors persisted into 1889 and beyond. As time passed, more individuals sought to discredit Lincoln's birth for various reasons. Others joined the list of his alleged sires until it reached a grand total of sixteen men.

Topping the list was Abraham Enloe, or more accurately, *Enloes*—for there were four Abraham Enloes said to be Lincoln's real father. Once again, the similarity of surname resulted in confusion when telling the story. The four men lived scattered across the country: Abraham Enlow of LaRue County, Kentucky; Abraham Enlows of Hardin County, Kentucky; Abraham Inlow of Bourbon County, Kentucky; and Abraham Enloe of North Carolina. It was this last claimant that the North Carolina gentleman who wrote me expressed an interest in.

Where did the rumors that Lincoln was illegitimate first begin? William E. Barton, a Congregationalist minister and early Lincoln scholar from Foxboro, Massachusetts, set out to answer this very question, and in the process he ran down all of the stories and the men alleged to be Lincoln's father. It was no small task. Barton prided himself as being an indefatigable researcher, and with justification. Born in 1861 (he died in 1930), Barton published the first of several books on Lincoln, *The Soul of Abraham Lincoln,* in 1920 at the age of fifty-nine.[14] His interests turned to Lincoln's ancestry, and he soon became caught up in the question of Lincoln's alleged illegitimacy. Barton's forte was researching old records long forgotten and using his research to demolish the myths that had grown up around Lincoln. Benjamin P. Thomas, Lincoln's best early biographer, said of Barton, "If he fell short of being a great historian, he was a great historical detective."[15]

In his second book, *The Paternity of Abraham Lincoln,*[16] Barton took on the spurious claims, tracing their lineage back to their beginnings. Barton traces the story of Lincoln's alleged illegitimacy back to Hodgenville and one of Thomas Lincoln's neighbors, Abraham Enlow (the LaRue County Enlow mentioned earlier). Enlow never claimed to be Lincoln's father. He did claim in later life that Lincoln was named after him in recognition of his help at the time of Lincoln's birth. Enlow was on his way to Kirkpatrick's mill on Saturday, February 11, 1809, when he happened to pass the cabin of Thomas Lincoln. Lincoln stopped Enlow and told him that his wife was in labor and asked Enlow to return home and bring his mother, who was a local midwife. Leaving his sacks of corn with Thomas Lincoln, Enlow returned to his home and gathered up his mother and his sister, Peggy Enlow Walters, and returned to the Lincoln cabin. Barton writes, "Some time after midnight, on the morning of Sunday, February 12, 1809, a little boy was born."[17]

According to Barton, it was Enlow who, in his later years, told how Thomas and Nancy named their son Abraham after him in recognition of his kindness in bringing the two midwives to the Lincoln cabin. Lincoln genealogists, however, believe differently. They believe that Lincoln was named for his grandfather, Captain Abraham Lincoln, not Abraham Enlow. The name Abraham was first introduced into the Lincoln lineage by Lincoln's great-great-great grandparents, Mordecai Lincoln and Sarah Jones. Sarah's father was Abraham Jones, and it is his name that Mordecai and Sarah gave to their first son.[18] It was the first of many Lincolns to be named Abraham. The name continued through the next four generations, including Thomas and Nancy's son.[19]

Abraham Enlow died in 1861, and when the old-timers living in Elizabethtown and the surrounding area remembered a Nancy Hanks who bore an illegitimate child, they soon began looking for the father. Abraham Enlow, President Lincoln's alleged namesake, became the likely candidate. After all, most people around the area had heard Enlow himself say that Lincoln was named after him. Lincoln, folks concluded, took his Christian name from his "real" father and his surname from his "adopted" father.[20]

Barton put the story to rest by proving that Abraham Enlow was fifteen years old when Lincoln was born (fourteen when Lincoln was conceived), and that Thomas Lincoln did not move to the birthplace cabin until several months after Nancy had already become pregnant.[21] They lived far from where Abraham Enlow lived at the time Nancy conceived. Underlying the Enlow story was the fact that no marriage record could be found for Thomas and Nancy. Of course, whether a minister married the couple or they were living a common law marriage has no bearing on Nancy Hanks Lincoln's alleged infidelity, but it did have a bearing on her character to the people living in the community. Even with the discovery of the marriage record in Washington County, the rumors persisted. Barton concluded that wherever there was an Abraham Enlow (Enloe, Inlow), the story was picked up, becoming a part of the local folklore. The most persistent myth, however, is the one mentioned in the letter I received from the congressional aide in 1997—that Lincoln was born in North Carolina, the illegitimate son of Abraham Enloe.

A RECENT HISTORY OF LINCOLN boldly proclaims that "the North Carolina account of his birth is far more genuine and believable than the trumped up, government manufactured story fed the American public these past one hundred and fifty years."[22]

The origin of Lincoln's North Carolina birth dates back to 1899, when it was first introduced in a book authored by James H. Cathy. Cathy wrote that he was familiar with the traditional story of Lincoln's North Carolina heritage, having heard it from the old-timers in the area. He was concerned that with the passing of the "older generation," the true story of Lincoln's birth would be lost forever. He set out to ensure that the "true" story would not die. Cathy interviewed several of the elder pioneers still living in western North Carolina. "[I] was conscious," Cathy wrote, "of the delicacy of the undertaking, but the implicit, unquestioned faith which I had in the truthfulness of the tradition gave me a courage which shrank not from the most formidable looking anti-traditional hobgoblin."[23] Cathy's "proof" of Lincoln's illegitimacy was a collection of statements from eleven individuals, born between 1809 and 1842, described variously by Cathy as "intelligent," "progressive," "being of perfect veracity," of "unquestionable integrity," of "upright character," and of "spotless reputation."[24] The statements differ little from person to person: a young girl named Nancy Hanks, herself born out of wedlock, is sent to live with her uncle Dick Hanks in western North Carolina. While living with her uncle she is hired out to the home of Abraham Enloe. She soon becomes pregnant, giving birth to a boy whom she names Abraham after the alleged father. The rest of the story diverges at this point and takes on two different endings. In the first story, Enloe talks his daughter and son-in-law, who live in Kentucky and are visiting the Enloes, to take Nancy and her baby back to Kentucky with them. Back in Kentucky, Nancy marries Thomas Lincoln, who agrees to assume the role of the boy's father. In the second version of the story, Thomas Lincoln is working as a carpenter not far from the

This standing portrait of Lincoln was taken on April 17, 1863, in Mathew Brady's studio in Washington, D.C. (Author's collection)

Wesley Enlow, son of Abraham Enlow, one of the alleged fathers of Lincoln. The similarity in physical appearance between the two men has been offered as evidence in support of their being half-brothers. (Author's collection)

Enloe home in North Carolina. Enloe, faced with an illegitimate son and an angry wife, strikes a deal with Tom Lincoln, to take Nancy and the boy off of his hands for the sum of $500.[25]

The question of Lincoln's illegitimacy slowly faded away, due in part to William E. Barton's second book on the genealogy of Lincoln entitled *The Lineage of Lincoln*.[26] Barton relied on extant documents to prove that Thomas Lincoln and Nancy Hanks were married and living in Kentucky prior to and after the birth of their son, Abraham. The question of Lincoln's illegitimacy remained an issue with only a handful of Lincoln detractors. Cathy's little book sold few copies and drifted into obscurity, along with the story it told. Then in 1940 the issue gained attention once again as a result of a new book authored by James C. Coggins entitled *The Eugenics of President Abraham Lincoln: His German-Scotch Ancestry Irrefutably Established from Recently Discovered Documents.*[27]

Coggins, like Cathy before him, relied on statements from several people living in North Carolina. One statement signed by fifteen local citizens reads: "This certifies that, for many years, we, the undersigned have heard the older people relate the current story, that 'Nancy Hanks, the mother of President Lincoln, was reared in Rutherford County,' and also that Lincoln was born here."[28] The statement, which Coggins refers to as an "affidavit," proves only that a group of people had heard stories (rumors) that Nancy Hanks was raised in Rutherford County and that her son, Abraham Lincoln, was born there.

Coggins's clincher, however, was a long-lost "manuscript" written by an alleged cousin of Nancy Hanks. The author of the manuscript, whose name is not given, writes that two brothers, Daniel and Michael Tanner, came to North Carolina from Virginia in the latter part of the 1800s.[29] While in Virginia, Michael Tanner's wife dies giving birth to a baby girl they name Nancy. Michael, now a single father with a baby girl, asks his brother and sister-in-law to care for the baby. Daniel and his wife agree, provided the baby's birth parents are kept a secret. Daniel and his family migrate to North Carolina, where the baby, now grown to young womanhood, commits an indiscretion (never explained), resulting in her banishment from the Tanner household. She is sent to live with her Uncle Richard Hanks and his family. But Uncle Dick is a habitual drunkard, and it soon turns out that he is unable to care for his children and Nancy, so the children are bound out and Nancy is sent to the home of Abraham Enloe of Rutherford County.

Nancy's life at the time is idyllic. She has a good home and young friends to play with. After a few years Enloe decides to pull up stakes and move to the beautiful Appalachian Mountains to the west. He settles at one of the most beautiful spots in the state, where Soco Creek joins the Ocona Lufta River. He still owns his homestead and farms back in Rutherford County and rents his house to tenants. Nancy, according to Coggins, is now a woman, between eighteen and twenty years old.[30]

It is in this new home in western North Carolina that Abraham Enloe visits young Nancy late one night. It soon becomes obvious to members of the Enloe household that Nancy is "increasing." It does not take long for Mrs. Enloe to come to the conclusion that her husband is the culprit. But instead of turning on him, she turns on poor Nancy. In a burst of purple prose, Coggins describes the scene: "Mrs. Enloe's private, personal, and domestic happiness had been ruined forever! Forbidden fruit had been partaken stealthily . . . the low-down Hanks girl had to go."[31] But Abraham Enloe's conscience will not allow the poor girl to be tossed out into the cold, so he asks the tenants renting his old homestead in Rutherford County to take the pregnant Nancy into their home. They agree, and Nancy returns to the place of her early years, where she gives birth to a baby boy. Grateful for Enloe's help in finding her a new home, she names the baby Abraham.

With Nancy safely out of his hair, Abraham Enloe settles back into his routine, eventually forgetting about Nancy and her baby. His troubles, however, are only just beginning. Because Nancy's move back to Rutherford County is carried out in secret, no one knows what happened to the young woman once living in his household. It isn't long before people begin to suspect foul play has taken place. Rumors soon spread that Enloe murdered Nancy and her unborn child. As the rumors spread, Enloe begins to fear for his life. Word somehow reaches his daughter and son-in-law in Kentucky. The couple make the trip to Enloe's new home and, learning of Nancy's relocation, offer to get Nancy and take her back to Kentucky, furnishing a new home for the wayward girl and her baby.

Michael Tanner, Nancy's real father, according to the legend, also hears of his daughter's plight and travels to the old Enloe homestead, where he finds Nancy and her baby. With tears in his eyes, he tells Nancy that he is her real father and the baby's grandfather. He has come to help her. Nancy packs up her meager belongings and, climbing up behind her father with little Abe in her arms, heads back to the Enloe household.

If you have been able to follow this sad tale of Nancy Hanks and her baby up to this point, you will be glad to know that it is almost at an end. Arriving at the Enloe household, Nancy is greeted by Enloe's daughter and her husband, Mr. and Mrs. Thompson, who traveled from Kentucky after hearing of the old man's plight. They tell Nancy that they will take her home with them to Kentucky. Michael Tanner agrees that his daughter would be better off returning to Kentucky with the Thompsons instead of staying with him. And so Nancy and little Abe finally land in Kentucky, which future generations will come to believe is the birthplace of Abraham Lincoln.

The story of Nancy Hanks, Abraham Enloe, and little Abe draws to a close when Enloe, back in North Carolina, pays Thomas Lincoln to marry Nancy and represent himself as the baby's father. Thomas agrees, and the bargain is struck.

Coggins fills the rest of his book on the eugenics of Lincoln with a discussion of Lincoln's eldest son, Robert Todd Lincoln. "It is impossible," Coggins writes, "for a man of superior intellect to come from an ancestor of inferior or 'subnormal mentality.'"[32] Coggins points out Robert's success as a businessman as evidence of his superior intellect, giving credit to the Tanner and Enloe gene pools brought together through the young Nancy Hanks.

Coggins brings his exposé to a close by citing the final piece of evidence that will settle the question of Lincoln's illegitimacy for all time. He claims that Robert Lincoln attached a codicil to his will that would provide the final proof of Lincoln's ancestry: "There was a little private box of his father's papers," Coggins writes, "of a personal character, which he wished and willed should not be opened or disturbed for twenty years."[33] This box, Coggins boldly proclaims, "contains the solution of the 'Lincoln mystery,' about which historians and writers have had so much to say for over a hundred years. Abraham Lincoln wanted the people to know the truth, the real facts about his origin."[34] Coggins goes on to write that Robert Lincoln knew that he was not any kin to the Lincolns and that "there was not a drop of Lincoln blood in him."[35] The contents of the box, Coggins claimed, would prove once and for all who Lincoln's father was.

Robert Lincoln was a reticent man. He had shunned the limelight throughout his entire life, even though he held several prominent appointments in government and private industry. Coggins attributes Robert's "reclusiveness" to the "sting of his great father's illegitimacy." Because of this, Coggins claims, Robert "walled himself in from the social world; to make himself a 'hermit.'"[36] Robert feared that the lurid details would become public if he were to allow himself to become a public figure. Offered the Republican candidacy for president, Robert turned it down, knowing what would happen if he were to accept.

Robert Lincoln died in 1926 at his summer home "Hildene," located in Manchester, Vermont. His will, written in 1919 and now in the collection of the Abraham Lincoln Presidential Library in Springfield, contains no codicil and no reference to his father's ancestry. It was a remarkably simple will for the size and nature of his extensive estate. The only reference to his father pertains to his father's papers, which Robert bequeathed to the Library of Congress. His stipulation was that they would not be made public until twenty-one years after his death. Coggins obviously confused this stipulation, believing the "papers" contained information about the secret paternity of Abraham Lincoln. Like so many claims made about Abraham Lincoln, the claim of a codicil explaining his paternity was a myth.

WHAT ARE WE TO MAKE OF THESE CLAIMS about Lincoln's father and mother? There is a thin thread that ties most of the claims together. Herndon, Cathy, and Coggins all share one thing in common. Their conclusions are based entirely on traditional stories without any documentary proof from public records. The absence of documentation is not a criticism. A great deal of history is founded on oral tradition, but not in place of the documentary record where it does exist. In the case of Lincoln's parentage, there are records extant that provide answers to the question of Lincoln's birth. We only need examine them to find the answers to our questions.

Interestingly, neither Cathy nor Coggins give dates for the various events they write about in their books. The one thing they do claim is that both Nancy and her baby lived in North Carolina at the time of the baby's birth. And, in one part of the tale, Thomas Lincoln is working as a carpenter near the Enloe farm when Enloe negotiates with him to marry Nancy and assume responsibility for little Abe.

Documents pertaining to Lucy Hanks, Nancy's real birth mother, and Nancy herself are rare, but there are a few that are relevant to fixing their place of residence at certain times critical to our story. We can fix the year of Nancy Hanks's birth to 1784 with reasonable certainty. The best source of information is Abraham Lincoln himself. Lincoln made several entries in the family Bible listing vital information for his mother and father. The Bible remained in family hands, and at some point after Lincoln's death his cousin Dennis Hanks tore the page from the Bible and kept it in his wallet, where it became worn and tattered over the years, resulting in a small piece being missing. The missing piece contained entries for the birth and marriage dates of Lincoln's parents. Fortunately, John D. Johnston, Lincoln's stepbrother, and John J. Hall, a grandson of Lincoln's stepmother, both made copies of the page for their own use. The missing entry reads: "Thomas Lincoln was born Jan. 6, 1778, and was married June 12, 1806, to Nancy Hanks, who was born Feb. 5, 1784."[37]

Most historians accept that Nancy Hanks was the illegitimate daughter of Lucy Hanks, and that Lucy was one of four sisters whose father was Joseph Hanks. Since Lucy was the unwed, pregnant daughter of Joseph Hanks, it is reasonable to believe that she would be under his and his wife's care at the time of her pregnancy and when she gave birth. Fixing Joseph's residence at the time of Nancy's birth should also fix the place of her birth.

To find Joseph Hanks's place of residence in 1784, we again draw on the research of William E. Barton. Barton uncovered a series of documents that formed a continuous time line from 1725, the year of Joseph Hanks's birth, to 1793, the date of his will, and presumably his death. Records for North Farnham parish in Richmond County, Virginia, show that Joseph Hanks was born on December 20, 1725.[38] For the next fifty-seven years of Joseph Hanks's life, Barton tracked his activities through courthouse documents up through 1782. Following that year, Hanks disappears from Richmond County records.

Barton discovered documentation that on February 28, 1787, five years after the last known record in Richmond County for Hanks, he purchased a farm on the Rolling Fork of the Salt River in Nelson County, Kentucky. On January 8, 1793, he recorded his last will and testament, naming his wife as principal benefactor and listing the names of his children and their inheritance. Having pieced together a paper trail in Virginia and Kentucky from 1725 through 1793, with the exception of the period from 1782 to 1787, Barton set out to fill in the missing gap.

Barton began his search with the U.S. Census Records, making up a who's who of Hankses from 1782 to 1790.[39] He found a single listing for a Joseph Hanks with a family of eleven white persons living in Hampshire County, Virginia (now West Virginia), in the year 1782. Barton was unable to find any other listings in the census of a Joseph Hanks for this period. He wrote, "This [family of eleven persons] was a family of precisely what it should have been to include Joseph Hanks, his wife, fives sons, and four daughters, including Lucy."[40]

Barton further bolstered his claim that Hampshire County was the interim home of Joseph Hanks and his family by finding a document in the Pension Office for Thomas Hanks, born 1759, who was drafted into militia service while a resident of Hampshire County. Both the dates of his birth and residence in Hampshire County fit the son of Joseph Hanks.[41] The last piece of evidence Barton located was a mortgage agreement that Joseph Hanks took out on his 108-acre farm on Mike's Run in Hampshire County on March 9, 1784.[42] Barton had filled in the gap from 1782 to 1787 and constructed a time line for Joseph Hanks and his family that began in 1725 and ended in 1793. Assuming Lucy was under her parents' care when she gave birth to her daughter Nancy, she was living in her father's cabin located on Mike's Run in Hampshire County, (West) Virginia.

The years between 1793 and her marriage to Thomas Lincoln in 1806 find Nancy Hanks living near Springfield, Kentucky, with the family of Richard Berry. From 1786 until 1803, Thomas Lincoln lived with his widowed mother and siblings a short distance from the Berry home.[43] We know that at the time Nancy Hanks married Thomas Lincoln she was living in Washington County, Kentucky, under the guardian care of Richard Berry and that her mother, Lucy, was living in Mercer County, Kentucky. Just how Lucy landed in Mercer County and Nancy landed in Washington County is not clear, but the most likely answer is that at the time of her marriage Lucy relinquished care of her illegitimate daughter to the Berry family. This practice of not bringing the illegitimate child into the home of the new husband was not uncommon in frontier America.

While the above evidence places Nancy Hanks in Hampshire County, Virginia (now West Virginia), in 1784 and in Washington County, Kentucky, in 1806, what proof exists for Abraham Lincoln's being born in Kentucky and not North Carolina? There is one piece of evidence that trumps all other claims in fixing Lincoln's place of birth. It comes from Lincoln's cousin and early playmate, Dennis Hanks. Dennis was the illegitimate son of Nancy Hanks, Nancy Hanks Lincoln's aunt (the sister of Lucy Hanks). Dennis was living with his aunt and uncle, Elizabeth and Thomas Sparrow, not far from the Lincoln cabin at Sinking Spring, in Hardin County, Kentucky, on February 12, 1809. In 1865, two months after Lincoln's assassination, Dennis Hanks wrote a lengthy letter to William Herndon in response to a series of questions Herndon posed to Dennis. He wrote the following account concerning Lincoln's birth: "I was born in Hardin Co Ky in 1799—May the 15—on Nolan Creek near Elizabethtown. I was ten years older than Abraham Lincoln and knew him intimately and well from the day of his birth to 1830—*I was the second man who touched Lincoln after his birth*—a custom then in Ky of running to greet the newborn babe."[44]

Dennis's appearance at the Lincoln cabin only an hour or two after the birth of Abraham Lincoln outweighs all the vagaries and contradictions associated with the North Carolina stories. Surely Dennis knew his cousin, Nancy Hanks Lincoln, as well as he knew his own mother. His testimony trumps the several traditions that continue to live on in Rutherford County, North Carolina.

While there may have been a woman named Nancy Hanks who lived in western North Carolina in the early years of the nineteenth century, and while she may have given birth to a baby boy fathered by a man named Abraham Enloe, neither the mother nor the baby had any relationship to Nancy Hanks Lincoln and her son, Abraham Lincoln. While the myth of Abraham Lincoln's illegitimacy has faded from the public's mind, it still thrives among those Lincoln detractors who attempt to use it to discredit Lincoln's place in American history. To their thinking, illegitimacy is a stain on the character of the mother and the baby. Like so many of the myths associated with Lincoln, the myth of his illegitimate birth refuses to die in spite of the facts.

CHAPTER THREE

ABE AND ANN

The Wilma Frances Minor Affair

> In matters like this the mind must shut itself against the will to believe.
> —Ellery Sedgwick, editor of the *Atlantic Monthly*

I N 1926, HARCOURT, BRACE AND COMPANY published the first two volumes of Carl Sandburg's Pulitzer Prize–winning biography of Abraham Lincoln entitled *The Prairie Years*.[1] These first two volumes covered from Lincoln's early life up to his leaving his hometown of Springfield as president-elect in February 1861. It would take Sandburg another thirteen years to finish the final four volumes, called *The War Years*.[2]

Sandburg's beautiful prose captivated readers in unprecedented numbers, pushing sales of *The Prairie Years* to an incredible 1.5 million copies.[3] Sandburg single-handedly moved Lincoln from the constrained world of the historian to the hearts of everyday people, and in the process helped turned Lincoln into an American icon. His biography launched a wave of books about Lincoln that continued unabated for the rest of the twentieth century.

Among the many colorful folktales Sandburg wrote about was the story of Lincoln's romance with the beautiful and talented Ann Rutledge. The romance took on a life of its own and became the best-known part of Lincoln's early life. The story rivaled the best of Shakespearean tragedy when the love affair ended in Ann's untimely death, leaving the heartbroken Lincoln so despondent that he nearly lost his mind. It was said by some that Lincoln threw himself into politics to fill the void left by Ann's death. While Sandburg's version of the relationship between Lincoln and Ann Rutledge became part of American folklore, it was rejected by most Lincoln scholars as more fiction than fact.

SHORTLY AFTER HIS TWENTY-FIRST BIRTHDAY the young Lincoln bid his family goodbye and set out determined to find his own way in the world. The hardscrabble life of the frontier did not suit the ambitious Lincoln, who set his sights on something more than dirt-farming. He landed in the pioneer village of New Salem, located on the banks of the Sangamon River in central Illinois. Here in New Salem, Lincoln spent many of his afternoons and evenings in the tavern of James Rutledge. It was there that he met Ann Rutledge, the tavern-keeper's eighteen-year-old daughter. Carl Sandburg wrote of how this "pink-fair face, and mouth and eyes in a frame of light corn-silk hair" would cause Lincoln to tremble when "she spoke so simple a thing as, 'The corn is getting high, isn't it?'"

Lincoln and Ann became friends. Sandburg told how they shared similar likes and spent time together talking, reading, laughing, and falling in love. It was not the first time the story had been told, but it was the first time it had been told to so large an audience in such an eloquent manner. Sandburg wrote, "He was twenty-six, she was twenty-two; the earth was their footstool; the sky was a sheaf of blue dreams; the rise of the blood-gold rim of a full moon in the evening was almost too much to live, see, and remember."[4] Lincoln, who had suffered tragedy years before in the deaths of his mother and older sister, was to suffer it once more. Ann became sick with fever, lingered for several days, then died, leaving a heartsick Lincoln to "ramble in the woods along the Sangamon River."[5]

A decade after the publication of Sandburg's *Prairie Years*, the public would again be exposed to this tragic love story in Twentieth Century–Fox's movie *Young Mr. Lincoln*, starring Henry Fonda as Abe Lincoln and Pauline Moore as the beautiful Ann Rutledge.[6] A year later, audiences would again be enthralled with the Lincoln-Rutledge romance in Robert Sherwood's *Abe Lincoln in Illinois*, starring Raymond Massey as Lincoln and Mary Howard as Ann Rutledge.[7]

Like most folktales, the story of Lincoln and Ann Rutledge's rela-tionship is a blend of fact and fiction neatly woven together to warm the hearts of most romantics. Ann Rutledge was a real person who was known for her beauty and cheerful nature. She lived in New Salem, where she and Lincoln first met in 1831. And while Ann may have been Lincoln's first love, Lincoln was not the beautiful Ann's first beau.

Ann's father, James Rutledge, founded New Salem along with John M. Cameron in the year 1829. That same year a man by the name of John McNeil opened a store in the fledgling village in partnership with Samuel Hill. McNeil was one of New Salem's more successful entrepreneurs. His mercantile business thrived, and he used his share of the profits to buy property in the surrounding area. He courted Ann, and within a year the two became engaged. Neighbors remarked how Ann seemed to glow with joy. The handsome and wealthy McNeil was quite a catch, especially in a sparsely populated village like New Salem.[8]

The couple's plans were abruptly put on hold when McNeil came to Ann in late summer with a startling story. He told her he had not told the truth about his personal circumstances. He even had lied about his name. His real name was not McNeil; it was McNamar. He told Ann that he had changed his name when he came to New Salem in 1829 to give him anonymity from his family back in New York State. His parents were poor, and McNeil had set out on his own to establish himself and earn enough money to eventually support his mother and father. Now that he had accumulated wealth, he needed to return to New York and his parents and make provisions for their care. He promised Ann he would return as soon as he could and the two would be married.[9]

McNamar left New Salem in the fall of 1832 and returned to New York. He wrote to Ann telling her that he had experienced a series of setbacks that would delay his quick return. His father had become ill shortly after McNamar's arrival back home and lingered for several months before dying. Weeks turned into months, and months into years. By the summer of 1835 McNamar had been absent for three long years. His letter writing became less frequent and then stopped altogether. The long absence had dulled whatever passion Ann may have felt for John.[10]

It was during the long interval of McNamar's absence that Ann and Lincoln became close friends. About the time of McNamar's departure from New Salem, Lincoln became a boarder at the Rutledge Tavern, where he saw Ann on a daily basis. She was bright and vivacious, a perfect foil for Lincoln's intellect. But the closeness of the two was brief. In May 1833, Ann's father sold the tavern and moved the family to the small community of Sand Ridge, some seven miles north of New Salem. Among the many properties McNamar had purchased with his store profits was a small farm located in Sand Ridge. After McNamar left for New York, James Rutledge moved his wife and ten children to McNamar's farm.[11]

Around the time of Ann's move, county surveyor John Calhoun hired Lincoln as his deputy. The new job frequently took Lincoln to the Sand Ridge area, where he and Ann continued their friendship. In soon became obvious to many of their neighbors that the couple had fallen deeply in love. Some even said they were secretly betrothed. But hovering in the background was John McNamar. Ann, now in love with Lincoln, felt honor-bound by her engagement to McNamar. She could not agree to marry Lincoln until she could secure her release from John, which was complicated by his long absence. Fate, however, would intervene, relieving Ann of her dilemma. In August 1835, the lovely Ann fell ill with fever. After lingering for several days, she died. Her death seemed to close this chapter of Lincoln's life—just one more tragedy among the many he would endure.[12]

THE STORY OF THE BETROTHAL of Abraham Lincoln and Ann Rutledge is one that has divided historians both past and present. The love affair so cruelly taken from the young Lincoln made him the great man he became by channeling his grief over the loss of Ann into politics. There were some who said Lincoln never loved again and ultimately married seven years later more for convenience than for love. Others, however, scoffed at the idea, claiming that there is no credible evidence to support any romance between the two. It was all a fiction and not part of the Lincoln story. They acknowledge that Ann Rutledge and Lincoln were real people. They lived together in New Salem and its surrounding environs. They enjoyed many of the same things, including an intellectual curiosity. It was only natural they would share many attractions, but romantic love was not one of them. Their alleged betrothal was just a fable meant for the amusement of the uninformed.

Following Ann's death in 1835 she slipped into obscurity. As Lincoln rose from pioneer youth to president of the United States, she was not part of his rise to prominence and perhaps would have remained unknown had it not been for Lincoln's unexpected and tragic death. Ann was rescued from oblivion by Lincoln's law partner and close friend, William Herndon. Following Lincoln's death in 1865, Herndon set his mind to writing a biography of his friend, one that would tell the true story of Lincoln. Herndon, like most others, saw Lincoln as a great man, but unlike so many others, Herndon knew Lincoln as a real person, not as an icon, and wanted to tell the story of the real Lincoln. Herndon began by contacting many of the people who had known Lincoln during his early years, including his New Salem neighbors. It didn't take long before he learned of the alleged love affair between Lincoln and Ann Rutledge. These same people even claimed the two were betrothed and planned to marry in the spring of 1836, after Ann had completed a year of schooling at the Female Academy in Jacksonville.

But not all of Herndon's informants believed the couple were in love, let alone engaged. These dissenters, however, did not deter Herndon from telling the love story of Abe and Ann, much to the chagrin of Mary Lincoln and several family friends.[13] Selecting his informants carefully, Herndon delivered a lecture to Lincoln's Springfield neighbors on November 16, 1866, in the courthouse. He titled his talk "Abraham Lincoln, Miss Ann Rutledge, New Salem, Pioneering, and the Poem."[14] Some historians believe Herndon deliberately used the information he gathered to settle a long-held animosity toward Mary Lincoln (the feeling was mutual on Mary Lincoln's part).[15] According to Lincoln historian John Y. Simon, Herndon "used Ann Rutledge for an irrelevant and baseless attack on Mary Lincoln which provoked counterattacks by her defenders." Herndon, Simon wrote, "mingled the evidence with speculation . . . insulting Lincoln's memory by exaggerating his [Lincoln's] grief to the point of madness."[16] While Herndon had gathered enough evidence to satisfy himself that a romance and betrothal existed between Lincoln and Rutledge, he damaged his case with most historians by his overzealous speculations that lacked veracity.

The argument over whether a romance and betrothal existed between Lincoln and Rutledge was more widely believed by the general public than by historians, thanks to Carl Sandburg's inclusion of the legend in his masterful work. Historians were more skeptical, and most dismissed the evidence gathered by Herndon. To them, the evidence did not rise to a high enough standard to be believable.

It was based on reminiscences recorded thirty years after the actual events took place. Furthermore, the evidence was entirely circumstantial and lacked a single contemporary letter or document of any sort that might support the claim of a love affair. Herndon appeared to have lost the battle. Then in the summer of 1928 a stunning discovery came to light that appeared to settle the question once and for all. The December issue of the prestigious *Atlantic Monthly* magazine published excerpts from a previously unknown cache of letters by Lincoln and Ann Rutledge that confirmed beyond any doubt that the two were not only deeply in love, but engaged to be married. Here was the documentary proof that even the most skeptical historian could not ignore.[17]

The story begins one July day in 1928 when Edward A. Weeks, the editor of the *Atlantic Monthly* book division (Atlantic Press), received a letter querying the magazine about the eligibility of a manuscript for the magazine's nonfiction book award of $5,000. The writer described the manuscript as "the true love story of Abe Lincoln and Ann Rutledge." It was based, the writer said, on a collection of materials that were among her mother's family papers and included love letters between Abraham Lincoln and Ann Rutledge. The letter was signed, "Wilma Frances Minor."[18]

Weeks, somewhat stunned by the letter, took it to the *Atlantic's* editor, Ellery Sedgwick. At first the two men were skeptical that a treasure so great as the letter alleged could still exist without being known, but they were equally intrigued, even excited. In his memoir published in 1973, Weeks wrote: "One could not shut out the possibility of what the letters would mean to the magazine and the *Atlantic Press* if they could be proved genuine."[19] Sedgwick wrote to Minor asking to see photostats of the documents. Minor sent copies of six of the letters in her possession. Weeks wrote, "Of course we concentrated on those signed 'Abe.' . . . The handwriting, admittedly, was more angular and crudely formed than the small, rounded script of Lincoln's presidential years, but these were dated 1834, when he was twenty-five and, if they were to be believed, written in the rustic surroundings of New Salem, perhaps by firelight—and as everyone knows, handwriting changes with the years!"[20] After some negotiation, the *Atlantic* received a full manuscript along with photostats of all of the supporting documents. In all there were fourteen letters (ten written by Lincoln, four by Ann Rutledge), several pages taken from the diary of Matilda Cameron (Ann Rutledge's cousin and close friend), a memorandum written by Sally Calhoun (daughter of John Calhoun, the county surveyor who hired Lincoln in New Salem), and four books owned by Lincoln with his signature, each sprinkled with insightful notations by Lincoln.

Impressed with the materials, Sedgwick invited Wilma Minor to visit the editors of the *Atlantic* at their expense and discuss how they should proceed. The fact, however, was that Sedgwick and Weeks wanted to size up Minor by personally meeting with her. They still had some doubts. Whatever doubts they had were quickly dispelled during that first meeting with the attractive Wilma. She arrived at the *Atlantic*'s office in September with her mother, Cora DeBoyer, and younger sister, Clover. Wilma was "a handsome woman with a curvaceous figure, seductive gray-green eyes, and an appealing ingenuous manner."[21] Her mother, Weeks wrote, was "tall, beady-eyed, with surprisingly black hair, who somehow reminded me of a fortune-teller."[22] Sedgwick was completely taken by Wilma, and the pair hit it off at once. A deal was soon struck, and Wilma was given a contract for her book and a $1,000 advance, with an additional $4,000 due at the time of publication.

Pending authentication of the documents, it was agreed that Wilma's manuscript would be published in three parts in the *Atlantic*. In looking for authentication, Sedgwick turned first to William E. Barton. Respected by his peers in history as a tenacious researcher who uncovered documentary material whether it resided in courthouses or other people's libraries, Barton had published several books on Lincoln dealing with every period of his life. Most important in this case was his book entitled *The Women Lincoln Loved*, published just the year before.[23] The book contained a lengthy chapter entitled "Ann Rutledge."

At Sedgwick's invitation, Barton made the trip to Boston from his summer home in nearby Foxboro, Massachusetts. Barton arrived in Sedgwick's office before Minor's original documents had arrived, but Sedgwick had the photostats Minor had sent him earlier, and he showed them to Barton. Barton examined the photographs carefully. He couldn't help thinking that both the number and content were "suspiciously high."[24] In fact, as an "unknown discovery," the collection

Wilma Frances Minor poses for
a publicity photograph for the
Atlantic Monthly. (Courtesy of
the *Atlantic Monthly*)

Above left: Ellery Sedgwick, editor of the *Atlantic Monthly.* Sedgwick told his
readers: "Here is the human Lincoln, before the sterility of his deification."
(Courtesy of the *Atlantic Monthly*)   *Above right:* Edward Weeks, editor of book
publications for the *Atlantic Monthly.* (Courtesy of the *Atlantic Monthly*)

was unique among Lincoln finds and could be considered the greatest find of Lincoln material ever. Despite his initial skepticism, Barton was satisfied. After looking over all of the photostats, he gave his approval. Barton told Sedgwick that the collection was "remarkably consistent and satisfactory."[25] The documents were real, Barton said.

Sedgwick, delighted with Barton's approval and convinced of the collection's authenticity, next turned to Ida M. Tarbell. Tarbell was famous for her investigative journalism, described at the time as "muckraking." Her investigation of big oil led her to write a popular history of John D. Rockefeller's Standard Oil Company, published in 1904. It won her acclaim as one of the country's top investigative journalists. Like Barton, Tarbell was well credentialed as a Lincoln scholar. Her four-volume biography of Lincoln was published in 1900 and was followed by several spin-off books resulting from her research.[26]

Unlike Barton, who only got to examine photostat copies of Minor's documents, Tarbell examined the originals—and like Barton, Tarbell expressed concern about a few minor points but gave her blessing to the collection. "My faith is strong that you have an amazing set of true Lincoln documents."[27]

Sedgwick next showed the photostats to the editor of the Massachusetts Historical Society, Worthington Chauncy Ford. Ford had retired as head of the Manuscript Division at the Library of Congress and was quite familiar with history involving Lincoln and New Salem. He had worked on completing Albert Beveridge's two-volume history of Lincoln's life before the presidency.[28] Beveridge had died before he finished the final touches on his Lincoln biography, and Ford completed the work. After examining the same photostats that Barton had pronounced authentic, Ford declared the letters to be forgeries. Lincoln did not write them, he said. They bear no resemblance to Lincoln's handwriting. At first Sedgwick was shaken. He soon recovered and simply ascribed Ford's negativity to jealousy. Sedgwick looked for another Lincoln scholar to counter Ford and bolster his own opinion.

He found it with Carl Sandburg. Sandburg visited Sedgwick's house over Thanksgiving, only one month before the *Atlantic* would come out with the first installment of Wilma Minor's articles. After examining the original documents, Sandburg was thrilled. He wrote a letter to Sedgwick stating: "These new Lincoln letters seem entirely authentic—and preciously and wonderfully co-ordinate and chime with all else known of Lincoln. Students of Lincoln's personal development will prize and love them for several known reasons and for intangible and inexplicable reasons. Thank you. Carl Sandburg."[29] Barton, Tarbell, and now Sandburg had given their stamp of approval. Only Ford disagreed, and his view didn't really count as far as Sedgwick was concerned.[30]

Sedgwick next sought to have the documents tested by a forensic chemist. Such tests are completely objective. All of the tests supported the documents' authenticity. The paper contained natural linen fibers, referred to as "rag content," which was consistent with the period when they were claimed to have been written. Later paper was made from wood pulp. The ink "was consistent" with the supposed age of the documents. The only element missing was an examination of Lincoln's handwriting by handwriting experts. There were no known examples of Ann Rutledge's handwriting or the handwriting of Matilda Cameron and Sally Calhoun, leaving only Lincoln's available for scrutiny. But three Lincoln experts familiar with Lincoln's handwriting through their extensive research had already given their approval to the documents' authenticity. To top matters off, Herbert Putnam, the Librarian of Congress, visited Boston to view the documents and told Sedgwick that he wanted to display them following publication. All this took place within one month of the *Atlantic*'s receiving the original documents.[31] Sedgwick was now ready to reveal Minor's wonderful articles to the world.

In the introduction to the magazine's opening article in the December 1928 issue, Sedgwick extolled the find: "This chapter out of the life of Lincoln has always been shrouded in mystery. With books on Lincoln running into the thousands it has long seemed impossible to unearth any new material about this greatest of our leaders. Imagine then, our incredulity when the Wilma Frances Minor collection first appeared, our amazement that authentic Lincoln letters had defied the most diligent research of the biographer, and our delight when the material passed test after test put to it by the country's most distinguished Lincoln scholars."

Sedgwick went on to praise the discoverer of the collection: "In this place [the editor] would like to put on record the *Atlantic's* gratitude for the kindness and helpfulness of Miss Wilma Frances Minor who, when a strange turn of fortune presented her with a treasure beyond price, felt instantly her responsibility."[32]

The first article appeared under the title "Lincoln the Lover: I. The Setting—New Salem."[33] It began by pointing out the schism among historians in accepting the relationship between Lincoln and Ann Rutledge: "Eminent students have denied altogether the reality of Lincoln's passion for Ann; others have accepted the tradition in general outline." Minor then put all doubt to rest: "Now it becomes possible to reveal in full light and at first hand the story—so full of tenderness and hope, so tragic in its close—which has hitherto rested on contestable report. Not only did Lincoln and Ann hold each other dear; the actual letters which passed between them remain."[34]

The seventeen-page article includes two letters from Lincoln to John Calhoun (the county surveyor who hired Lincoln as an assistant) and date from Lincoln's time as a congressman (1848), three excerpts from Sally Calhoun's diary (John Calhoun's daughter) dated 1848, and quotations from several books once owned by Lincoln with his annotations sprinkled throughout—each one giving insight into some aspect of Lincoln's character. In the letter to Calhoun, Lincoln writes of his stepmother, Sarah Bush Lincoln: "God bless my Mother the part that is best in me, and the ability to give it to the world, is my inheritance from her, that is the reason John I will never stop in my endeavor to achieve that which is best for the people as I see it."[35] In his second letter to Calhoun, Lincoln writes about his feelings on slavery: "I never have forgotten a single instance of my memorable stay in New Orleans which was so marked by the atrocious cruelty practiced by many slave holders. . . . I guess it takes a queer fellow like me to sympathize with the put upon and down trodden."[36] Next we hear from Sally Calhoun: "Father predicts great things in the future for Lincoln, for he says Lincoln has character."[37] The material was almost too good to be true. It affirmed in Lincoln's own words what heretofore had been handed down second and third hand.

In the second installment (published in January 1929), entitled "The Courtship," Minor introduces her readers to Matilda "Mat"

Cameron, Ann Rutledge's cousin and close confidante.[38] To Mat's diary we owe much, for in it we have proof of Abe and Ann's deep love affair. Mat wrote on July 10, 1833: "I am so happy coz now that Abe Lincoln and my deerest frend Ann are a ingaged cupel . . . ," and further on: "Abe and Ann are awful in love he rites her leters."[39]

Finally, eight pages into the second article we find our first love letters between Ann and Abe. Ann's letters are more expressive than Lincoln's, but that is consistent with his introverted nature in dealing with emotion. Ann begins her letter, "My beloved Abe," and ends it with "all my hart is ever thine." Abe answers: "My Beloved Ann," and ends with: "I am happy to ask you to accompany me later to literary they have planned for you to sing and I am to recite. I could write to you forever but Nance will not wait that long [to mail this letter]. With great affection, Abe."[40]

With James Rutledge's move to Sand Ridge, Ann and her sisters were forced to hire out to earn money to keep the family together. Ann took a job with Lincoln's good friend "Uncle Jimmy Short," whose farm was near the Rutledge place at Sand Ridge. Lincoln wrote to Ann from New Salem lamenting her situation of having to work like some scour maid, blaming himself:

> My beloved Ann: I am filled with regret over the defect of the conduct of a fate that has bourne down so heavily upon you and yours. I try to persuade myself that my unlucky star has not overshadowed you. Molly Prewitt told me about you going to work for James Shorts family, you are too frail for that hard work. my *treasured one* I should now be standing between you and such trials. O! when will success crown my untiring efforts. I sicken at my many failures especially as no more am I lazy in the discharge of my duties. forgive this long-faced letter, as I should now be upholding you in hope for the future, for I but today have been greatly assured of my election as member to the *Legislature*. So perhaps our dreams will come true. I am borrowing Jack's horse to ride over to see you this coming Saturday. Cutting my foot prevents my walking. I will be at your pleasure to accompany you to the Sand Ridge taffy-pull. I will be glad to hear your good Father's sermon on the Sabbath. I feel unusually lifted with hope of relieving your present worry at an early date and likewise doing myself the best turn of my life. With you my beloved all things are possible. Now James kindly promises to deliver

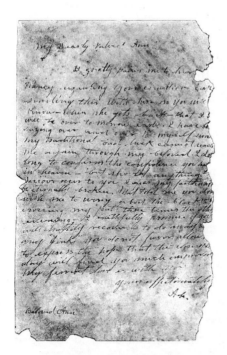 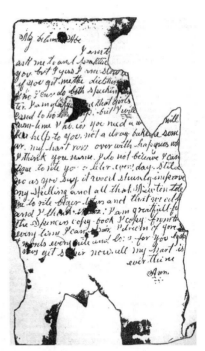

Above left: "My Dearly Valued Ann," Lincoln writes to Ann Rutledge in 1835, shortly before her death. Lincoln signs his letter, "Yours affectionately Abe." (Courtesy of the *Atlantic Monthly*)   *Above right:* Ann writes, "My beloved Abe," ending with "ever thine." (Courtesy of the *Atlantic Monthly*)

into your dear little hands this letter. May the good Lord speed Saturday afternoon.

Affectionately A. Lincoln[41]

The February 1929 issue of the *Atlantic* carried the final installment of Minor's three articles. Part 3, entitled "The Tragedy," began with the year 1834.[42] It is Lincoln's third year in New Salem and Ann's second at Sand Ridge. Ann and Abe continue their correspondence and visits whenever possible. Ann sends Lincoln her mother's Bible, writing: "Dear Abe It was my mothers she giv it to me. I love it so much that I want you to hav it. Ples read it all. It will make you feel diferent. Ann."[43]

Minor writes, "Not only was it a lover's gift from Ann to Abraham, but it has been marked with Lincoln's own writing, and he has left in it impulsive traces of his thought or emotion."[44] At the bottom of the title page Abe has written: "I will be diligent in my reading A. Lincoln."[45] Minor points out that Ann's statement that "it will make you feel diferent" refers to Lincoln's "independence toward the accepted religious convictions of the village."[46] She supported this view by pointing out to her readers that Lincoln penned the following phrase "a good precept I would say" next to the verse from the book of Judges that reads: "In those days there was no king in Israel: every man did that which was right in his own eyes."[47]

The article contains more excerpts from Mat Cameron's diary and Ann's last letter to her "beloved Abe." The letter was written during August 1835, and Ann alludes to her falling ill with "a cole" and tells her beloved Abe not to "cum to-nite." She asks him to "Cum tomoro nite eny-way."[48]

Lincoln wrote an ominous letter to Ann in return, foreshadowing the tragedy to come: "My Dearly Valued Ann I have been saying over and over to myself surely my traditional bad luck cannot reach me again through my beloved. I do long to confirm the confidence you have in heaven—but should anything serious occur to you I fear my faith would be eternally broken. . . . My fervent love is with you. Yours affectionately Abe."[49]

Unfortunately, Ann succumbed to "brain fever" (probably typhoid fever) after lingering for several days "between life and death." Racked with fever, Ann sent for Lincoln to come to her. Lincoln was ushered into the sickroom where Ann lay feverish, and the two lovers were left alone to console each other. It was apparent to the fatalistic Lincoln that Ann would not get better. She died on August 25, 1835. Her wasted body was clothed in her finest dress and a yellow ribbon was fastened in her hair. She was buried in the Old Concord Cemetery, a mile from where she was living on Sand Ridge.[50]

With Ann's death, Lincoln fell into a deep depression, so much so that his friends feared he would take his own life. Mat Cameron wrote of Abe's behavior in her diary: "The kin ses Abe is luny. I think he is braken-harted. He wants me to keep his 5 leters from her coz he is perswaded he will sune foler her I expect he will."[51] Despite Abe's deep depression ("Abe is luny"), he had the foresight to give Ann's love letters to Mat Cameron for safekeeping, suggesting to her that he may kill himself. There were tales of Lincoln's visiting the cemetery and throwing himself on her grave to protect her from the harsh rains in summer and driving snows in winter. He couldn't bear the thought of her delicate corpse suffering the ravages of storm. For those who doubted such behavior, Minor produced a verse from one of Lincoln's treasured books, *Kirkham's Elocution*. The verse reads: "The sorrow for the dead, is the only sorrow from which we refuse to be divorced. Every other wound, we seek to heal—every other affliction, to forget; but this wound, we consider it a duty to keep open—this affliction we cherish." In the margin below the verse Lincoln had written: "Wait, Wait my Beloved for me, Abe."[52]

And so the beautiful love story of Ann and Abe came to its tragic end. Lincoln eventually recovered and continued his steady rise to greatness—some say, thanks to Ann. In 1837 he left New Salem and Ann behind and moved to Springfield, where he took up the practice of law and politics. In 1842 he married the vivacious Mary Todd, and together they had four sons. Two years after Lincoln abandoned the pioneer village, only a few people remained. New Salem became a ghost town, sinking beneath the prairie sod. All that remained were the depressions in the ground where cabins once stood. In 1906 William Randolph Hearst visited the abandoned site and was so moved that he purchased the sixty-two-acre tract for $11,000 and donated it to a local association intent on restoring the old village as a memorial to Abraham Lincoln and the early pioneering days that existed in New Salem.

The story of Ann and Abe's love affair was confirmed at long last thanks to the precious collection of letters and documents brought to light by Wilma Frances Minor and published for all to read by Ellery Sedgwick and the *Atlantic Monthly*. The tragic love story warmed the hearts of Americans, but only until the fourth and final article in the series was published in the April 1929 issue. The article, written by a young and able Lincoln scholar named Paul Angle, exposed the collection as a fabrication and its owners as frauds. The *Atlantic* and its readers had been the victims of a bad hoax.

By the time the second article appeared in the January 1929 issue of the *Atlantic*, a growing chorus of dissenters had begun to emerge. Worthington Chauncy Ford had dismissed the documents as forgeries at the outset. He was determined to go public with his view in a press release. Sedgwick, to his credit, told Ford he would publish Ford's press release as a letter to the editor in the *Atlantic* carrying the first installment. Ford declined, not wanting to wait. Oliver R. Barrett, a lawyer and one of the country's major Lincoln collectors, and Paul M. Angle, secretary of the Abraham Lincoln Centennial Association, joined with Ford in denouncing the collection. Sedgwick's support was crumbling rapidly. Now he began to lose his earlier supporters. Barton, who was the first to give his approval, was having second thoughts, and so was Carl Sandburg. Barrett had been conducting his own careful examination of the documents and concluded the Lincoln letters were not in Lincoln's handwriting, nor was the "composition" of the letters in Lincoln's style. Sandburg now reversed his earlier position, acknowledging the expertise of Barrett and Angle.

Handwriting analysis and review of the style and composition of the documents are legitimate tools in determining authenticity, but they are entirely subjective tools. In the final analysis, the opinions of Barton, Tarbell, Sandburg, Ford, and Barrett were based on a subjective interpretation of the evidence, and on its appearance. One person who disagreed with the experts from the very beginning was Paul Angle. Angle, a young historian who would become one of a select group of recognized Lincoln authorities, looked at the content of the materials, analyzing those items that could be, or could not be, authenticated.

Angle's first revelation was devastating to Sedgwick's claim of authenticity. Angle concluded that Mat Cameron, Ann's cousin and dear friend, did not exist. To make matters worse for Minor and Sedgwick, neither did Sally Calhoun. They were figments of someone's imagination. It was an amazing claim by Angle. While some may have believed the documents were fabricated, no one considered that the historical figures were also fabricated. Angle showed that the Cameron family Bible listing all of the Cameron family members lacked a Matilda "Mat" Cameron. Likewise, Angle could find no contemporary record that contained a "Sally" or "Sarah" Calhoun. But Angle understood that a negative result is not proof. It is only supportive. For proof, Angle pointed to Mat's Cameron's diary, allegedly written in the 1830s (the period covering New Salem), where Mat writes about her friend, Martha Calhoun. Martha Calhoun was real enough, but not before 1843, when she was born—ten years after Mat's diary entries.[53] Angle continued with his amazing exposé.

In one of her letters, Ann writes of using Spencer's copybook: "I am greatfull for the Spencers copy-book I copy frum that every time I can spair."[54] Ann died August 25, 1835, but *Spencer's Copybook* was not published until 1848, thirteen years after her death.[55]

Angle next turned to the letters allegedly written by Lincoln. In a letter to John Calhoun, the surveyor who hired Lincoln as his assistant during his New Salem days, Lincoln writes: "Dear friend John if you have in your possession or can tell me where you left the Certificate of Survey of Joshua Blackburn's Claim, there seems some controversy between him and Green concerning that North East quarter of Section 40—" Section 40? No such survey designation exists. Townships were laid out as a square six miles by six miles, with each section being one square mile. This yields only thirty-six sections, the highest number any section can have. Both Lincoln and John Calhoun were excellent surveyors. Using modern methods, many of their surveys have been checked and found to be without error.[56] In the same letter Lincoln wrote, "The Bixby's are leaving this week for some place in Kansas."[57] At the time of Lincoln's letter (May 9, 1834) Kansas did not exist. Kansas became a state on January 29, 1861, and was not organized as a territory until 1854. Prior to that, it was Indian Territory and referred to as such.[58]

Angle's analysis of the internal data gleaned from the documents leaves no doubt that the collection was a fabrication. The fabricator was knowledgeable about many things in the history of New Salem and the speculations that surrounded the romance of Lincoln and Ann Rutledge, but not knowledgeable enough to fool a scholar of Angle's expertise. Sedgwick, however, was not yet ready to throw in the towel. He had gone to Arizona to visit his son and gain some peace from all of the controversy now swirling about his head. While Sedgwick was in Arizona, members of his staff, deeply concerned that he and the magazine had been duped, hired a detective agency in Los Angeles to investigate Wilma and her mother, and a handwriting expert to examine the Lincoln letters. The results were the final straw for Sedgwick and the staff of the *Atlantic*. Wilma and her mother (who was acting as Wilma's advisor) had quite a checkered past. Wilma's mother had been married at least five times, while Wilma had been married twice before and had given false information on one of her marriage licenses. But the real bombshell came when it was learned that Wilma had first approached a publisher in San Diego with an entirely different history of her Lincoln collection.[59]

Working as a columnist for the *San Diego Union* newspaper, Wilma had approached James Ashe, the head of a San Diego publishing house, asking him to arrange interviews with some of his authors for use in her weekly column titled "Sidelights on Life."[60] Ashe obliged, and Wilma began interviewing several of his authors. One of her interviews, it turned out, was with Scott Greene, the son of William "Billy" Greene, of New Salem. Greene and Lincoln had been hired by Denton Offutt to run his store in 1831. The two became fast friends, and years later, when Lincoln was president, he appointed Greene the federal tax collector for Peoria, Illinois.[61]

Following her interview with Greene, Wilma told Ashe that Greene had a large collection of Lincoln letters, including several written by Ann Rutledge (Wilma told Sedgwick that the collection descended through her mother's family). A few weeks later Wilma told Ashe that she had persuaded Greene to sell her the collection and she was going to write a book based on the documents. Ashe said he suggested to Wilma that she submit her manuscript to the *Atlantic* book division and try and win the $5,000 award for the best manuscript. Clearly Wilma had written to the *Atlantic* with an entirely different story of how she came into possession of the collection. The clincher came in the form of the handwriting expert hired by the *Atlantic* staff. The conclusion was that the author of documents in Wilma's collection was none other than Wilma herself.[62]

The head of the Los Angeles detective agency went to San Diego with orders to confront Wilma and her mother. When the two women were shown the evidence that the documents were forgeries, Wilma and her mother were "stunned." They said they had been deceived and denied having anything to do with the fraud, the implication being that Billy Greene's son had put one over on Wilma and her mother. No amount of evidence could persuade the two ladies to confess.[63]

In the meantime, Sedgwick, rather than attack Angle's evidence, decided to attack Angle. In what can only be considered a mean-spirited effort, Sedgwick got hold of a letter Angle had written to his parents about the whole affair and his efforts to show the documents

William Greene was a close friend and partner of
Lincoln's in New Salem. In one of Wilma's scenarios
she claimed she purchased the love letters from Greene's
son, Scott. Later, she claimed that the letters descended
through her mother's family. (Courtesy of the Library of
Congress)

were forgeries. Much to Angle's chagrin, the letter was published
in his parents' hometown newspaper. In his letter, Angle boasted
about his good fortune resulting from his research debunking the
Minor collection. Angle wrote: "I was going at it in a leisurely way,
intending simply to write the editor a letter. But Monday noon Oliver Barrett came in the office. He insisted that I give the story to
the press. That's what I had wanted to do, knowing that it would be
great advertising for me, and good publicity for the Lincoln Memorial Association." Angle gave the story to the local Springfield paper that published it. No sooner had it appeared in the Springfield
paper than it ran into trouble: "It went out of Springfield, but some

Associated Pressman in Chicago killed it, afraid of a libel suit. Nevertheless we did get it out East. A friend of Mr. Hay [president of the Lincoln Memorial Association] owns the *Philadelphia Record*. Mr. Hay called me and I wired 1200 words which the *Record* printed in a big story."[64]

Angle went on to write that once the *Record* broke the story in the East, several prominent papers followed suit. He ended his letter boasting to his parents of his success: "It's the biggest thing that ever happened to me. One doesn't get a chance very often to put the magazine of the country [the *Atlantic Monthly*] in the frying pan and cook it brown."[65] The *Atlantic* added a sarcastic remark aimed at embarrassing Angle: "It seems fair that Mr. Angle should have the advertising which means so much to him."[66]

Sedgwick's little ploy to discredit Angle failed. The editor was still on the defensive. On his way back to Boston from Arizona, he agreed to stop in Chicago and meet with Angle. Angle graciously put aside Sedgwick's attempt to embarrass him and met with him. Angle suggested that he and the *Atlantic* work together and publish an article critiquing the collection and exposing the hoax. Sedgwick, persuaded by his staff, finally agreed. Angle wrote the article in a matter of a few days, meeting the deadline for the April issue.

Meanwhile, Wilma and her mother continued to hold to their story that they had been the victims of a hoax. In July, well after the furor had died down, Wilma was paid a visit by Teresa Fitzpatrick, the *Atlantic* staff member who arranged for the handwriting expert to examine the collection. Fitzpatrick was able to coax Wilma to tell her story of how she came to acquire the collection, for all to know, suggesting that it would make a wonderful story. Wilma, sensing another opportunity to stand in the spotlight, agreed. Her account of how the collection came to be was a story in itself.[67]

When Wilma and her mother first visited Sedgwick and Weeks in September 1928, Weeks had written in his memoir that Wilma's mother reminded him of a "fortuneteller." Little did Weeks realize how perceptive he was. After Wilma had interviewed Scott Greene in San Diego, a lightbulb went off in her head. Wilma went to see her mother, who, among her many talents, was also a "medium," with the ability to act as an intermediary between the spirit world and the real world. Wilma said to her mother, "Mama at last our faith of a lifetime has led to something." She then asked her mother, "Don't you think I have earned the right to be the channel to tell that real story [of Lincoln and Ann] to the world?" Wilma's mother said, "We can try."[68]

A few days later, while "Mama" was in a trance receiving messages from Wilma's dead uncle, Wilma asked him, through her mother, if she might be the "instrument" to tell the real story of Lincoln and Ann Rutledge's tragic love affair. Of course, Wilma's dead uncle didn't know but said he would go and find out. The following week Wilma's mother fell into another trance. Wilma's uncle was back once again chatting with Wilma's mother. Acting as a "guide" between Wilma's mother and Lincoln and Ann Rutledge, the uncle brought good news and bad news. The good news was that Lincoln and Ann had agreed to tell their story through Wilma's mother, the whole story. The bad news was that Wilma must commit herself "to months and months of systematic labor." It would be physically exhausting, but well worth the effort. Wilma agreed. She prepared a long list of questions that her mother would ask her dead uncle, who would then provide the answers, which her mother would write down. Actually, her mother was merely holding the pen. The guide would write the answers down, Wilma's mother serving as the instrument through which the guide would write.[69]

The "sessions" went on for several weeks. Wilma's mother would phone Wilma and tell her "a message came through last night." Wilma would hurry over to her mother's apartment and pick up the "message" and transcribe it. Wilma pointed out to Fitzpatrick that "every word in Matilda Cameron's diary is verbatim as given by her uncle. Every word written through my mother as the medium." At one point Wilma told Fitzpatrick that she asked her uncle where she could get old paper to write on. He told her she could find plenty of the appropriate paper in old books. "He gave me a list of books that Lincoln used at that period of his life." Wilma told Fitzpatrick that she went to used bookstores and had no difficulty finding the old books, and by removing the endpapers had a ready supply of old paper. In an unusual moment of candor, Wilma said the guide told her that she should consult published books to gather the well-known facts that she would need in "understanding the story." Wilma closed her remarkable confession by telling Fitzpatrick that "Ann Rutledge sent through this message to me, 'I want in the next three years time, for you to tell the world exactly how you got this.' She thought it was a wonderful test case."[70]

Once all the evidence was in, Sedgwick considered the case closed. He wanted to hear no more about the hoax or Wilma Minor. The *Atlantic* eventually recovered from the embarrassing affair. While it had been fooled into accepting a dreadful hoax, it had come away in the end with a fascinating story of forgery and fraud that would surely delight its readers. The details were given to a staff writer, who prepared an article covering Minor's confession. In the end, however, Sedgwick killed the story. He claimed that the *Atlantic*'s lawyers had advised against publishing any details about the hoax. This was probably not true, but no one challenged Sedwick's decision to bury the whole affair.

In the end, Paul Angle had the last word. He closed his April 1929 article writing, "To me, at least, a belief in the common authorship of these documents and the Gettysburg Address was impossible—and I much prefer the Gettysburg Address."[71]

CHAPTER FOUR

ANN RUTLEDGE'S RESTING PLACE

The Myth of Ann Rutledge's Gravesite

I am Ann Rutledge who sleep beneath these weeds
—Edgar Lee Masters

THE STORY OF THE RELATIONSHIP between Abraham Lincoln and Ann Rutledge has had an uncertain history. Historians have been unable to agree on little more than that both Ann and Abe lived part of their early lives together in the village of New Salem and shared a common interest in learning grammar. There are no documents that link the two directly.[1] Only the reminiscences of friends and neighbors breathe life into the relationship. Despite the ongoing debate of whether or not the two were romantically involved and betrothed to marry, Ann Rutledge was a real person. The man she was engaged to marry, John McNamar, described her as "a gentle Amiable Maiden . . . winsome and Comly withal a blond in complection with golden hair, 'cherry red Lips & a bonny Blue Eye.'"[2] Her brother Robert said she "possessed a remarkably amiable and loveable disposition."[3] William Greene, who together with Lincoln operated a store in New Salem, becoming fast friends, described Ann Rutledge as "a woman of Exquisite beauty. . . . She was beloved by evry body and evry boody respected and lovd her—so sweet & angelic was she."[4]

Perhaps the most puzzling aspect of the Lincoln-Rutledge story is that although no new evidence has come to light, some historians have changed their positions on the alleged romance in recent years—a kind of historian flip-flop. One historian has changed his position three times, from disbelieving the story to believing to disbelieving to believing.[5] In each instance the evidence remains the same, only the evaluation changes. Historians, however, do not determine the public's perception when it comes to dearly held stories. The majority of Americans get their history from the movies, television, and novels—and the romance of Abe and Ann is the stuff novels and movies are made of.

Whatever the real relationship between Lincoln and Ann Rutledge, it came to a tragic end in the summer of 1835. In August of that year Ann came down with a fever. While mild at first, the fever persisted, and as days passed Ann's condition worsened. Those who tended her frail body believed she would die. According to the legend, Ann asked to see Lincoln, and while the family demurred at first, it eventually sent word for him to come to the Rutledge home. Abe and Ann were left alone to say their goodbyes. The meeting must have been heart wrenching. Years later, Lincoln's law partner and biographer, William Herndon, gave a lecture in which he said, "Lincoln loved Ann Rutledge better than his own life." About their final meeting, he wrote, "Heaven only knows what was said by the two. God only knows what was thought."[6]

Ann died on August 25. A coffin fashioned out of local pine was carried into the bedroom where Ann's body lay recently clothed in her finest dress. Her hair was fixed with a yellow ribbon. Her body was carefully placed inside the wooden box and carted off to the Old Concord Cemetery, where she was buried among her New Salem neighbors.

The memory of Ann Rutledge would eventually fade, along with the village of New Salem and the rugged pioneers who lived there. The village and its people would have become little more than a footnote in history were it not for their association with Abraham Lincoln. Lincoln lived in New Salem from the summer of 1831 until the spring of 1837. In New Salem he won election to his first political office, owned a store in partnership, served in the Black Hawk War as a member of the state militia, became postmaster, worked as county surveyor, and took up the study of law, eventually earning his license. New Salem, it could be said, was where Lincoln passed to manhood, learning several important lessons in life. Today the village is restored to its original state as a memorial to its famous citizen, the only village dedicated to an individual.[7]

The years following Lincoln's assassination fixed his image in the national memory as the country's savior and our greatest president.

THIS MARKS THE ORIGINAL GRAVE
OF ANN RUTLEDGE, BORN JAN. 7, 1813
AND DIED AUG. 25, 1835

A modern-day sign marks the original gravesite in Old Concord Cemetery where Ann Rutledge was buried following her death on August 25, 1835. Residents of New Salem said Lincoln came here on several occasions to grieve over her grave. (Author's collection)

There was a thirst for learning everything there was to know about the man. In his 1866 lecture on Lincoln and Ann Rutledge, Herndon told his audience that Lincoln was devastated by Ann's death. It affected Lincoln's mind: "He sorrowed and grieved, rambled over the hills and through the forests, day and night. . . . He slept not, he ate not, joyed not. This he did until his body became emaciated and weak and gave way. His mind wandered from its throne."[8] Herndon told how one of Lincoln's close friends had heard him say, "I cannot endure the thought that the sleet and storm, frost and snow of heaven should beat on her grave."[9]

Herndon had given life to the legend of Ann Rutledge and Abraham Lincoln's love affair. Old Concord became immortalized as the resting place of Ann Rutledge—its soil wet from the tears of Lincoln's grief poured out at her graveside. The burying ground remains one of those mystical places that haunt the Lincoln story. And yet, were Lincoln to return in search of his first betrothed he would not find her. He would be told that she is gone, taken from her grave and carried off to the nearby town of Petersburg, where her remains now rest in Oakland Cemetery. The story of Ann's removal from the Old Concord Cemetery adds yet another layer to the myth surrounding this young girl and her love affair with Abraham Lincoln.

Ann's grave remained undisturbed in the Old Concord burying ground for fifty-five years, until 1890, when a Petersburg entrepreneur named Samuel Montgomery came up with an imaginative sales ploy. Montgomery, an undertaker and furniture dealer, was an officer and part owner of Petersburg's Oakland Cemetery. Cemetery plots were not selling nearly as well as the owners would have liked. Montgomery conceived the idea of using Ann Rutledge as a marketing tool. He proposed to move Ann's remains from Old Concord Cemetery to a prominent spot in the Oakland Cemetery. Her place in the cemetery, and her connection to Abraham Lincoln, would draw visitors and help sell lots.[10]

Characterized by those who knew him as "a very honourable man, well educated, trustworthy, and very religious,"[11] Montgomery had no qualms about moving Ann to Petersburg, where he could show off her grave. It was a clever plan, but to bring it off Montgomery needed the approval of Ann's closest kin to exhume and move her remains. The Rutledge family had long ago left the New Salem area, scattering across the country. All, that is, except James McGrady Rutledge, Ann's favorite cousin who still lived in Petersburg.

Montgomery went to McGrady Rutledge with his idea. Mc-Grady was resistant at first, believing it would be wrong to disturb Ann's grave. He didn't want to be responsible for digging her up. But Montgomery was persuasive. He argued that by moving Ann to Petersburg her grave would get perpetual care as well as visibility for all her admirers who wished to visit her. At Old Concord it would be neglected, covered by weeds and vines. Moving Ann would be good for Ann and, of course, for Petersburg. Surely McGrady could see how moving Ann would be good for her and for the residents of the town. McGrady finally succumbed to Montgomery's pressure and reluctantly gave his approval to move Ann's remains.

On May 15, 1890, fifty-five years after Ann's death, the exhumation took place. Montgomery had brought his furniture-store wagon and two gravediggers, together with McGrady Rutledge and the young son of one of the diggers, to Old Concord Cemetery. McGrady was

Ann Rutledge's alleged gravesite in the Oakland Cemetery in Petersburg, Illinois. The modern stone carries the famous words of poet Edgar Lee Masters: "I am Ann Rutledge who sleep beneath these weeds, Beloved of Abraham Lincoln." (Author's collection)

present at Ann's funeral in 1835, and he showed Montgomery the location of the unmarked grave. He knew that Ann's brother, David, who died in 1842, was buried beside his sister, but McGrady wasn't sure on which side. He knew a small child was buried on one side of David Rutledge and Ann on the other. Montgomery set the two men to digging. Several feet down they found a small coffin still intact. It contained the remains of a small child. Montgomery had picked the wrong side. At least it confirmed what McGrady had told Montgomery. Montgomery pressed ahead and told the two men to start digging on the other side.

After digging down several feet the men came to a piece of rotted wood. They had struck a wooden coffin, or what remained of a wooden coffin. Only part of the sides were left; the lid and ends had mostly rotted away. Removing the few small pieces of wood that were left from the lid, Montgomery peered into the dark hole. James Hollis, the nine-year-old son of one of the gravediggers, later described what Montgomery found. He said he had no trouble

James McGrady Rutledge,
Ann Rutledge's favorite cousin.
McGrady reluctantly gave in to
Montgomery's pressure to relocate
Ann's remains to Petersburg.
(Courtesy of the National Park
Service)

remembering what he saw. The incident "is as vivid in my memory as though it happened yesterday."[12]

According to Hollis's statement, made in 1958 at the age of seventy-seven, "the top and ends of the wooden coffin had been rotted away but the sides of the coffin were still in fairly good condition . . . there were two bones found, one a thigh bone [femur] and the other the left upper arm bone from the elbow to the shoulder [humerus]. Some hair was also found, and Hollis said that "the hair was rolled up."[13] Montgomery placed these items in a small box along with a shovelful of dirt from the grave and carried them to his store, where he kept them overnight. The next day the small box was interred in Oakland Cemetery, including the shovelful of dirt.

Statements from individuals who were not at the actual exhumation but spoke later with those that were said that some buttons from a dress, a buckle, a piece of cloth, and a roll of hair were removed. While some disagreement exists as to the exact number of items taken from the grave, it appears that no more than two bones, one to three buttons, a buckle, a piece of black lace, a ribbon, and a roll of

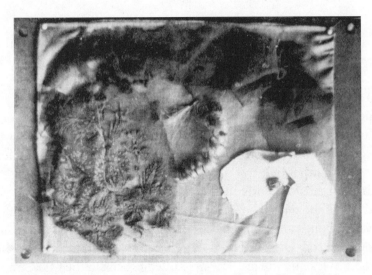

Relics recovered by Montgomery from Ann's grave. He withheld them from reburial. They remain in the Rutledge family to the present time. They consist of a yellow satin bow and an acorn button (*bottom right*), a piece of black lace (*bottom left*), and a large lock of Ann's hair (*center*). (From the *Menard, Salem, Lincoln Souvenir Album,* 1893)

hair, along with a few pieces of the wood from the sides of the coffin, constituted the total of Ann's "remains" that were removed.

The items Montgomery buried at Oakland Cemetery raise serious doubt that a "reburial" took place. The removal of Ann's remains is further compromised by the fact that certain articles removed from the grave never found their way to Petersburg. In 1969, Gary Erickson published the results of his investigation into the circumstances surrounding the exhumation and reburial. He wrote that he located "a lady in Menard County who claims she has a lock of Ann's hair and buttons from Ann's dress, acquired from members of her family to whom they were given at the time of Ann's exhumation. But, since there is not an affidavit, these items would be very difficult to verify."[14]

Fortunately, the lady was later located, and the items removed from the grave were still in her possession. Author John Evangelist Walsh in his book *The Shadows Rise* identifies her as Margaret Richardson, a descendant of Jasper Rutledge, brother of McGrady

Rutledge. The articles in Ms. Richardson's possession are a small, acorn-shaped button covered by cloth, a bow four inches long made of yellow satin-like ribbon, a strip of black lace, and a lock of hair two inches long. Walsh photographed the items and published the picture in his book.[15] The items, it turns out, appeared a hundred years earlier in a similar photograph in a *Souvenir Album of Menard County* (Illinois) published in 1893, only three years after the exhumation. The items in the two photographs closely match, leaving little doubt as to their authenticity.

If the items currently in the possession of Ms. Richardson were held out of the reburial of Ann Rutledge in 1890, it would mean that only two bones and some pieces of rotted wood along with a small amount of soil from the original grave were interred in Petersburg Cemetery, leaving the rest of Ann Rutledge back in the Old Concord grave. Montgomery's effort hardly represents a reburial.

Whether the alleged love affair and betrothal of Ann Rutledge and Abraham Lincoln is a historical fact or simply the false reminiscences of fading memories, one thing seems certain: the removal of Ann Rutledge to the Petersburg Cemetery is a hoax. Two bones, part of a coffin, and a handful of soil hardly constitute Ann's remains. Even if soil conditions were such that most of the organic material decomposed over the fifty-five years of her internment, the attempt to recover the remains was insufficient.

Sam Montgomery's effort to relocate the remains of Ann Rutledge to Oakland Cemetery fell far short of his intentions. Perhaps he was satisfied to recover anything at all from the original grave, justifying his claim that he had relocated Ann to the Oakland Cemetery. Today, a large tombstone sits inside a small iron fence that surrounds the Petersburg grave. The stone bears the words of Edgar Lee Masters's beautiful poem paying tribute to Ann:

Out of me unworthy and unknown
The vibrations of deathless music!
"With malice toward none, with charity for all"
Out of me forgiveness of millions for millions,
And the beneficent face of a nation
Shining with justice and truth.

I am Ann Rutledge who sleep beneath these weeds,
Beloved of Abraham Lincoln,
Wedded to him, not through union,
But through separation.
Bloom forever, O Republic,
From the dust of my bosom!

Sam Montgomery certainly had no intention of deceiving the public with his attempt to relocate Ann's remains to Oakland. He was correct in claiming that her grave would be better cared for and more accessible to a curious public. But despite Montgomery's effort, it seems certain that whatever remains of Ann Rutledge, most of it still rests among her friends and neighbors in her original resting place in Old Concord Cemetery. If Abraham Lincoln still walks at midnight and visits with those of his past, it is in Old Concord, and not Petersburg, where he walks with Ann.

CHAPTER FIVE

WAS LINCOLN BAPTIZED?

The Religious Conversion of Abraham Lincoln

Mr. Lincoln had made all the necessary arrangements . . . to be received into the membership of said church, by confession of his faith in Christ, on Easter Sunday following the Friday night when Mr. Lincoln was assassinated.

—Mrs. Sidney I. Lauck, New York Avenue Presbyterian Church

Mariah, I've been baptized . . . the Reverend Elkins came in the night time and baptized me . . .

—Attributed to A. Lincoln, December 1860

O N MARCH 4, 1861, the Sunday following his inauguration as president, Lincoln attended services at the New York Avenue Presbyterian Church in Washington.[1] The church sits on a small triangular piece of land at the point where New York Avenue intersects H Street. It is an easy walk from the White House along New York Avenue to the church. Ever since Lincoln's presidency the church has been known as "The Lincoln Church." This is all the more impressive when one realizes that the church's history is rich with religious and political personalities. It is the church of Peter Marshal, one of the country's more famous theologians, immortalized in a bestselling book and film of the same name, *The Man Called Peter*. And it is the church that inspired the addition of the phrase "under God" to the Pledge of Allegiance in 1956. It has served as the church of several presidents, although none more famous than Abraham Lincoln.

Before coming to Washington, Lincoln had heard good things about the church's pastor, a scholarly theologian by the name of Phineas Gurley. Lincoln had pursued an intellectual interest in religion for much of his adult life, and while he never joined a church,

New York Avenue Presbyterian Church in Washington, D.C. (Author's collection)

he occasionally attended church as much for the sermons as for the liturgy. He was interested in hearing Gurley preach. Stories abound in the voluminous Lincoln literature dealing with his faith—or lack thereof, depending on the source. While religion has always had a place for Lincoln, there was a view among certain of his detractors that Lincoln did not have a place for religion, at least for Christianity.

Lyon G. Tyler, the son of President John Tyler, held a particular dislike for Lincoln. In a pamphlet published in 1928 entitled "Confederate Leaders and Other Citizens Request the [Virginia] House of Delegates to Repeal the Resolution of Respect to Abraham Lincoln, the Barbarian," Tyler nailed Lincoln to a bitter cross. He wrote: "Lincoln's apotheosis has been rightly described as 'the most amazing climbing vine in the garden of history.' Rhodes in his history shows Lincoln an infidel, if not an atheist. He nowhere ever professed the slightest faith in Jesus as the Son of God. He never told anyone that he accepted Jesus as the Christ."[2]

Tyler offers no proof to support his claims, but if we believe those closest to Lincoln, he was correct in claiming that Lincoln did not believe that Christ was the Son of God. Lincoln never openly

The Lincoln pew preserved in its original place in the New York Avenue
Presbyterian Church in Washington, D.C. (Author's collection)

professed such beliefs, but then, he was an extremely private person
when it came to such personal matters as religion.

Shortly after Lincoln's death, William Herndon began gathering
material for a biography he hoped to write about his beloved friend.
It was to be an honest biography that portrayed Lincoln in a truthful
light.

Herndon had compiled many notes in recording his own reminiscences of Lincoln. They were to provide the background for his
book. Among the notes that have survived is an essay dated August
21, 1887, entitled "Lincoln's Philosophy and Religion." In it Herndon
notes: "Lincoln did not believe that Jesus was God, nor a special
child of him. . . . Mr. Lincoln was a thoroughly religious man, not
a Christian, a broad, liberal-minded man, was a liberal, a free reli-
gionist, an infidel, and so died." Herndon's description of Lincoln
and his religious thoughts were received much like his claims about
Ann Rutledge being the only woman Lincoln ever loved. They were
viewed as disparaging to Lincoln's memory.[3] It appeared that the

country was not ready to read about the "true Lincoln" as revealed by Billy Herndon.

Another close friend and legal colleague, Ward Hill Lamon, supported Herndon in his views. Lamon wrote in his 1877 biography of Lincoln that he "never . . . let fall from his lips or pen an expression, which remotely implied the slightest faith in Jesus as the Son of God and the Savior of men." Lamon, like Herndon, felt the sting of Lincoln's closest supporters, who tried to suppress publication of their biographies. The two men became the focus of strong animosity borne by Robert Todd Lincoln and Mary Lincoln as well as those who felt that anything perceived as negative about Lincoln was desecration.[4]

In 1846, while running for Congress against the Methodist circuit rider Peter Cartwright, Lincoln had been publicly labeled a "scoffer of Christianity" and an "infidel."[5] Lincoln had to respond or risk losing the election. But typical of Lincoln's compulsion against deception, he answered his detractors with carefully chosen words. He explained his position on church membership and religion in a handbill published on July 31, 1846: "That I am not a member of any Christian church is true; but I have never denied the truth of the Scriptures; and I have never spoken with intentional disrespect of religion in general, or of any denomination of Christians in particular." He concluded his defense by writing: "I do not think I could myself be brought to support a man for office whom I knew to be an open enemy of, or scoffer at, religion. Leaving the higher matter of eternal consequences, between him and his Maker, I still do not think any man has the right thus to insult the feelings, and injure the morals, of the community in which he may live."[6] In answering his detractors, Lincoln chose not to profess his personal belief in Christianity, but rather to express tolerance for another man's beliefs.

The dilemma of Lincoln's religious beliefs for doctrinaire Christians is in the requirements of their faith. According to orthodox Christian belief, to enter the kingdom of heaven one must embrace the most fundamental tenets of the Christian church: acceptance of Jesus Christ as the son of God, of his virgin birth, and of his rising from the dead and ascension into heaven. To be a Christian one must confess his faith by joining the church, and seal his faith by baptism. The fundamental tenet of Christian faith is stated in the gospel of

St. John (14:6): "Jesus saith unto him, I am the way, the truth, and the life; no man cometh unto the Father, but by me."[7] Herein lay the rub. If Abraham Lincoln did not accept Christ as the Son of God, there could be no apotheosis, no ascension into heaven, no way unto the Father. This is unacceptable to many of Lincoln's devoted followers, especially his twentieth-century followers. If a person like Lincoln, who abided by the teachings of Christ in his personal life, was barred from entering heaven, there was little hope for millions of others.

For most of the nineteenth century the question of Lincoln's stand on orthodox Christian beliefs was avoided, or when written about, mischaracterized.[8] Lincoln was perceived to have been a good man, a man of compassion and great humanity—a man whose life reflected the teachings of Christ as evidenced in the words "With malice toward none; with charity for all."[9] His apotheosis went unchallenged save for Herndon and Lamon and a few postwar Confederates like Tyler who felt that if the South were ever to rise again it must do so at Lincoln's expense. As scholarship increased, however, and every aspect of Lincoln's early life and presidency came under intense study, the problem of his failure to formally affirm his belief in Christian doctrine became more problematic to some people. Even Lincoln's supporters began to wonder just what was it that Lincoln believed.

Lincoln's religious roots can be found in the Baptist religion practiced in Kentucky. He was born in a part of Kentucky that was still considered wild frontier and the heart of southern Baptism. His parents were practicing members of a Baptist denomination known as "Free Will Baptists." These Baptists took their doctrine literally from the Bible and did not believe in the administrative offices or accoutrements that normally arose among church congregations. They did not subscribe to missionary work, Sunday schools, or to financial associations with other churches, but believed that each individual was free to associate with the church based solely on the teachings of the Bible. The only sacraments of the church were those that Christ himself participated in; these were baptism, foot washing, and Holy Communion. And baptism was by total immersion, adhering to the practice of the early church. Members were "free" of all of the man-made church associations and interactions. This was the religious environment that surrounded Abraham Lincoln for the first twenty-one years of his life.

Perhaps the most important aspect of this early church was its policy on slavery. The year Lincoln was born, fifteen members of the local Baptist church near his birthplace in Kentucky walked out of the existing church because of their opposition to slavery. They organized a new church, which became known as the Little Mount Anti-Slavery Baptist Church. It was this church that Thomas Lincoln subscribed to as a member and in which he was baptized. This church was ministered by William Downs and David Elkins, two antislavery Baptist preachers whose views influenced Thomas Lincoln and later his son, Abraham. Fifty years later the Reverend David Elkins would figure prominently in the religious mythology surrounding President-elect Abraham Lincoln.

In 1816 Thomas Lincoln moved his family from Kentucky to the community known as Little Pigeon Creek in southern Indiana. Two years later Nancy Hanks Lincoln died of an illness known as the "milk sickness," caused by a neurological toxin found in the milk of cows that had eaten a wild plant known commonly as snakeroot.[10] Nancy Lincoln's death left the family in despair. The children became dirty and disheveled, and their home deteriorated into a hovel without the daily care of a mother. Leaving the young children to fend for themselves, Thomas Lincoln returned to Elizabethtown, Kentucky, and asked Sarah Bush Johnston to marry him. Sarah, a widow who had known Thomas for many years, agreed on the condition that Thomas pay off her debts. He agreed, and the two were married in Elizabethtown before heading to the Lincoln farm in Indiana. Sarah had three children from her first marriage and welcomed young Abraham and his sister as her own. She cleaned up the children and cabin and brought a loving spirit to young Lincoln at a critical period in his life.

Both Thomas Lincoln and Sarah joined the Little Pigeon Creek Baptist Church on June 7, 1823. Lincoln, then fourteen years old, did not join the church at that time, nor did he join during the next seven years that the family lived in Indiana. In fact, Abraham Lincoln never became a member of any denomination of organized religion throughout his entire life, although he was afforded ample opportunity. Interestingly, neither his father nor his stepmother forced religion on the young Lincoln, instead letting him find his own way.

ALMOST A HUNDRED YEARS AFTER HERNDON compiled his notes, Everett Dirkson, the senior senator from Lincoln's own state of Illinois, took up the cause of civil rights, proclaiming to his colleagues that it was the duty of every member of Congress to "get right with Lincoln." While true for politicians, this maxim was given a new twist by certain religious groups who sought to have Lincoln "get right with Christ." If Billy Herndon was right, Lincoln was not a Christian. He not only failed to join an established church, but he also never accepted Christ through baptism. No baptism, no apotheosis. Several individuals set out to correct this serious omission in Lincoln's life on behalf of their own churches. Lincoln would become a Christian whether he wanted to or not, and the first step would be his formal baptism.

In the early 1900s, a series of stories began to emerge claiming Lincoln had professed his desire to join a church and undergo baptism. There are common elements running through each of the stories of Lincoln's alleged conversion. First, the sacrament is always performed in secret during the time he is president-elect because Mary Lincoln would never approve of her husband joining a church other than her own. Second, Lincoln wants to avoid the spectacle that would surely attend the president-elect of the United States being dunked in a river. Third, no local minister can be trusted to keep such a secret; hence, the minister travels from a distant community. And fourth, there are no eyewitnesses. In each of the stories the minister arrives by train, and the two men travel to the banks of the Sangamon River, where the baptism takes place. The majority of these stories are easily dismissed because the internal evidence fails time and again.

Then, in 1995 an extraordinary historical chronicle appeared that caught the history community's and public's attention. The chronicle's title underscored its significance: *Lincoln's Unknown Private Life: An Oral History by His Black Housekeeper Mariah Vance, 1850–1860.* The book was a compilation of first-person accounts made by the woman who worked for the Lincoln family for the ten years leading up to Lincoln's election as president. It was not only an eyewitness account of the Lincoln family during the important pre-presidential months, but it covered many of the tantalizing personal subjects for which few facts are known. And, importantly, one of the editors was a well-known and respected member of the Lincoln community, Lloyd Ostendorf. It was truly history come alive.

The book was based on a series of interviews of Mariah Vance by a woman named Adah Sutton (1884–1972), who became a close friend of Vance in Vance's twilight years. Mrs. Vance (1819–1904) had worked as a maid for the Lincoln family part-time from 1850 until 1858 and then full-time until 1860. Years later while living in Danville, Illinois, she became acquainted with Adah Sutton, a seventeen-year-old girl. Sutton had moved to Danville from Attica, Indiana, in 1900 to take a position as a clerical worker in a shoe store. Sutton needed someone to do her laundry and found Mrs. Vance, who lived not far from her apartment. From 1900 until her death in 1904 at the age of eighty-one, Mariah Vance took in Sutton's laundry. The two women soon became good friends, spending their free hours chatting about life in general and the Lincoln family in particular. It was during these times together that Vance regaled Sutton with wonderful stories about "de Lincolumns." Realizing that Vance was an eyewitness to history, Sutton decided to begin writing down Vance's reminiscences. Sutton later transcribed her notes into a narrative that eventually became *Lincoln's Unknown Private Life*. In the book's preface, Sutton explains how she came to record Vance's stories: "Becoming so interested in Mrs. Vance's stories, I thought it would be nice to take these stories and incidents down, to tell them to my parents. She willingly repeated the ones she had already told, which I jotted down on any bit of paper available."

After Vance's death in 1904, Sutton set her bits of paper aside until the mid-1950s, when she became acquainted with Lloyd Ostendorf, a well-known Lincoln scholar and respected photograph historian. Ostendorf quickly realized the importance of Sutton's material and encouraged her to transpose her notes into a narrative of Vance's reminiscences. Sutton, having never written anything more than a letter, agreed to try. "I went over every note carefully. Many were badly worn, brittle, and writing so erased that they were not legible. First I pasted [the legible notes] on large sheets of paper. Rearranging as best I could in sequence and according to dates of historical facts which she [Mariah Vance] often mentioned."[11]

Reaching back over fifty years, Sutton began writing her manuscript. She attempted to simulate Mariah's dialect and even developed a small "dictionary" where Vance's word appears next to the English version. For instance, "babsized" was Vance's word for "baptized," "ribber" stood for "river," "de Lincolumns" was "the Lincolns," and so on. By the time Sutton finished, she had composed twenty-three separate stories, which became the chapters for the finished book. Ostendorf, lacking editorial expertise, solicited the help of Walter Oleksy. Oleksy had been a feature writer with the *Chicago Tribune* newspaper who turned to writing books. With Ostendorf providing his knowledge of Lincoln, Oleksy reworked Sutton's rough narrative into a finished product.

Among the many interesting incidents that form the chapters in *Lincoln's Unknown Private Life* is Mariah's tale of Lincoln's baptism, entitled "Mistah Abe's Secret Baptism at Night." In her introductory remarks to the chapter Sutton writes: "In my heart and mind I know, every story that Mariah Vance told was as true as there is a God in Heaven."[12] Sutton then quotes Vance as telling her, "He always wanted to be babsized."

Shortly after his election as president on November 6, 1860, Lincoln came to Mariah and asked, "Mariah, do you think it has helped save your soul to be baptized?" Mariah explained to Lincoln the importance of baptism since it was one thing that Christ had done. "He let John babsize him in de Ribber Jordan," Vance said. She was able to convince Lincoln of the necessity of being baptized. As the account goes, Lincoln confided in Mariah a few days after their discussion that he decided he was going to be baptized and that he would do it before leaving for Washington. Once again he sought her council: "Do you think it would be sinful if I was baptized and not let on to Missy Lincoln?" It seems that Mary Lincoln would in all probability not agree with her husband's ideas, or Mariah's, about baptism unless it could be done publicly and in her own church (the First Presbyterian Church of Springfield). Mary would settle for nothing less. Immersion in "de Ribber Jordan," or any "ribber" for that matter, was out of the question. Lincoln was also concerned about such a personal religious sacrament turning into a public spectacle. After all, Lincoln was the president-elect, and his every move was being scrutinized by the press of his day: "Gossips and sightseers would most likely come in mobs. Not to show reverence but to mock and

The Sangamon River near Springfield, Illinois, where Lincoln was allegedly baptized by immersion in December 1860 while president-elect. (Author's collection)

beguile my intentions. I don't like show of any kind, when it can be helped. I'd like to know just how to help it."[13]

It seems that Lincoln had promised his mother, Mariah said, "when a little tyke 'way back there in Indiani when he was old enough to know the meanings, he would be babsized." So once again Lincoln turned to Mariah for guidance, "Mariah, you've got a good head for planning. Just how can I be baptized so Mother [Mary Lincoln] won't be upset." Mariah had the answer: "Mistah Abe, you can think and think, but there's only just one way. You got to go at night."[14]

Lincoln was shocked, then sad. He walked away muttering, "God help us," only to return shortly and exclaim in a cheerful manner, "Mariah you saved the day for me. I'm not going to Washington without doing all I can to keep this one of Christ's commandments. I couldn't expect God to help me lead the nation so full of woes, if I failed him. I'll write to Parson [David] Elkins and have him come, if he will. Let's pray he will."[15]

David Elkins was a Baptist minister who was well connected to the Lincoln family. Years earlier, in Kentucky (1808–1816), Elkins had ministered to the Lincoln family at the Little Mount Baptist Church near Hodgenville. In 1816 Thomas Lincoln and his family migrated to Indiana, and two years later Nancy Lincoln died suddenly from the "milk sickness" and was buried without a Christian funeral. Legend persists that the nine-year-old Abraham wrote a letter to Elkins in Kentucky and asked if he would come to Indiana and perform a proper burial service for his mother. Shortly after receiving young Abe's letter, Elkins, during a planned trip to Indiana, visited the Lincolns and recited the funeral service over Nancy's grave. It left an impression on the young boy that would stay with him all his life.

Lincoln was able to overcome two major obstacles, thanks to Mariah's smart thinking. By holding the baptism at night it could be kept secret—Mary Lincoln and the public need never know. And by having Parson David Elkins perform the baptism there would be no need for a local minister who might "blab" about Lincoln's conversion. Elkins was an old and dear friend of the Lincolns and could be trusted to keep the secret.

According to Ostendorf and Oleksy, Lincoln witnessed the baptism of his stepmother, Sarah Bush Johnston Lincoln, in Little Pigeon Creek in Indiana.[16] It so impressed Lincoln that he was determined to undergo immersion at the hands of a Baptist minister in the Sangamon River. Lincoln's father, Thomas, had been baptized by immersion in Knob Creek while the family still lived in Kentucky. Following their removal to Indiana in 1816, Thomas and his second wife, Sarah, joined the Baptist church at Little Pigeon Creek. Thomas Lincoln's baptism along with his and Sarah's joining the church were described years later by Sarah Lincoln's granddaughter's husband, A. H. Chapman.[17] By having Elkins perform his baptism, Lincoln would keep faith with his mother, his stepmother, and his father. Elkins had moved to Indiana, where he continued his ministering as a Free Will Baptist. Now all Lincoln had to do was get Reverend Elkins to Springfield and then back home to Indiana without anyone finding out the purpose of his secret mission.

Sutton wrote that Mariah put her discussion with Lincoln completely out of her mind until one morning after she fixed "Mistah Abe" some breakfast of mush cakes and sorghum. Finishing his breakfast, Lincoln pushed away from the table, rocked back on the legs of his chair, and let fly, "Mariah, I've been baptised . . . the Reverend Elkins came in the night time and baptised me and went back in the night time." Mariah was thrilled. She wanted to know all the details. Lincoln described how the two men had walked through "persimmon scrub, hazel brush, and wild grape vine" before reaching the banks of the Sangamon. They entered the river together, and Lincoln was immersed. "The parson and I had a mighty sacred charge to keep, and deep inside of me I was praying. Now I really praise my Lord and my God I took the right step. You know, Mariah, many weeds have to be trampled to reach the right path."[18]

Later that same day, after Mariah prepared the noonday dinner, she went to the barn for the mule and cart, and there was "Mistah Abe's wet shoes, shirt, long underwear, and pants hanging up drying." The next time she visited the barn the clothes were gone, and two new sets were in the wash for her to clean, Mistah Abe's and Parson Elkins's.[19] Mariah sealed her lips, telling no one for the next thirty-five years, until she unsealed them for the young Adah Sutton, who brought soiled clothes to her for washing. Once told, however, she never told it again. Apparently Sutton was the only person who knew of Mariah Vance's incredible story.

After writing the story of Lincoln's baptism in the Sangamon River, Sutton had second thoughts about Parson Elkins's being the minister who performed the baptism, although she did not make a change in her original manuscript: "I've always thought, especially since I read somewhere that Elkins was the name of the minister who presided at (Lincoln's) mother's grave, that Mariah got the names mixed."[20] Why would Sutton think Vance "got the names mixed"? She accepted everything else Vance allegedly told to her.

Adah's misgivings stemmed from having read two other accounts of Lincoln's alleged baptism. Neither account named Elkins as the minister who performed the baptism. The first account appeared forty-eight years before Sutton's manuscript was published. It appeared in a book entitled *Maryland and Pennsylvania Historical Sketches,* published in 1947 by the Reverend Freeman Ankrum.[21] Ankrum, a Brethren minister (Disciples of Christ), wrote that when Lincoln was president, Daniel P. Sayler, an elder of the German Baptist Church (known as Dunkards) often visited him in the White House. Ankrum claimed that Lincoln was especially interested in the desolation surrounding the Dunkard Church at Antietam following that great battle in September 1862 because "While still in Spring-field, Illinois, Lincoln sent for a minister of the German Baptist church, commonly called 'Dunkards' and was baptised by him in the [Sangamon] river."[22]

Here was a second claim of Lincoln's baptism. Since Elkins was a Baptist minister, this story was at variance with the one originally written by Sutton on behalf of Mariah Vance. Ankrum does not identify the minister other than to write that he was "a minister of the German Baptist church." Nor does Ankrum claim that Sayler was the man who baptised Lincoln, only that they were good friends who visited in the White House. Unfortunately, Ankrum cites no authority for his statement that Lincoln was baptized.

The second account that Sutton mentions in her book is taken from a letter written to her in 1956 by Mrs. Anna Wagner Deal. Mrs. Deal wrote to Sutton that her father, David E. Wagner, told her in 1935 that an elder of the German Baptist church named Isaac Billheimer told him a story that had been told to Billheimer by a minister who claimed to have actually baptized Lincoln in 1860. El-der Billheimer had long ago forgotten the name of the minister but remembered the story:

> The minister who baptized Lincoln was a member of the German Bap-tist Church. Lincoln sent this minister word to come to Springfield on a certain train, which arrived there after night. (Lincoln had sent him twice as much money as he needed.)
>
> Lincoln met him and they went to the river where Lincoln was baptized, yet that night. Lincoln had brought extra clothes needed for both, and having changed clothes they went and waited for the train to arrive, and the minister left after midnight. Lincoln promised that after his term of office expired he would conform to the church.[23]

Mrs. Deal's account of her father's story bears a resemblance to Rev-erend Ankrum's story. However, a new element is added. The minis-ter travels to and from Springfield by train the same night. The min-ister arrives after nightfall and leaves after midnight. As in Ankrum's account, the minister's name is forgotten—but not for long. Further light was cast on the identity of this minister through the efforts of one of the editors of the Sutton manuscript. Lloyd Ostendorf did his own investigating into Lincoln's alleged baptism and published parts of a letter he had received from a minister of the East Dayton Church of the Brethren in Dayton, Ohio. The minister of this church, the Reverend Calvin Bright, knew of the story and was able to identify the unknown minister who baptized Lincoln. He told Ostendorf he had heard the story from another church elder, Albert Harshbarger, who learned as a young boy about Lincoln's secret baptism: "Harshbarger claimed that it was Bishop Daniel P. Sayler [of Carroll and Frederick counties, Maryland] who actually performed the baptism, and though it was supposed to be kept secret, he told certain people in the town of Cerro Gordo where he changed trains on his trip back home to Indiana."[24]

Two new elements are introduced by Harshbarger's story: the name of the minister (Bishop Daniel P. Sayler) and the fact that the minister changed trains in Cerro Gordo, where he told several fellow Brethren that he had baptized the president-elect of the United States. The minister identified in this story is the same Daniel P. Sayler who visited Lincoln in the White House, mentioned earlier by Ankrum.

Reverend Bright went on to write in his letter: "No written record was made of the baptism, not only because it was to be kept secret, but because the baptized person was not to become a member of a local meetinghouse congregation, therefore his name would not have been recorded in their records. Thus, it remained an oral tradition."[25]

There is yet another account of Lincoln's baptism, which appeared in a publication titled *Christian Evangelist* in 1942. This account is not mentioned in *Lincoln's Unknown Private Life*. It tells of a man named G. M. Weimer, a member of the Disciples of Christ, who told of an interview he had with John O'Kane, a minister of the Disciples of Christ. In this interview Weimer quotes O'Kane as saying: "Yes, Brother Weimer, I know all about the affair [secret baptism]. On the night before Lincoln was baptized his wife cried all night. So the matter was deferred as she thought. But soon after, Lincoln and I took extra clothing and took a buggy ride. I baptized him in a creek near Springfield, Illinois. We changed to dry clothing and returned to the city, and by his request I placed his name on the church book. He lived and died a member of the Church of Christ."[26]

The story told by Weimer of John O'Kane's baptizing Lincoln bears a striking similarity to Sutton's reconstructed tale. One new

Reverend John O'Kane, who it was claimed baptized Lincoln in the Sangamon River on a cold December evening in a secret ceremony. (Author's collection)

feature is O'Kane's reference to a "buggy ride." O'Kane does not explain how he arrived in or left Springfield. We know from Sutton's account that the minister arrived by train at night and left by train the same night, albeit early morning—"after midnight." At this point we are left with three ministers who are alleged to have baptized Lincoln: David Elkins (Baptist), John O'Kane (Church of Christ), and Daniel Sayler (Dunkard).

There are common threads running through all of the stories of Lincoln's baptism. The baptism occurs in the winter of 1860, just before Lincoln leaves for Washington; it is kept secret; it takes place at night; it involves total immersion in the Sangamon River; Lincoln selects the minister; and the minister arrives and returns home by train all in the same night. While all the participants vow to keep the sacrament secret, they eventually break their vow.

In sorting out these tales of Lincoln's secret baptism, let us begin with David Elkins. According to Sutton, Vance claimed it was Elkins who baptized Lincoln. The time of the baptism, December 1860, saw Springfield temperatures average near freezing for the entire period. Orville Hickman Browning, a close political friend of Lincoln and wartime senator from Illinois, made several entries in his diary for the month of December noting weather conditions for the region encompassing Springfield. During the month it snowed on eight days, and Browning describes five days as "hard frozen."[27] The Sangamon was frozen with ice part of that time. During the same period, Thomas D. Jones, a sculptor who traveled from Cincinnati to Springfield on Christmas Eve, 1860, to begin sculpting a bust of Lincoln, wrote in a letter dated December 25, "It was the first time I ever beheld a real Prairie, and even in winter, covered with snow, it is a rare scene."[28] Central Illinois was experiencing a typical winter of freezing temperatures and snow. Wading into the Sangamon River would test the faith of the most devout Christian, let alone a man like David Elkins, who would have been in his eighty-first year—had he been alive at the time. Born in 1779, Elkins died in 1857, mercifully avoiding a winter dunking in the freezing Sangamon in 1860. Elkins is buried in a small cemetery southwest of Bedford, Indiana, in a grave now marked with a stone provided by the citizens of Mitchell, Indiana.[29] The 1850 census for Lawrence County, Indiana, lists David Elkins, age seventy-one, a Baptist minister, and his wife, Elizabeth, age sixty-nine, living in Marion Township, Indiana. Neither Elkins nor his wife appear in the 1860 census.

It is not clear whether Adah Sutton or the editors of *Lincoln's Unknown Private Life* were aware that Elkins died in 1857. In any event, his death did not deter the story of Lincoln's baptism since other ministers, like Daniel P. Sayler and John O'Kane, were ready to step in and fulfill Lincoln's desire to undergo the sacrament of baptism. O'Kane claimed that following Lincoln's baptism, "I placed his name on the church book. He [Lincoln] lived and died a member of the Church of Christ."[30] Lincoln's name does not appear "on the church book" of the Church of Christ in Springfield, and neither does John O'Kane's, for that matter.[31] At the time of Lincoln's alleged baptism, O'Kane was not a resident of Springfield but was living in Indiana and ministering in the counties of Rush, Fayette, Union, and Wayne.[32] While Lincoln was acquainted with the Disciples of Christ church in Springfield, there is no evidence to support O'Kane's claim that he either baptized Lincoln in Springfield or that he entered Lincoln's name on the church record in that city. There are other problems with Weimer's story claiming O'Kane baptized Lincoln.

A few months after Weimer's story was published in the *Christian Evangelist*, he wrote a letter to a friend in which he describes the circumstances of his meeting with O'Kane and of hearing O'Kane's story of Lincoln's baptism. Weimer wrote that he was living in Eureka, Illinois, at the time of his meeting with O'Kane so that his two sons could attend college there. According to Weimer, O'Kane stayed with the Weimer family during a state church convention in Eureka, and it was during this visit that he told Weimer about his having baptized Lincoln. Weimer describes what O'Kane told him:

> I am going to tell you folks all about the matter. I have kept it in my own memory because when he [Lincoln] first had me to arrange to baptize him, his wife assumed a bitter resentment—that it would ruin their social status. So it was postponed for a while (10 days) till the "storm" was over. Then he and I took a buggy ride one day with a change of clothing under the seat. I then baptized him in a small river near Springfield, Ill. Of course, he became a member of the Church of Christ. But I have kept it a secret as far as humans are concerned on account of his home condition.[33]

Weimer gives his age in his letter, dated 1942, as "almost 86 years of age." This would place his birthdate in 1857. John O'Kane died January 5, 1881, which would mean Weimer would have been twenty-four years old at the time of O'Kane's death. Remember that Weimer claimed he had two sons attending college at the time of O'Kane's visit, which would be impossible. There were four state conventions held in Eureka, Illinois, between 1860 and the date of O'Kane's death in 1881: 1866, 1874, 1876, and 1878.[34] Weimer's age would have been nine, seventeen, nineteen, and twenty-one respectively. This raises serious questions about Weimer's statement that he lived in Eureka at the time of O'Kane's visit. Weimer's move to Eureka occurred several years after O'Kane's death, and O'Kane could not have visited Weimer in Eureka.[35] These inconsistencies cast further doubt on Weimer's story.

There are similar difficulties with all of the other stories of Lincoln's baptism. An important element in each of the stories has the minister traveling round-trip from Indiana to Springfield all on the same night. In the account of Sayler's alleged baptism of Lincoln, he changed trains in Cerro Gordo on his way back to his home in Fairview, Indiana. To travel from Indianapolis to Springfield in 1860 required traveling on three different railroads: the Lafayette and Indianapolis, the Toledo and Wabash, and the Great Western.[36] Anyone traveling between Indianapolis and Springfield would have to use these three railroads and transfer twice, but not at Cerro Gordo. Cerro Gordo did not become a transfer point until several years after Lincoln's death.

Rail connections are not the only problem in attempting to verify these stories. According to all accounts, the entire episode occurred the same night, with the minister leaving sometime after midnight. According to the version recounted by Sutton, the two men walked the entire distance to and from the river and, if Lincoln is to be believed, walked cross-country through fields. According to Sutton's account, Lincoln told Mariah:

> We didn't go the regular cow path, just waded through persimmon scrub, hazel brush, and wild grapevine. I knew if that parson felt as I did, he was as glad to get in that river [the Sangamon] as I.
>
> Now Mariah, I don't mean I wasn't pondering and considering, but I swear the needles were thicker on us than dog fleas on Rover. . . . You know, Mariah, many weeds have to be trampled to reach the right path.[37]

The distance from the Great Western depot to the closest point on the Sangamon River was four and a quarter miles. Under the best of conditions the shortest route to the river would have taken over two hours to walk in each direction. Walking across farm fields through wild grapevine, persimmon scrub, hazel brush, and farm fences would add to the time required. If we allow for time to wade into the river, perform the baptism, and change into dry clothes, a minimum of five hours is not unreasonable to accomplish the baptism. Was there enough time for the minister to arrive "after night" and leave the same night?

In 1860 only one weekday train departed at night from Springfield heading east to Indiana. This occurred at 9:44 P.M. Since no train is listed as arriving in Springfield on Sunday, it can be assumed that the minister traveled on a weekday and would have taken the 9:44 P.M. train back to Indiana. Clearly, Anna Wagner Deal's statement that "the minister left after midnight" is in error.

If we allow five hours to carry out the baptism, the latest arrival time in Springfield would have to be at 4:45 P.M. to allow time for the minister to catch the 9:44 P.M. train back to Indiana. Was there a train arriving in Springfield from Indiana before 4:45 P.M.? According to a train schedule published in the *Danville Republican* newspaper for 1860, there were two daily trains departing Danville for Springfield, one at 11:12 A.M. and one at 9:50 P.M.[38] The 11:12 A.M. train out of Danville arrived in Springfield at approximately 5:00 P.M. This arrival time barely fits the minimum time necessary to carry out Lincoln's baptism under the best of conditions; it requires a precision that leaves no room for error. More importantly, it is at variance with an arrival "after night" and a departure "after midnight."

Stories of Lincoln's secret baptism persist in the literature today. In a recent issue of the *Louisiana Lincolnator*, a newsletter of the Louisiana Lincoln Group, Walter Oleksy defends the story of Lincoln's baptism in an article entitled "Was Abraham Lincoln a Christian?" In his article Oleksy repeats the claim that Lincoln was baptized and cites the Mariah Vance story in *Lincoln's Unknown Private Life* as proof of his baptism. Oleksy, however, dismisses David Elkins as the minister who baptized Lincoln, concluding that it was Daniel P. Sayler.

It has often been said, "The devil is in the details." In the story of Lincoln's secret baptism such details include a dead minister, a frozen river, a train connection that did not exist, and too many ministers with their hands in the water. It is important to realize that none of the people who are credited with baptizing Lincoln ever made such a claim on their own behalf. Adah Sutton told the alleged memoir of Mariah Vance. G. M. Weimer told John O'Kane's story. Elder Albert Harshbarger (as repeated by the Reverend Calvin Bright) told Bishop Sayler's story. All three accounts of Lincoln's baptism contain too many errors to make them believable. But more importantly, those closest to Lincoln, including his wife, deny that Lincoln ever joined a church, let alone submitted to baptism. The story of Lincoln's baptism as allegedly told by Mariah Vance to Adah Sutton is not the only story in *Lincoln's Unknown Private Life* that crumbles under scrutiny. The book contains twenty-three chapters, each one allegedly based on Mariah Vance's oral recollections of the "Lincolumns" as recorded by Adah Sutton, and like the tale of Lincoln's secret baptism, they fail under close examination.[39]

What can we make of all of these claims of Lincoln's baptism? For the one hundred years following Lincoln's tragic death in 1865 there has been an effort by some of Lincoln's most devout supporters to "Christianize" him.[40] Unable to do it in life, it became easier to do it in death. Interestingly, none seemed to be concerned about what Lincoln really believed and how those beliefs served him in dealing with the nation's greatest crisis. Whatever Lincoln's religious beliefs were, or were not, there is no evidence to support his conversion and subsequent baptism.

CHAPTER SIX

THE MOLE IN THE WHITE HOUSE
Mary Todd Lincoln

It is untrue that any of my family holds treasonable communication with
the enemy.

—Attributed to Abraham Lincoln

THE YEAR 1862 ENDED in yet another crushing defeat for Union
forces. On December 13, Major General Ambrose P. Burnside
hurled the full strength of the Army of the Potomac against Robert
E. Lee's entrenched veterans occupying a ridge overlooking the city
of Fredericksburg. Wave after wave of Union troops bravely clawed
their way up the heights, only to be cut down by a withering fire
from the Confederate soldiers safely entrenched behind a stone wall.
It was out of character for most Union army commanders to show
such aggression in battle, misplaced as it was. Having served under
George B. McClellan not once, but twice, this army had been led
with timidity and caution, not forced into suicidal charges. When
the fighting ended, Union forces had suffered nearly thirteen thousand casualties as a result of inept leadership. Burnside withdrew his
battered forces back across the Rappahannock River and hunkered
down, not quite ready to admit defeat.

In Washington, Congress was becoming increasingly dissatisfied
with the war's progress. A committee of three senators and four congressmen sat in judgement of the military leaders and of the administration. The committee, called the Joint Committee on the Conduct
of the War, had been established a year earlier on December 10, 1861.
Its task was "to inquire into the conduct of the present war."[1] Un-
happy with the way the war was being waged, Congress had decided
to take a hand in its operation. Chairing the committee was Senator

Benjamin F. Wade of Ohio, a leader of the Radical Republicans and a thorn in the president's side.

Wade represented the wing of the Republican Party that felt the war was progressing much too slowly and the fault was Lincoln's. Lincoln lacked the "will and purpose" to force the military to act.[2] The committee had no direct power to require the president or the military to do its bidding, but it was influential nonetheless. Its members felt that Lincoln had appointed too many inept generals and not enough of the generals the Radicals wanted him to appoint. Lincoln was well aware of his problem with inept generals, but the pickings were slim and he needed these "War Democrats," such as Major General Benjamin Butler and Major General Nathaniel Preston Banks, in his corner. They brought not only political clout but also thousands of badly needed troops so necessary to continue the fight to restore the Union.

While there were times when Lincoln was the target of the committee's displeasure, the attacks were never personal. However, rumors began to filter throughout the political back rooms of the city that there was a Southern spy in the White House "giving important information to secret agents of the Confederacy."[3] The Southern spy was none other than the president's wife, Mary Todd Lincoln.

Slanderous accusations against Mary Lincoln began the day she entered the White House and continued through the fours years and five weeks she and her husband were its occupants. Her mail became so spiteful and offensive that William Stoddard, an assistant secretary to the president, was given the official task of screening both the president's and her mail. Stoddard was especially upset at the vicious attacks leveled at her.[4]

That Mary Lincoln had Confederate sympathies was believable. Like her husband, she was born in Kentucky, a Southern slave state, and also like her husband, she had relatives serving in the Confederate army.[5] While Lincoln's Confederate "connections" were distant relatives several generations removed who had never met the president, Mary's connections were close to home—very close. Her brother George Rogers Clark Todd served as a surgeon in the Confederate army. Three of her half-brothers, Alexander, David, and Samuel, served in the Confederate infantry, and her two brothers-in-

Mary Todd Lincoln, from an original carte de visite.
(Photograph by Mathew B. Brady, ca. 1861; author's
collection)

Opposite Page Top Left: Emilie Todd Helm, Mary Lincoln's younger stepsister.
Emilie was the wife of Confederate general Ben Hardin Helm. In December
1863, following Helm's death, Lincoln invited Emilie to spend several months
with her sister in the White House. Despite Lincoln's graciousness, Emilie
remained bitter toward him, writing in 1864, "Your minie bullets have made
us what we are." (Courtesy of Lloyd Ostendorf)   *Opposite Page Top Right:*
Confederate general Ben Hardin Helm while a cadet at West Point. Helm
was killed at the battle of Chickamauga on September 20, 1863. (Courtesy
of the Katharine Helm Collection, Filson Historical Society, Louisville,
Kentucky)   *Opposite Page Lower Left:* Alexander H. Todd, aide-de-camp to

Ben Hardin Helm and Mary Lincoln's youngest stepbrother. Todd was killed at Baton Rouge in August 1863. (Courtesy of the Katharine Helm Collection, Filson Historical Society, Louisville, Kentucky)   *Lower Right:* Captain David Todd, Mary Lincoln's stepbrother. Todd served for a time as warden of Libby Prison in Richmond, where prisoners later told of his brutality to Union prisoners of war. (Courtesy of the Katharine Helm Collection, Filson Historical Society, Louisville, Kentucky)

law Ben Hardin Helm and N. H. R. Dawson were Confederate officers. Helm, a West Point graduate and brigadier general, was married to Mary's favorite stepsister, the beautiful Emilie Todd. Helm was killed at the battle of Chickamauga in 1863. Sam Todd died at Shiloh in Tennessee, and Aleck Todd died at Baton Rouge in Louisiana. Mary's family paid a heavy toll for its convictions.

In December 1863, three months after her husband's death, Emilie came to the White House at Mary's (and Lincoln's) invitation. The two stepsisters, once gay and lighthearted, had been deeply scarred by death: Emilie's husband, and Mary's young son Willie. Emilie was especially embittered, and although Lincoln had welcomed her to the White House and provided her with safe conduct through Union lines and a letter allowing her to recover cotton she claimed to own, she showed no signs of gratitude. Returning to Lexington, Kentucky, Emilie wrote an unforgiving letter to Lincoln asking him to grant her a license to sell six hundred bales of cotton. Lincoln would readily grant her request, provided she complied with the requirement all such persons met, taking an oath of allegiance to the Constitution and the Union. Emilie refused, believing such an oath would be a sacrilege on her dead husband's honor. She ended her letter to Lincoln writing, "I remind you that your minie bullets have made us what we are."[6] It was the last communication between Emilie and her brother-in-law and stepsister.

The wife of a rebel general staying in the White House under the protection of the president confirmed the suspicions of Lincoln's enemies that his wife was sympathetic to the Confederate cause. Others went even further, whispering that she was actually passing military information to Confederate agents milling about Washington.[7]

Rumors continued to grow against the president's wife. Carl Sandburg wrote of the unprecedented event that followed: "The talk of a Southern spy in the White House arrived at the point where Senate members of the Committee on the Conduct of the War arranged a secret session for discussing reports that Mrs. Lincoln was a disloyalist."[8] Margaret Leech, whose book *Reveille in Washington, 1860–1865* remains among the essential works required for understanding Civil War Washington, wrote: "Reports of Mary Lincoln's treason were persistent enough to cause Senate members of the Committee on the Conduct of the War to gather in secret session to consider them."[9]

The committee was about to open its investigation into the question of the First Lady's disloyalty when suddenly "the officer stationed at the committee room door came in with a half-frightened expression on his face. Before he had an opportunity to make [an] explanation, we understood the reason for his excitement, and were ourselves almost overwhelmed with astonishment. For at the foot of the Committee table, standing solitary, his hat in his hand, his tall form towering above the committee members, Abraham Lincoln stood."[10]

It was an unprecedented event, a tense moment for everyone including the president. As the committee members sat in stunned silence, Lincoln spoke: "I, Abraham Lincoln, President of the United States appear of my own volition before this committee of the Senate to say that I, of my own knowledge, know that it is untrue that any of my family holds treasonable communication with the enemy." Lincoln paused, then turned and left the hearing room. The members of the committee sat in stunned silence, "Then by tacit agreement, no word being spoken, the committee dropped all consideration of the rumors that the wife of the President was betraying the union. . . . We were so greatly affected that the committee adjourned for the day."[11]

If Sandburg and Leech preserved the story of Lincoln's appearance before the committee, Lowell Weicker, a Republican senator from Connecticut, elevated it to national prominence. In July 1973, one year after the break-in of the Democratic National Committee headquarters in the Watergate building, Weicker read Carl Sandburg's account of Lincoln's appearance before the committee into the Watergate proceedings and before a national television audience.[12] It was Weicker's purpose to show the country and the current president, Richard M. Nixon, that Lincoln had set a precedent for presidents by willingly testifying before a congressional committee, one that was investigating his wife's alleged treason in the White House. President Nixon ignored Weicker's ploy, but the senator had made his point. After all, Lincoln was the first Republican president. Surely President Nixon, also a Republican, could follow his example.

Where does the dramatic story of Lincoln's appearance before the joint committee come from? The story first appeared in 1905 in an article in a Washington, D.C., newspaper written by E. J. Edwards.[13]

Thomas L. James, postmaster general in the Garfield administration. James appears to be the source of the story that Lincoln appeared before the joint committee in defense of his wife. (Courtesy of the Lincoln Museum, Fort Wayne, Indiana)

Edwards, it turns out, gave permission to a Lincoln admirer and collector, Gilbert A. Tracy, to republish his article as a pamphlet in 1916.[14] Edwards attributed the story to Thomas L. James, postmaster general in James Garfield's administration. According to Edwards's account, one of the members of the Senate Committee on the Conduct of the War told the story to James (the committee was actually a joint committee of the House and Senate and had members from both bodies). James, in turn, told the story to Edwards.

The description of Lincoln's appearance before the committee as told to Edwards is worth repeating: "The pathos that was written upon Lincoln's face, the almost unhuman sadness that was in his eyes as he looked upon us, and above all an indescribable sense of his complete isolation—the sad solitude which is inherent in all true grandeur of character and intellect—all this revealed Lincoln to me and I think to every member of the committee in the finer, subtler light whose illumination faintly set forth the fundamental nature of this man."[15]

It seems reasonable to assume that Edwards, Sandburg, Leech, and Weicker believed the story to be true. As Mark Neely, a professor of history at Penn State University and winner of the Pulitzer Prize in history, observes in his 1975 article about the myth, Weicker elevated the story from relative obscurity to a moral precedent pointed directly at President Nixon.[16] Perhaps the most widely seen and heard version of the episode occurred on NBC's six-hour series titled *Sandburg's Lincoln,* adapted from Carl Sandburg's six-volume Lincoln biography. The show was a considerable success. In part 3, titled "Mrs. Lincoln's Husband," John Hay, Lincoln's private secretary, alerts the president that the Joint Committee on the Conduct of the War is holding an afternoon session to investigate his wife. Lincoln walks in on the secret meeting, taking the members by surprise. Lincoln stands before the committee and says: "I would like to give testimony gentlemen." When one of the members begins to tell Lincoln the purpose of the committee, Lincoln cuts him off by saying, "I am aware of the purpose of this committee. I am here to assist you." Then Lincoln says, "It is untrue that any of my family holds treasonable communication with the enemy. I know that of my own knowledge."[17] Sandburg's influence continues to hang heavy over the image Americans have of Lincoln.

With all the problems Lincoln faced during his presidency, defending his own wife against charges of treason must have fallen heavily on his shoulders. Lincoln, it seems, could find no respite from scurrilous attacks even from members of his own party. The story of his surprise visit before the committee and its embarrassment leading to its dissolution is another of the wonderful stories that seem to follow Lincoln wherever he goes. The story, however, is untrue. It never happened.

The first point in evaluating this story is to remember that the committee was a joint committee of the House and Senate. Edwards writes that "a member of the Senate committee" told the story to James. It was not a Senate committee. While Sandburg quotes heavily from Edwards's article, he gets around this sticky point by writing

"Senate members of the committee."[18] The second point is that Edwards writes that James heard the story during his tenure as postmaster general under Garfield. Six senators served on the committee: Benjamin F. Wade, Zachariah Chandler, Andrew Johnson, Joseph A. Wright, Benjamin F. Harding, and Charles R. Buckalew. By 1881, when James was postmaster general, four of the six were dead. Wade died in 1878, Chandler in 1879, Johnson in 1875, and Wright in 1867. That leaves Harding and Buckalew as the only possible sources of the story. Both died in 1899. Harding, a Republican, left the Senate at the end of his term in 1862 and returned to his home state of Oregon. He never served again in any national office, and as far as we know never returned to Washington. The remaining senator, Charles Buckalew, a Democrat, served only one term and returned to his home state of Pennsylvania.[19]

Neely points out that the committee did not need a quorum to meet, and all of its sessions were held in secret. The Republican senators could meet secretly without the Democratic members (Johnson and Buckalew), as Neely believes they would have in investigating so delicate a matter as treason in the White House: "It seems very doubtful indeed that Republicans would have invited Buckalew to be present at a meeting discussing rumors which, if true, would have doomed the Republican administration and probably destroyed the party."[20] If Harding, the only Republican senator still alive in 1881, were the source of the story, he would have had to travel to Washington or James would have had to travel to Oregon, both unlikely. Both Buckalew and Harding had been out of office for at least fifteen years at the time of the alleged story telling, making them improbable candidates as the source of the story.

Like so many myths, Lincoln's appearance before the Joint Committee cannot be traced to its origin. Edwards was the first to publish the story, but Edwards claimed he heard it from James, who claimed to have heard it from a "member of the Senate committee on the conduct of the war" while serving in Garfield's cabinet. James may have been an innocent conduit, having heard the story from someone else that served in Congress during Lincoln's administration. As of this writing, however, the myth remains an orphan, but an interesting one. Lincoln never appeared before the committee.

CHAPTER SEVEN

YOU CAN FOOL ALL OF THE PEOPLE SOME OF THE TIME . . .

Lincoln Never Said That

IT SEEMS THERE IS NO PHASE of Abraham Lincoln's life or death that has not been written about in detail. The subject matter runs from his eating habits to his sex life.[1] There are books devoted to his personal finances, psychological state of mind, portrayal in the movies, and even his favorite jokes.[2] The area that has attracted the most attention by scholars over the years deals with Lincoln's words, both written and spoken. Entire works have been written on Lincoln's Gettysburg Address, a speech consisting of only 272 words that lasted all of three minutes.[3] Other writings by Lincoln have been singled out for high praise, including his speech at the Cooper Union in New York City, which Lincoln later said made him president.[4] His letter of condolence to the widow Bixby has been immortalized both in print and in film,[5] while his second inaugural is considered by one scholar as his "greatest speech."[6]

Lincoln's mastery of words is unequaled among American presidents, or world statesmen for that matter. While generalizations are often misleading, it can be said with confidence that Lincoln ranks among the most quoted individuals in history, with the possible exception of William Shakespeare. It can also be said with reasonable assurance that Lincoln is the most *misquoted* individual in history. The plethora of quotations attributed to Lincoln is a measure of his stature throughout the western world.

How can we be sure which words attributed to Lincoln are authentic and which are not? For written documents our only concern is whether or not the documents are authentic. For speeches and other pronouncements we judge the source and look for independent corroboration. In recalling the words of Lincoln, some auditors have greater credibility than others. Judging credibility is subjective at best, and in the absence of proof we can only establish probability rather than certainty.

Fortunately, there are two excellent sources on which we can rely. The first is the work of Roy P. Basler, who undertook the task of collecting, and verifying, all of the known writings and utterances of Lincoln. The result is an eight-volume work titled *The Collected Works of Abraham Lincoln,* published by the Rutgers University Press.[7] The second is a study by a husband and wife team, Don and Virginia Fehrenbacher, titled *The Recollected Words of Abraham Lincoln.*[8] The Fehrenbachers sifted through several hundred statements by individuals whose only requisite was having recorded a reminiscence of having heard Lincoln. From William A. Aiken to Charles S. Zane, the Fehrenbachers selected quotations traceable to known individuals who claimed to have heard the words directly from Lincoln. Interestingly, the Fehrenbachers did not include only those statements attributed to Lincoln that could be substantiated with certainty, but also statements for which there was little or no proof that Lincoln ever said them. The Fehrenbachers established five categories of Lincoln quotations. In evaluating a quotation, they assigned a letter grade (A, B, C, D, and E) reflecting their opinion on the reliability of the quotation coming from Lincoln. A, for example, is "a quotation cast in direct discourse and recorded contemporaneously," while E is "a quotation that is probably not authentic."[9]

This last category (E) is of interest to this chapter. Why did the Fehrenbachers include the more dubious quotations instead of simply omitting them? "Because," the Fehrenbachers write, "the legendary Lincoln, created in part out of dubious recollected material, may have been in the long run, as powerful an influence in American life as the historical Lincoln."[10] That so much has been attributed to Lincoln is a testament to the stature of Lincoln in our culture.

While the Fehrenbacher's *Recollected Words* serves as a reference for many of the quotations attributed to Lincoln, there are hundreds more that are not included in their book. Many of these can be found in two other publications devoted to Lincoln quotations: *The Lincoln Encyclopedia* by Archer H. Shaw, and *The Lincoln Treasury* by Caroline Thomas Harnsberger.[11] The difficulty with relying on these latter two compilations is that they contain forgeries and must be used with caution.

Lincoln's relationship with the natural world during his formative years in Kentucky and Indiana provided him with a reservoir of examples to draw on in his speeches and writings. His imagery was filled with metaphors and similes. He rivaled Aesop in the telling of parables, a favorite method for getting his point across. Even when it seemed he was joking, his words more often than not were meant to make his position clear. There are those who, knowing the powerful attraction of Lincoln, borrow him as a spokesman for their cause or to shore up their beliefs. At the Republican National Convention in 1992, former president Ronald Reagan recited from a list of quotations he attributed to Lincoln known as his "Ten Points," or "The American Charter." Reagan read them as if they were the Republican creed originated by the party's first president.

The American Charter
1. You cannot bring about prosperity by discouraging thrift.
2. You cannot strengthen the weak by weakening the strong.
3. You cannot help small men by tearing down big men.
4. You cannot help the poor by destroying the rich.
5. You cannot lift the wage-earner by pulling down the wage-payer.
6. You cannot keep out of trouble by spending more than your income.
7. You cannot further the brotherhood of man by inciting class hatred.
8. You cannot establish sound security on borrowed money.
9. You cannot build character and courage by taking away a man's initiative.
10. You cannot really help men by having the government tax them to do for them what they can and should do for themselves.[12]

While some of the ten points have a Lincoln-like ring to them, they are not Lincoln's words. They were the creation of the Reverend William J. H. Boetcker. Born in Germany in 1873, Boetcker immigrated to the United States in 1891. He was ordained a Presbyterian minister in 1897 and began his ministry in Brooklyn, New York. In 1903, Boetcker moved to Toledo, Ohio, where he became the director of an antistrike organization known as "The Citizens' Industrial Alliance," a position he held at the time he composed his "American Charter." Boetcker never claimed Lincoln composed the ten points, but he did pair them with Lincoln. In 1916, he published a leaflet entitled "Lincoln on Private Property." In it he placed Lincoln's words on one side and his own ten points on the reverse. At some point, the reprinting of the ten points resulted in dropping Boetcker's name, leaving the reader to conclude the ten points were Lincoln's. Even when it became generally known that Boetcker wrote them, some people still chose to attribute them to Lincoln.

Carl Sandburg, the author who more than any other writer introduced Lincoln to the public, wrote: "On the afternoon of September 8th at Clinton [Illinois], Lincoln told the people, 'You can fool all of the people some of the time, and some of the people all of the time, but you cannot fool all of the people all of the time.'"[13] The quotation has become one of the favorites attributed to Lincoln. It has a singsong cadence that one finds in many of Lincoln's statements, and it sounds like something Lincoln would say. But did he?

John Nicolay and John Hay, Lincoln's two secretaries, made an early attempt to gather and publish Lincoln's papers and speeches. Their effort resulted in a ten-volume series published in 1894. Nicolay and Hay include Lincoln's speech delivered at Clinton, Illinois (which they misdate as occurring on September 8, 1858; it actually occurred on September 2), and raise the question of the famous epigram in a footnote. They write that the "question remains unsettled as to Lincoln's having made the remarks during his speech." Their source for the text of the speech is the *Bloomington Pantograph* newspaper, which they point out did not include the famous quotation.[14]

The Fehrenbachers, in preparing *Recollected Words,* were unable to find the origin of the epigram in any contemporary accounts. They write that during the centennial celebration of Lincoln's birth in 1909, two acquaintances of Lincoln, William P. Kellogg and Richard P. Morgan, independently claimed to have heard Lincoln use the quotation in a speech at Bloomington, Illinois, in 1856, two years before the Clinton speech.[15] The Fehrenbachers point out that the quotation had already appeared prior to 1909 in a book by Alexander K. McClure titled *Lincoln's Yarns and Stories.*[16] McClure wrote that Lincoln made the remark to an anonymous caller at the White House. Including the famous epigram in their book, the Fehrenbachers assign it a "D," "a quotation about whose authenticity there is more than average doubt."[17]

The best overall discussion of the evidence both for and against Lincoln's being the originator of the famous epigram is in an article by Thomas F. Schwartz, secretary of the Abraham Lincoln Association, in its newsletter, *For the People*.[18] Schwartz ends his article by pointing out that *Hoyt's New Cyclopedia of Practical Quotations*[19] attributes the quotation to the great American showman Phineas T. Barnum. "If the epigram is Lincolnian in sentiment," Schwartz writes, "one could equally argue that it is Barnumian."[20] To date, the quotation remains one of the favorites attributed to Lincoln, but it is unlikely that he actually used it.

To MANY PEOPLE, discrediting a Lincoln quote is a disturbing thing. Most of us want to believe in the truth of claims concerning Lincoln's recollected words. Imagine the effect if it was discovered that Secretary of State William Seward wrote Lincoln's second inaugural address, or that Lincoln's secretary John Hay wrote the Gettysburg Address. Those two works are part of the foundation of Lincoln's literary and political greatness. While it is certain that Lincoln did write his second inaugural and the Gettysburg Address, doubt has been raised about another writing of Lincoln that is considered a masterpiece of both composition and compassion, the Bixby letter.

The Bixby letter is one of Lincoln's writings that holds a special place among his literary works. It is a letter that Lincoln sent to a Boston widow by the name of Lydia Bixby who had five sons killed in the Civil War. The letter is often cited along with Lincoln's other great masterpieces as a tour de force of his writing skills. It received special attention when it was read on-screen to millions of viewers during the 1998 Academy Award–winning film *Saving Private Ryan*. In the film, General George C. Marshall, on being informed of the deaths of three Ryan brothers and that a fourth brother was part of the Normandy invasion, reads the Bixby letter to a group of officers gathered in his office. The scene was written into the original film script at the request of Steven Spielberg, the film's director.

Unfortunately, the letter has also become the focus of considerable controversy. Serious questions have been raised concerning Lincoln's authorship of the letter. Claims have been made most recently that Lincoln's personal secretary John Hay wrote the letter on behalf of Lincoln.[21]

The original letter has never been found, although a facsimile did appear around 1900 and was included in a collection of Lincoln's writings edited by Nicolay and Hay.[22] This facsimile has been ruled a forgery, and no serious scholar today accepts it as the original letter. And, while Mrs. Bixby had five sons, not all five died in the war. Mrs. Bixby, a woman of questionable character, may well have been behind the claim that all five of her sons died in the war.

The letter's origin can be traced to another letter written by a father who, like Mrs. Bixby, had five sons that served in the Union army. On September 21, 1864, Massachusetts governor John A. Andrew received a letter from Otis Newhall of Lynn, Massachusetts, asking that his recently wounded son be discharged from service. Newhall wrote that one of his sons was a prisoner, one was killed in battle, and two were still fighting at the front. He pointed out that his wounded son's regiment had mustered out of service while his son was recovering in a hospital from wounds he received during the battle at Spotsylvania. Once recovered, the son was sent back to the front even though his regiment had been discharged. Andrew, on learning that Newhall had five sons in service, wrote to William Schouler, the adjutant general of Massachusetts, asking whether the request could be granted. In his report to Andrew, Schouler points out that the discharge would require the approval of the War Department. Schouler also notes that another constituent of Andrew, a Boston widow named Lydia Bixby, also had five sons in service and that tragically all five had been killed. In forwarding Schouler's report to the War Department in Washington, Andrew added a personal note about the widow Bixby and her loss of five sons: "This is a case so remarkable, that I really wish a letter might be written her by the President of the United States, taking notice of a noble mother of five dead heroes so well deserved."

Schouler's report with Andrew's notation moved through the War Department's chain of command, eventually winding up on the desk of Secretary of War Edwin Stanton. Stanton took the request, together with the records of the five sons, to Lincoln, who agreed to write a letter to Mrs. Bixby. The letter, dated November 21, 1864, was hand-delivered to the widow on the morning of November 25, and the full text of the letter was printed in the *Boston Evening Transcript* the same day:

> Executive Mansion,
> Washington, Nov. 21, 1864
>
> To Mrs Bixby, Boston, Mass.
>
> Dear Madam,
> I have been shown in the files of the War Department a statement of the Adjutant General of Massachusetts that you are the mother of five sons who have died gloriously on the field of battle. I feel how weak and fruitless must be any word of mine which should attempt to beguile you from the grief of a loss so overwhelming. But I cannot refrain from tendering you the consolation that may be found in the thanks of the republic they died to save. I pray that our Heavenly Father may assuage the anguish of your bereavement, and leave you only the cherished memory of the loved and lost, and the solemn pride that must be yours to have laid so costly a sacrifice upon the altar of freedom.
> Yours very sincerely and respectfully,
> A. Lincoln.

While Lincoln believed the widow mother had lost five sons in combat, it turned out that only two had been killed. Of the remaining three sons, two had deserted and one had been honorably discharged after the date of the letter. Mrs. Bixby may have been part of the problem. In his report to Governor Andrew, Schouler wrote: "Mrs. Bixby came to my office and showed me five letters from five different company commanders, and each letter informed the poor woman of the death of one of her sons." This seems rather strange since Schouler, as the adjutant general of Massachusetts, would have the records for all of the soldiers in Federal service from his state. At the time of her visit to Schouler, Mrs. Bixby knew that two of her sons were dead and believed a third son was killed near Petersburg,

Executive Mansion
Washington, Nov 21. 1864

To Mrs Bixby, Boston, Mass,
Dear Madam,

I have been shown in the files of the War Department a statement of the Adjutant General of Massachusetts that you are the mother of five sons who have died gloriously on the field of battle I feel how weak and fruitless must be any word of mine which should attempt to beguile you from the grief of a loss so overwhelming. But I cannot refrain from tendering you the consolation that may be found in the thanks of the republic they died to save I pray that our Heavenly Father may assuage the anguish of your bereavement, and leave you only the cherished memory of the loved and lost, and the solemn pride that must be yours to have laid so costly a sacrifice upon the altar of freedom

Yours very sincerely and respectfully,
A. Lincoln

A facsimile of the famous Bixby letter. Such facsimiles can be traced to Michael Tobin, a New York dealer in prints and engravings, who sold them as souvenirs. Tobin had the text of the letter engraved by a lithographer simulating Lincoln's handwriting. Over the years, the facsimile has fooled many individuals who believed they had discovered the "lost copy" of Lincoln's famous letter. From time to time these facsimiles appear for sale on the Internet auction eBay. (Author's collection)

Virginia. She did not find out until several days after she received Lincoln's letter that her third son was alive, having been captured and a prisoner of war.

While Schouler's records may have been incomplete or in error, the War Department's should have been able to give Lincoln an accurate accounting for all five sons, but didn't. Whatever the cause of the foul up in the War Department's records concerning the five brothers, Lincoln acted in good faith. He began his letter with what seemed to him to be the facts, "I have been shown in the files of the War Department a statement of the Adjutant General of Massachusetts." Lincoln had every reason to believe that Mrs. Bixby had lost five sons in battle.

Son number one, Private Arthur Edward Bixby, was mustered into the 1st Regiment, Massachusetts Heavy Artillery, on August 6, 1861, and deserted nine months later in May of 1862. While he was a deserter, his mother wrote to the War Department claiming that her son was fifteen years old at the time of his enlistment and signed up without her permission, and she added that he had temporary fits of insanity. An order was issued for his discharge, but he was already a deserter somewhere unknown at the time.

Son number two, Sergeant Charles N. Bixby, enlisted July 28, 1862, in Company D of the 20th Massachusetts Infantry and was killed at Fredericksburg on May 3, 1863. Son number three, Corporal Henry C. Bixby, enlisted August 13, 1862, in Company K, 32nd Massachusetts Infantry. Captured, he was eventually paroled in March of 1864 and mustered out of service on December 17, 1864. Schouler's records had him listed as being killed at Gettysburg. Son number four, Private Oliver Cromwell Bixby, enlisted in Company E, 58th Massachusetts Infantry, and was killed near Petersburg, Virginia, on July 30, 1864. Son number five, Private George A. Bixby, enlisted under the false name George Way on March 19, 1864, in Company B, 56th Massachusetts Infantry. He was captured at Petersburg on July 30, 1864. Schouler's records list Bixby (Way) as being killed at Petersburg, but later Pension Office records show that he was taken prisoner and deserted to the enemy in October 1864. The War Department listed him as killed in action, and the published records in *Massachusetts Soldiers, Sailors, and Marines in the Civil War* include both accounts under his name. His true fate remains a mystery.

Although the original letter has long been lost, no one doubts its authenticity. Its publication in the *Boston Evening Transcript* the same day the letter was delivered to Mrs. Bixby confirms its one-time existence. The most reasonable explanation for its not still existing is that Mrs. Bixby, an ardent Confederate sympathizer who disliked Lincoln, destroyed the letter. A granddaughter remarked how surprised she was when her mother told her how much Mrs. Bixby resented receiving the letter from Lincoln.[23]

The facsimiles that now exist of the letter can be traced to a New York dealer in prints and engravings, Michael Tobin, who applied for a copyright of an engraving of the Bixby facsimile in 1891.[24] It is assumed that the dealer had the text of the letter engraved by a lithographer simulating Lincoln's handwriting. The format of the letter was simply the engraver's best guess. The lithograph was reproduced in unknown numbers as a "souvenir" item and not meant to deceive anyone purchasing it. Tobin sold his souvenir lithograph of the Bixby letter for $2. Over the years, the facsimile has fooled some individuals, who believed it was the famous "Bixby Letter." From time to time these lithograph facsimiles have appeared for sale on the Internet auction site eBay.

The most serious question concerning the letter is whether Lincoln was its author; or was it the work of his secretary John Hay, as has been claimed most recently by Lincoln scholar Michael Burlingame? Hay, in responding to a series of questions concerning Lincoln's habits as president, wrote to William Herndon: "He wrote very few letters. He did not read one in fifty that he received. At first we tried to bring them to his notice, but at last he gave the whole thing over to me, and signed without reading the letters I wrote in his name. He wrote perhaps half-a-dozen a week himself—no more."[25] Advocates of Hay's having written the Bixby letter begin by citing this statement, drawing the conclusion that Hay wrote most of Lincoln's correspondence. Even so, according to Hay's own statement, Lincoln wrote somewhere around three hundred letters a year, leaving ample room for his writing the Bixby letter.

More definitive proof that Hay was the author of the letter can be traced back to Nicholas Murray Butler, a renowned educator who was president of Columbia University from 1902 to 1945. In his autobiography, *Across the Busy Years*, published in 1940, Butler wrote the following:

Theodore Roosevelt admired the Bixby letter greatly and had a framed photograph of it in one of the guestrooms at the White House.[26] John Morely occupied this room while the guest of President Roosevelt in 1904. His attention was attracted to the Bixby letter, of which he had never heard, and he too admired it greatly.

John Hay, Lincoln's assistant secretary. Lincoln scholar Michael Burlingame has made a strong case for Hay as the real author of the Bixby letter. (Author's collection)

One morning during his visit to Washington, Morely called on John Hay, then Secretary of State, whose house was on the opposite side of Lafayette Square from the White House. Morley expressed to Hay his great admiration for the Bixby letter, to which Hay listened with a quizzical look upon his face. After a brief silence, John Hay told Morley that he had himself written the Bixby letter and that this was the reason it could not be found among Lincoln's papers and why no original copy of it had ever been forthcoming. Hay asked Morely to treat this information as strictly confidential until after his (Hay's) death. Morley did so, and told me that he had never repeated it to anyone until he told it to me during a quiet talk in London at the Athenaeum on July 9, 1912. He then asked me, in my turn, to preserve this confidence of his until he, Morley, should be no longer living.[27]

It appears that Hay failed to follow his own rule of secrecy, allegedly telling two other individuals, W. C. Brownell and Walter Hines Page, that he authored the letter. In each instance, Hay swore his confidants never to tell his secret while he was alive. And in each instance, the claim that Hay was the author was made thirdhand or worse. Hay told Morley who later told Nicholas Murray Butler; Hay told W. C. Brownell who told Rollo Ogden who wrote about it in an editorial in the *New York Times*; and lastly, Hay told Walter Hines Page who told Lady Strafford who told the Reverend G. A. Jackson.[28] Such testimony is interesting but leaves the skeptic wanting something more substantive before accepting the hearsay claims that Hay authored the letter. Such evidence was uncovered by Michael Burlingame.

It seems that Hay, who became ambassador to Great Britain and later secretary of state under President William McKinley, was a poet and historian of some note. A graduate of Brown University, Hay donated most of his papers to that institution following his death in 1905. Included in Hay's papers was a scrapbook of 110 pages that contains many of his poems and clippings of reviews and commentaries on his various writings. Also included in the scrapbook is a clipping of the Bixby letter.[29] Burlingame makes the point that "it is difficult to understand why Hay would have pasted the Bixby letter" in this scrapbook if he were not the author of the letter. It is a compelling argument, especially when considered with the other evidence. As a result of Burlingame's discovery, the debate shifted in favor of Hay being the author of the Bixby letter. As Burlingame points out, his conclusion "does not affect Lincoln's literary reputation," which "will long command the world's admiration."[30] Maybe so, but the Bixby letter has long been admired as one of Lincoln's greatest literary achievements.

In March 2006, Jason Emerson, an independent historian, uncovered what may be the definitive answer to the long debated question of who wrote the Bixby letter. While gathering material for a planned biography of Lincoln's only surviving son, Robert Todd Lincoln, Emerson uncovered six letters written by Robert on the very subject of the Bixby letter. The letters were written to Isaac Markens, a historian who was writing a biography of Abraham Lincoln at the time. Markens queried Robert Lincoln about the Bixby letter, and Robert answered in a series of letters. As Robert Lincoln explained it, he had expressed an interest in the Bixby letter sometime between 1901 and 1905. Robert's interest was not in who wrote the letter—that controversy did not emerge until 1925, a year before Robert's death—but where the original letter was located. Robert told of receiving a lithograph copy of the letter from the Republican Club of New York intended as a memento of the evening dinner celebrating Lincoln's birth. Assuming the lithograph was made from the original letter, Robert made an attempt to find out where the original was located. Contacting the organizer of the dinner, Robert asked where the lithograph came from. The member did not know but promised to find out and pass the information on to Robert. Unfortunately, Robert never heard from the member and eventually dropped his investigation under the press of business.

Sometime later Robert visited John Hay in Washington and showed him the lithograph. According to Robert, Hay knew nothing about the source of the lithograph and pointed out to Robert that there were sufficient photographs of original Lincoln manuscripts available that anyone could construct the lithograph by mimicking other examples of Lincoln's handwriting. Hay gave no indication that he had written the original draft of the letter. Satisfied that Hay's suggestion was probably correct and that a lithographer simply created the letter by taking the text from printed versions, Robert ended his search.

In a letter to Markens dated February 17, 1917, Robert put an end to the debate with the following statement: "Your suggestion that neither Nicolay or Hay probably had any special knowledge of the [Bixby] letter at the time is correct. *Hay himself told me so*; [emphasis added] when I took the matter up Nicolay had died and it was he who had compiled the collection of papers."[31] So here is a definitive statement by Hay himself, albeit through Robert Lincoln, that he had no knowledge of the letter at the time it was written.

While the real author of the Bixby letter never intended a hoax, he did help to inadvertently create a myth that can safely be put to rest in Lincoln's favor.

CHAPTER EIGHT

THE WORLD WILL LITTLE NOTE . . .

The Myths of Lincoln's Gettysburg Address

A day or two before the dedication of the National Cemetery at
Gettysburg, Mr. Lincoln told me that he would be expected to make
a speech on the occasion; that he was extremely busy, and had no time
for preparation.

—Ward Hill Lamon

He wrote it in a few moments, while on the way to the celebration, on
being told that he would be expected to make some remarks.

—Harriet Beecher Stowe

Not a hand was lifted in applause. Slowly the big, awkward man slouched
back across the platform and sank into his seat, and yet there was no
sound of approval, of recognition from the audience.

—Mary Raymond Shipman Andrews

W HILE SEARCHING THE INTERNET one afternoon under the
word "Lincoln" with nothing in particular in mind, I was
surprised to find a copy of Mary Raymond Shipman Andrews's *The
Perfect Tribute*. What surprised me was the 1956 publication date. I
thought the date must surely be a mistake. The book, first published
over a century ago, was well past its prime and no longer relevant in
this modern, sophisticated age of Lincoln studies. What surprised
me even more, however, is that the book is currently available over
the Internet as an "eBook" and can be downloaded as a PDF file at
no cost, thanks to something called "Project Gutenberg."[1] Project
Gutenberg is a nonprofit educational corporation whose primary objective is the free distribution of electronic works in formats readable
by the widest variety of computers.

This fascinating little book was first published as an article in *Scribner's Magazine* in 1906. The story so captivated the reading public with its charming tale of President Lincoln, the Gettysburg Address, and a young Confederate soldier that Charles Scribner's Sons published the tale as a small book edition the following year. The book went through *fifty-seven editions* and in the process became required reading in nearly every school in the country. Before its run came to an end, it had sold over 500,000 copies, eclipsing every Lincoln title published during its run. I was surprised that after one hundred years this once popular story could possibly still hold anyone's interest sufficiently enough to justify yet another printing.

The story as told by Mrs. Andrews had all the elements of a warm and fuzzy tale that embraced the emotions of young and old alike. It is the story of Lincoln's Gettysburg Address: how Lincoln received an invitation to attend the dedication of the cemetery, how he wrote the words that became so famous, and how he learned afterward, from a dying Confederate soldier, how important his words were to the people of the North and the South.

Mrs. Andrews begins her story by writing how Lincoln, along with most of the elite members of his administration, boards a train especially arranged by the military to take them to the small Pennsylvania town where the president will take part in the consecration ceremonies. The weary president slouches in one of the hard, wooden seats of a passenger coach staring out of a window as the beautiful fall countryside slips past. Andrews writes with a heavy pen, "The weight on his shoulders seemed pressing more heavily than he had courage to press back against it, the responsibility of one almost a dictator in a wide war-torn country came near to crushing, at times, the mere human soul and body."[2]

The president knows that the main feature of the dedication ceremonies will be the speech from one of the country's greatest orators, Edward Everett. Lincoln was extended an invitation to give a "few appropriate remarks" mostly as a courtesy. And yet, he knows the people are entitled to the best he can give them, and he will do his best to meet their expectations. Reaching into his coat pocket, he feels around with his long, bony fingers for a pencil, finding only a short stub of one to write with. Examining the point, he sees that it is worn down to the wood. Removing a small, silver penknife from

Often referred to as "the Gettysburg Lincoln," the above photograph was taken by Alexander Gardner on Sunday, November 8, 1863, eleven days before Lincoln spoke at the dedication ceremonies. It is believed he was already working on a draft of his speech at the time. (Courtesy of the Library of Congress)

his pocket, he opens the blade and begins shaving the wood around the stub, carefully whittling away until he has fashioned a long, sharp point to the tip. Looking around for something to write on, he sees Mr. Seward, the secretary of state, unwrapping a small package of books. A piece of brown wrapping paper falls to the floor of the coach and lies at the secretary's feet. Reaching across the aisle, Lincoln picks up the piece of paper and says, "Mr. Seward, may I have this to do a little writing?" Seward protests, telling Lincoln he will find him some paper more suitable, but Lincoln insists on using the piece of brown paper that had been used to wrap the package of books.

For the rest of the trip through the Pennsylvania countryside the president carefully works his words into sentences, attempting to sanctify the holy ground that is to be consecrated the next day. Andrews describes it this way: "As a sculptor must dream the statue prisoned in the marble, as the artist must dream the picture to come from the brilliant unmeaning of his palette, as the musician dreams a song, so he who writes must have a vision of his finished work before he touches to begin it." But Lincoln finds the sentences that come to him "colorless and wooden."[3] He struggles on, cutting "here and there an adjective, here and there a phrase," and when he finishes he reads the speech "and dropped it from his hand to the floor and stared again from the window."[4] He is disappointed with his effort.

The next day, as the throng of people gathers around the speakers' platform, Edward Everett holds their rapt attention for two straight hours. They are fascinated by this silver-haired orator's lesson in classical history. Everett is the great orator of the nineteenth century. Born in 1794, he has become one of the nation's more esteemed citizens. His long public career has included service as a congressman (1825–1835), governor of Massachusetts (1836–1839), minister to England (1841–1845), and senator (1853–1854). He taught Greek literature at Harvard and served as its president (1846–1849).[5] Invited two months before Lincoln received an invitation, it is clear that Everett is the headliner on the program. Because of Everett, Lincoln will have a large audience. But it will be because of Lincoln that anyone will ever remember that Everett even spoke at the solemn dedication.

At the end of Everett's oration, the people break into "a long storm of applause, for they knew they had heard an oration that was an event."[6] Now it is Lincoln's turn. The gaunt figure raises itself up from the small, wooden chair set on the stage, then slowly shuffles across the platform until he stands alone facing the audience. A quiet falls over the gathering; all eyes focus on the figure standing at center stage. "A quivering silence settled down . . . every ear alert to catch the first sound of his voice. Suddenly the voice came, in a queer, squeaking falsetto . . ."[7]

Four score and seven years ago our fathers brought forth on this continent a new nation, conceived in liberty and dedicated to the proposition that all men are created equal.

"A suppressed yet unmistakable titter caught the throng, ran through, and was gone."[8]

Now we are engaged in a great civil war, testing whether that nation, or any nation, so conceived and so dedicated, can long endure. We are met on a great battlefield of that war. We have come to dedicate a portion of it as a final resting place for those who here gave their lives that that nation might live. It is altogether fitting and proper that we should do this.

But in a larger sense we can not dedicate, we cannot hallow, this ground. The brave men, living and dead, who struggled here, have consecrated it far above our poor power to add or to detract. The world will little note nor long remember what we say here, but it can never forget what they did here. It is for us, the living, rather, to be dedicated here to the unfinished work which they who fought here have thus far so nobly advanced. It is rather for us to be here dedicated to the great task remaining before us—that from these honored dead we take increased devotion to that cause for which they here gave the last full measure of devotion—that we here highly resolve that these dead shall not have died in vain, that this nation, under God, shall have a new birth of freedom, and that government of the people, by the people, for the people shall not perish from the earth.[9]

"There was no sound from the silent, vast assembly. . . . Not a hand was lifted in applause. Slowly the big, awkward man slouched back across the platform and sank into his seat, and still there was no sound of approval, of recognition from the audience; only a long sigh that ran like a ripple on an ocean through rank after rank."[10]

Andrews goes on to describe how the saddened Lincoln concludes his few words were a failure. "'It must have been pretty poor stuff,' he said half aloud; 'Yet I thought it was a fair little composition. I meant to do well by them.'"[11]

Lincoln returns to Washington and his crushing schedule of work. The day following his return he works from early in the morn-

Executive Mansion,

Washington, _____, 186_.

Four score and seven years ago our fathers brought
forth, upon this continent, a new nation, conceived
in liberty, and dedicated to the proposition that
"all men are created equal"

Now we are engaged in a great civil war, testing
whether that nation, or any nation so conceived,
and so dedicated, can long endure. We are met
on a great battle field of that war. We have
come to dedicate a portion of it, as a final resting place for those who died here, that the nation
might live. This we may, in all propriety do. But, in a
larger sense, we can not dedicate— we can not
consecrate— we can not hallow, this ground—
The brave men, living and dead, who struggled
here, have hallowed it, far above our poor power
to add or detract. The world will little note, nor long
remember what we say here; while it can never
forget what they did here.

It is rather for us, the living, we here be dedicated
to the great task remaining before us—
that, from these honored dead we take increased devotion to that cause for which
they here, gave the last, full measure of devotion— that we here highly resolve these
dead shall not have died in vain; that
this nation, shall have a new birth of freedom, and that government of the people by
the people for the people, shall not perish from the earth.

The first draft, or "Nicolay Copy," of the Gettysburg Address. The first page is written in ink, while the second page is written in pencil, suggesting the original second page was discarded in favor of the edited page in pencil. It is believed Lincoln completed the address at the Wills house sometime on the night of November 18 or on the morning of the 19th. Compare Lincoln's neat penmanship of this draft with that of his "Farewell Speech" (p. 114), which was written on a train. (Courtesy of the Library of Congress)

ing straight through to four o'clock in the afternoon without any break. At four he stops, feeling the need for a breath of fresh air. Lincoln leaves the White House alone and begins a slow stroll, his mind consumed in thought, unaware of where he is walking. Suddenly "at a corner, from behind a hedge, a young boy of fifteen years or so came rushing toward him and tripped and stumbled against him."[12]

The collision jars Lincoln from his daydream. The boy is crying. What is the matter? Why are tears running down his red cheeks? His older brother, a captain in the Confederate army, lies dying in a prison hospital. The soldier has told his younger brother he knows he is going to die and wants his brother to find him a lawyer so he can complete his will. It is very important to the dying boy. It is something he must do. Lincoln listens to the soldier's younger brother as he sobs out his tale. The dying soldier is engaged to be married and as an honorable man wants to make sure his fiancée gets everything he has. Lincoln tells the boy he can help him. He is, after all, a lawyer. The young boy, now happy, takes Lincoln by the hand and leads him to the hospital where his brother is being cared for.

The soldier is unaware that the "lawyer" his brother found is really the president of the United States. The two chat amiably. "My name is Lincoln," the tall stranger says. "That's a good name from your standpoint—you are, I take it, a Northerner?" the soldier answers. "I'm on that side of the fence," Lincoln answers. No matter, the soldier likes the gaunt man and watches as Lincoln drafts his will. The business done, the two men chat briefly once again. The conversation soon turns to the dedication at Gettysburg and the speech of the president. The soldier tells Lincoln that he read the speech in the morning paper and it will become "one of the greatest speeches of history."[13]

Lincoln is stunned. Can it be true? The dying soldier talks on, "It will live, that speech. Fifty years from now American schoolboys will be learning it as part of their education."

The prophetic words Mary Andrews gave to the soldier could not have been more true. Fifty years after Lincoln delivered his few remarks, they were being memorized by all the schoolchildren in the country as part of their education. Andrews's little book became an overwhelming success and was incorporated into educational systems throughout the North and even parts of the South.

The book is complete fiction, from beginning to end. There is not a word of truth in it. And yet, its words became rooted in the public mind. Today, it is perhaps one of the more enduring myths about Abraham Lincoln that he wrote his remarks on the "back of an envelope." The speech, like Lincoln's invitation to speak, was almost an afterthought, scribbled down on a piece of discarded paper during the train ride to Gettysburg.

By the summer of 1863 the war was already in its third year. The year began in the shadow of a crushing Union defeat at Fredericksburg, Virginia, that took place on December 13. The battle cost Union commander Ambrose Burnside his job and the Union army 12,653 casualties. With the coming spring, the Union suffered another disastrous defeat at Chancellorsville, Virginia, under a new army commander, Joseph Hooker. Once again, Lincoln was forced to replace his commander. If anything hopeful could be said about the terrible outcome, it was that the man Lincoln chose to replace Hooker, General George Gordon Meade, was head and shoulders above all of his predecessors combined.

Only four days on the job, Meade turned a rejuvenated Army of the Potomac against Robert E. Lee's Army of Northern Virginia at the small Pennsylvania town of Gettysburg. For three days the two armies battled. Meade, his troops holding the high ground, fended off repeated attacks by the best Lee had to offer, culminating in what has become the Valhalla of Southern mythology—Pickett's Charge. On the third day of battle, Lee chose to attack the center of the Union lines, believing it to be their weakest point. Three divisions, with Confederate general George Pickett's three brigades in the lead, marched into withering Union artillery and musket fire. Reaching a stone wall that represented the objective of the Confederate advance, Pickett's men were decimated. As the remnants of the three divisions withdrew back to the safety of their lines, Lee could only mumble, "All this has been my fault."[14]

The tide had turned. What future historians would refer to as the "high-water mark" of the Confederacy would become the holy ground for future generations of Americans who sought to honor the "brave men, living and dead, who struggled here."

The carnage left behind was overwhelming to the inhabitants after the armies moved away. The bodies of 5,747 dead soldiers lay scattered across the bloody landscape.[15] After caring for the nearly twenty thousand wounded left behind, the burial of the dead was of greatest necessity.

The Federal government was already keeping records of deceased soldiers and their place of burial under an order issued by the secretary of war in September 1861. Gettysburg, however, presented an overwhelming problem with so many dead in and around the town and little resources locally to deal with gathering the bodies, attempting to identify them, and providing an adequate burial. Meade wired Washington that he had no time to pick up the debris laying on the battlefield. The debris included the corpses of the two armies that were everywhere, many in graves so shallow that summer rains easily exposed them. Gettysburg had become a huge open morgue.

In February 1862 the Pennsylvania legislature passed a resolution providing for the burial of her soldiers who fell in battle.[16] Pennsylvania governor Andrew Curtin took it upon himself to visit Gettysburg a few days after the battle to see what arrangements could be made to fulfill the provisions of the legislation. Curtin met with Gettysburg attorney David Wills and appointed him his agent, authorizing Wills to take charge of the burials. But this authority pertained only to the 526 Pennsylvania soldiers out of a total number of 3,555 Union dead.[17]

It was during these first days following the battle that the concept of a national cemetery emerged. The idea was first put forward by Andrew B. Cross of the U.S. Sanitary Commission. Cross was not the only one thinking of establishing a national cemetery, and soon other representatives from other states joined the call. After several false starts, David Wills was appointed to head the effort. A plot of land adjoining the town's Evergreen Cemetery was purchased, and William Saunders, a landscape architect with the Department of Agriculture, was hired to come up with an appropriate design. Bids were let for exhuming the bodies and burying the soldiers in the designated section of the new cemetery. Thirty-four bids in all were received, ranging from a low bid of $1.59 to a high of $8.00 per body. The contract went to the low bidder, F. W. Biesecker.[18] The 3,555 interments were divided by states as follows: Unknown, 979; New York, 866; Pennsylvania, 526, Michigan, 171; Massachusetts, 159; U.S. Regulars, 138; Ohio, 131; Maine, 104; Indiana, 80; New Jersey,

The home of attorney David Wills. Lincoln stayed in the corner bedroom on the second floor facing onto the circle or diamond. (From a postcard, ca. 1895)

78; Wisconsin, 73; Vermont, 61; Minnesota, 52; New Hampshire, 49; Connecticut, 22; Maryland, 22; Delaware, 15; Rhode Island, 12; West Virginia, 11; and Illinois, 6.

With the design of the cemetery completed and the interment underway, Wills began making arrangements for a special program to consecrate the hallowed ground. He sent a letter to Edward Everett inviting him to be the featured speaker on the selected day, October 23. Everett wrote back to Wills that he could not refuse such an honor, but asked that the date be changed to November 19, the earliest date he felt he would be ready, needing the extra month to prepare his two-hour talk. Wills agreed to reschedule the ceremonies out of deference to Everett.

On November 2 Wills wrote a letter to Lincoln inviting him to attend the ceremonies and give "a few appropriate remarks."[19] The date of Wills's letter, barely two weeks before the scheduled dedication, has led many historians to conclude that Lincoln's inclusion in the ceremonies was an afterthought. But Governor Curtin's visit with Lincoln in the White House on August 28 to inform him of the plans in all likelihood included an invitation. Wills, after all, was acting as Curtin's representative and on behalf of all of the states

Journalist Noah Brooks later reported that Lincoln told him several days before the trip that his speech was written but not finished. (Author's collection)

when he wrote Lincoln on November 2.[20] The fact that no answer has ever been found to Wills's written invitation suggests that Curtin extended an invitation and Lincoln accepted at the time of the August 28 meeting.

Everything we know about Lincoln tells us that he began writing his speech well in advance of the scheduled day of the dedication. Lincoln was a meticulous writer who took great care with his words whether giving a formal speech or writing a letter. He seldom gave extemporaneous remarks. On most occasions when he found himself in a situation where he was asked to speak without formal preparation, he would decline, explaining that it would not be good for him, as president, to speak on any subject of a serious nature without first thinking it through. In all the collected works of Lincoln, it is difficult to find any instance where he spoke "off the cuff" or without careful consideration of what he wrote or said.

There is evidence to show that Lincoln began composing his thoughts about what to say at Gettysburg well in advance. Noah Brooks, a correspondent for the *Sacramento Daily Union* and a friend of Lincoln who was scheduled to become one of his secretaries in Lincoln's second term, wrote of visiting Lincoln on November 15, and of Lincoln commenting on his presentation. Brooks asked Lincoln if his speech was written and reported Lincoln as saying, "Well, no, it is not exactly written. It is not finished, anyway. I have written it over, two or three times, and I shall have to give it another lick before I am satisfied. But it is short, short, short."[21]

Added to Brooks's recollection are those of Ward Hill Lamon and James Speed. Speed, who would become Lincoln's attorney general in the final weeks of his presidency, said Lincoln told him, "The day before he [Lincoln] left Washington, he found time to write about half of a speech. He took what he had written with him to Gettysburg; then he was put in an upper room in a house, and he asked to be left alone for a time. He then prepared a speech but concluded it so shortly before it was to be delivered he had not time to memorize it."[22] Lamon, writing in 1887, said: "From his [Lincoln's] hat (the usual receptacle of his private notes and memoranda) he drew a page of foolscap, closely written, which he read to me, first remarking that it was a memorandum of what he intended to say. It proved to be in substance, and I think, in *haec verba* [in the same words], what was printed as his Gettysburg speech."[23] Clearly, Lincoln had prepared at least the major part, if not all, of his speech while in Washington.

What about the physical evidence? The claim that Lincoln wrote part or all of the speech while riding to Gettysburg aboard a train is easily dismissed for obvious reasons. It is simply not possible to write on a train that is swaying and jarring as much as trains were famous for in the 1860s and produce any writing that is not badly distorted. The best evidence of this can be seen in the one time that Lincoln did write out a speech while riding in a moving train. It happened on February 11, 1861, following Lincoln's famous "Farewell" speech to the citizens of Springfield. As the train pulled out of the Western Depot in Springfield at the start of Lincoln's trip to Washington, Lincoln attempted to write out the words of his remarks at the request of a newspaper reporter. Fortunately, the document survives to this day, showing the effect of the train's jarring as it slowly gains speed leaving the depot. It is a graphic record of the effect of the train's motion on Lincoln's handwriting. It should dispel any doubts as to whether Lincoln wrote his famous address aboard the train to Gettysburg.

Lincoln wrote this draft of his "Farewell Speech" to the citizens of Springfield while aboard the special train that began his inaugural journey to Washington as president-elect. Lincoln wrote out the speech at the request of a newspaper reporter. The effect of the train's rocking motion as it gained speed is evident as one reads down the page. A comparison with the graceful penmanship seen in the first draft of the Gettysburg Address is proof that the latter was not written aboard the train during Lincoln's trip to Gettysburg. (Courtesy of the Library of Congress)

Mary Raymond Shipman Andrews's delightful little story of Lincoln's Gettysburg Address was never meant to be a factual account of Lincoln's most famous speech. Nonetheless, her story became so popular that it created an enduring myth about Lincoln writing his speech on the back of an envelope, or on a discarded piece of paper, and despite all of the evidence to the contrary, it will continue to live on because of its touching portrayal of Lincoln.

CHAPTER NINE

THE "LOST" DRAFT OF THE GETTYSBURG ADDRESS

Real or Hoax?

> This sixth copy—the Wills draft page in Lincoln's handwriting, the paper held by Lincoln at Gettysburg—is the ultimate Lincoln collector's top treasure, and I thank God for letting it come my way.
>
> —Lloyd Ostendorf

THE COLLECTING OF LINCOLNIANA can be traced back to the year 1860, when an eighteen-year-old newsstand operator named Osborn H. I. Oldroyd read a campaign biography of Lincoln, became enthralled with the presidential candidate, and began seriously collecting memorabilia pertaining to him. After serving four years in the Union army, Oldroyd returned to private life and, devoting himself to collecting Lincolniana, amassed the largest collection in the country. Purchased by the U.S. government, the collection now resides in the custody of the National Park Service and is on display at Ford's Theatre.

Lincoln became one of the more popular subjects of collecting, and over the next half century a group of collectors, known as the "Big Five," acquired many of the historic documents associated with Lincoln and his administration. These included the original draft of the Emancipation Proclamation, Lincoln's letter to Grace Bedell concerning his growing a beard, his scrapbook with articles and personal commentary on the 1858 debates with Stephen Douglas, the Thirteenth Amendment to the Constitution abolishing slavery, and copies of what to many is the Holy Grail of Lincoln documents, the Gettysburg Address.

There are today five known copies of the Gettysburg Address in Lincoln's hand that are without challenge. All five now reside in public institutions. This constitutes the five accepted copies whose provenance is well established. There is another copy consisting only of the second page that was discovered in the early 1990s, but this copy is believed by some to be a clever forgery (more on this later). The five copies are known by the names of their donors: the Nicolay Copy (Library of Congress), the Hay Copy (Library of Congress), the Everett Copy (Illinois State Historical Library), the Bancroft Copy (Cornell University), and the Bliss Copy (White House).

The Library of Congress believes the copy known as the "Nicolay Copy" is the first draft, and the draft from which Lincoln delivered his speech.[1] The draft consists of two pages, the first being on "Executive Mansion" stationery, written in ink, while the second page, made of bluish-gray foolscap, is written in pencil (see illustrations in chapter 8). Because the first page is written in ink and ends in an incomplete sentence, it is assumed there was a second page, also written in ink, that was discarded when Lincoln revised his concluding remarks on a new second page in pencil at the Wills house in Gettysburg. The fact that the draft is in ink on stationery marked "Executive Mansion" supports the belief that the draft was written in the White House before leaving for Gettysburg. The troubling aspect that suggests this draft may not be the reading copy is that several words are left out of the first page: "here to the unfinished work which they have, thus far, so nobly carried on," and "under God."[2] Those who believe the Nicolay draft was Lincoln's reading draft conclude that he simply "interpolated" the missing words at the time he gave his speech.

The "Hay Copy," or second draft, is also controversial. It is written entirely in ink on two pieces of the same bluish-gray foolscap as the second page of the Nicolay copy, and historians are divided on whether Lincoln wrote the copy before leaving Washington or after returning. The fact that the paper is identical to the second page of the Nicolay copy supports the idea that Lincoln wrote it at the Wills house in Gettysburg, reflecting the changes he made to the Nicolay copy. If the draft was written on his return to the White House, why is it missing the words "under God," which appear in the newspaper accounts? Arguing against the Hay copy being the reading copy is the absence of any fold marks. There is irrefutable evidence that Lincoln removed the reading copy from his coat pocket and unfolded it before he delivered his speech. The Hay copy may, in fact, be just that—a copy Lincoln drafted for John Hay at Hay's request.

The "Everett Copy," or third copy of the Gettysburg Address, came about through a request by Edward Everett for Lincoln's reading copy. Everett, the lead speaker at the dedication of the National Cemetery at Gettysburg, had donated his own copy of his oration to Mrs. Hamilton Fish, wife of the governor of New York and head of the Ladies' Committee of the New York Metropolitan Fair. Everett had the copy he later received bound with his own address, but there is no record of the two speeches being sold to help support the fair. A Boston merchant, Carlos Pierce, purchased the manuscripts. They descended through the Pierce family through his sister, Mrs. Henry Keyes, and in 1930 the Gettysburg Address manuscript was sold to an autograph dealer. The copy was eventually purchased with money donated by Marshall Field of Chicago and an imaginative fundraiser involving the schoolchildren of Illinois. In 1944, the Everett copy was transferred to the Illinois State Historical Library, where it resides to this day. The words "under God" appear for the first time in this iteration of the five copies.

The fourth copy, known as the "Bancroft Copy," is without controversy of any sort. At the urging of Colonel Alexander Bliss, the famous educator and historian George Bancroft requested a copy from Lincoln to be used as a facsimile along with other great American documents in a bound volume titled *Autograph Leaves of Our Country's Authors*. Lincoln willingly agreed to provide Bancroft (and Bliss) with a copy of his address and wrote it after his return to Washington. The book was sold at Baltimore's Sanitary Fair to aid needy veterans who fought in the war, and the original copy eventually made its way to Cornell University.

The Bancroft copy resulted in the fifth copy, or "Bliss Copy." When the Bancroft copy was given to the editor of the *Autograph Leaves* book, it lacked sufficient margins for reproducing and also lacked a heading. Bancroft asked Lincoln to draft another version, this time according to certain specifications. Lincoln complied, sending what became known as the "Bliss Copy," the earlier copy remaining with Bancroft. The Bliss copy differs from the others in being written with a special heading and copied onto three sheets of paper rather than two. The copy remained in the Bliss family until sold at auction on April 27, 1949, to Oscar B. Cintas of Havana, Cuba. Escaping from Cuba to the United States when Fidel Castro came to power, Cintas left the document to the people of the United States, specifying that it be permanently displayed in the Lincoln Bedroom in the White House, where it remains today.

CONTROVERSY CONTINUES TO THIS DAY over which copy was the reading copy and whether Lincoln ever honored David Wills's request for the reading copy so that it might be included with all the other documents pertaining to the dedication ceremonies. If the Nicolay copy (first draft) is really the reading copy, why did Lincoln not send it to Wills? If he did send a copy to Wills, what happened to it? The reading draft of Lincoln's Gettysburg Address was a highly honored document the minute he completed giving it. It is not likely that it was discarded or lost once in Wills's care, if Wills ever had possession of it. The question of the "missing" Wills copy erupted into a full-fledged controversy in 1990 when a second page of the alleged Wills copy showed up in the hands of an individual who sought anonymity.[3] The individual brought the document to Lloyd Ostendorf, a respected artist and photograph historian who specialized in Lincoln and was a known collector of Lincoln memorabilia. Ostendorf possessed several items of exceptional quality and was amazed at the document, but he was not sure if it was authentic.

There were several things that Ostendorf noted that supported the document's authenticity. It was written in ink on bluish-gray foolscap that appears to be identical to that used during the period. It had a watermark consistent with the period in question. It was in Lincoln's hand and possessed all the characteristics peculiar to his handwriting. There was an endorsement on the back, "For Hon. Judge David Wills from A. Lincoln Nov. 19. 1863." And, the words "under God" were interpolated with a caret between the words "nation" and "shall," consistent with newspaper reports of the speech. The document looked to be authentic. If so, it was the find of the century.

The anonymous individual claimed to have found the document, absent the first page, between the pages of a book titled *The Lincoln Memorial: A Record of the Life, Assassination, and Obsequies of the Martyred President*, published in 1865. This sort of provenance is fa-

Lloyd Ostendorf's "Lost Draft" of the second page of the Gettysburg Address. According to Ostendorf, this second page was found in a book that purportedly belonged to attorney David Wills. Wills did request a copy of the address from Lincoln. The reverse bears the inscription: "For Hon. Judge David Wills from A. Lincoln Nov 19. 1863." (Author's collection)

mous among forgers and frauds and raised questions among several experts. Ostendorf satisfied himself that the document was real and negotiated a purchase price with the owner that included a combination of cash and several desirable photographs from Ostendorf's extensive collection of Lincoln images. In addition, the seller insisted he remain anonymous, and that authentication of the document would fall exclusively on Ostendorf. Ostendorf agreed and the deal was struck.

As a first step, Ostendorf set about having the document examined by other Lincoln scholars, followed by certain forensic-type tests. Three Lincoln scholars familiar with Lincoln's handwriting and who have handled numerous Lincoln documents found nothing to indicate the document was not authentic. Subjected to forensic tests, the ink, paper, and remnants of a small glue mark were consistent with an 1860s date. However, while these tests were encouraging, ink, paper, and glue from the 1860s are readily available to sophisticated forgers.

Most convincing of all the tests carried out, perhaps, was an analysis known as Scanning Auger Microscopy, or SAM. While a forger may have access to ink and paper dating from the 1860s, joining them together to create a forgery would, of course, be recent. The SAM method can give a fairly accurate estimate of a document's age. The scientific principle is relatively new and not widely used. It is based on detecting the migration of certain ions originating in the ink into the fibers of the paper. The older the ink-to-paper application, the greater the migration of ink molecules.[4] The technique is a complement to carbon dating, which can estimate the age of the individual specimens (ink and paper) but can say nothing as to the question of when the two specimens came into contact with each other. Ostendorf arranged to have his document subjected to analysis by Roderick McNeil, the expert who developed the SAM methodology at the Rocky Mountain Laboratories in Montana. McNeil reported that the document "showed a median age of 1869, plus or minus 10 years" and concluded that the manuscript page "was created in the time period purported by the document."[5]

The results of the SAM testing appear to support the age of the document to the time period between 1859 and 1879. Ostendorf and his supporters were confident the "missing" copy of the Gettysburg draft had been found—at least the second page. Even with these data in hand, however, a few of the experts still disagreed. There were other data that suggested the document might be a forgery. How could this possibly be, unless the forgery occurred around the time of the dedication in 1863?

Richard Sloan, an authority on Lincoln's assassination and the editor and publisher of *The Lincoln Log*,[6] a newsletter devoted to the assassination, performed a rather simple but revealing experiment. Sloan noted the striking similarity of the Ostendorf page to the Hay draft. Supplied with an accurate copy of the controversial page, Sloan made a transparent Xerox of the Hay draft and laid it on top of the Ostendorf page. Sloan wrote, "Most of the words were a perfect match. Short words, that is. The first two or three letters of long words and the last two or three letters were also matches. The words were stretched in the middle, though, so that the entire word wouldn't match."[7] Sloan concluded, as did others, that the Ostendorf copy was "a forgery—a tracing."[8]

While the two copies appear to be a perfect match, there is one anomaly that is not consistent with Lincoln's handwriting. Lincoln appears to have crossed his t's from right to left, while some of the t's in the Ostendorf copy appear to be crossed in the conventional manner—from left to right.[9] If true, this anomaly supports those who claim the Ostendorf draft is a forgery. As we shall see shortly, there is another explanation not considered by any of the experts.

There was still the matter of the results obtained with the Scanning Auger Microscopy. The ink and the paper, when analyzed as a "unit," date from the 1860s. The first clue came from the paper itself. While it was accepted by its proponents and critics alike as being of the right type and age, it exhibited fluorescence under ultraviolet light. Fluorescence appears as a bright reflection emitted by the paper when exposed to ultraviolet light. This is a telltale clue of paper produced well after the period in question. Since the paper was authentic, the fluorescence could only come about as a result of the paper being treated chemically to artificially "age" the ink. The ink commonly used throughout the period is known as "iron gall" (or "nut gall"), or to use the correct scientific name, "iron-gallotannate ink." This ink when fresh is black but with age slowly oxidizes to a brown color. To the average person the great majority of documents written during Lincoln's life appear to be written in brown ink. The oxidation from black to brown can be "speeded up" by chemical treatment. The presumption is that the draft was written with ink of the correct composition on authentic paper and then treated in some manner to "age" the ink and the paper's appearance. As a result the paper became fluorescent.

There may be another explanation for the perfect match and for the correct age of the ink and paper. In a separate experiment the author reversed the Sloan test, making a clear plastic photocopy of the "missing" draft and overlaying it on photographic copies of the Hay draft. As indicated by Sloan, individual letters and individual words

On close examination, the Ostendorf copy is an exact copy of the Hay manuscript, suggesting that the Ostendorf copy is a tracing. Placing a clear photocopy of the Ostendorf version over the Hay version forms a composite, and a certain amount of "slippage" is evident reading from left to right across the page. While individual words match perfectly, those at the end of the line are out of register. In the above illustration the words "for us to be here" align perfectly while the rest of the sentence "slips." (Courtesy of the Library of Congress and Lloyd Ostendorf)

match identically even to the smallest anomalies found in the pen strokes. This suggests that the "missing" draft is, as Sloan concluded, a tracing of the Hay copy. The one exception to this perfect match is that when one examines the entire composite made with the over- lay and Hay copy there is "slippage" as one reads from left to right across the entire page or down the page. That is, the kerning, or space between letters and words, as one moves across a sentence from left to right is off ever so slightly, so that while individual words match perfectly, those at the end of the line are out of synchrony.

How can one explain the perfect match of every pen stroke for every letter yet show this slight anomaly in kerning? As noted, most experts who feel the document is a forgery conclude the document is a tracing of the Hay draft. This is supported by close magnifi- cation, where slight "tremors" or "shakiness" can be seen in certain pen strokes. Experts in the field of handwriting often refer to this phenomenon as "forger's tremor." Even so, it seems extreme to be- lieve an individual can trace an entire page letter for letter without introducing a telltale slipup at some point. A second, more obvious explanation, which occurred to this author, is that the "missing" draft was made with a high-quality autopen, using a photograph facsimile of the Hay draft as the template. An autopen is a device that uses an original signature, or writing, as a template for making multiple cop- ies that are exact copies of the original. One anomaly of the autopen, however, is that one sees the occasional tremors or "pen skipping"

Similarly, the words "for which" in this illustration align while "they here gave" are out of register. (Courtesy of the Library of Congress and Lloyd Ostendorf)

that often occur in handwritten forgeries—a kind of "stutter" under close magnification. This is seen in some of the pen strokes in the Ostendorf draft. The autopen explanation would also account for the slight imperfection in kerning as the two pens scan across the page from left to right.

As noted earlier, the crossing of some of the t's in the Ostendorf copy appear to be made from left to right rather than right to left, as was Lincoln's habit. The horizontal marks appear thicker at the right side rather than at the left side of the pen stroke. Such an anomaly would occur if the user of the autopen crossed the t's in the conventional left to right manner rather than right to left.

Joe Nickell, a senior research fellow of the Committee for the Scientific Investigation of Claims of the Paranormal and author of *Detecting Forgery: Forensic Investigation of Documents,*[10] discusses in his book the anomalies of the Ostendorf draft. He points out that Maureen C. Owens, a forensic document examiner, concluded the document was a copy: "The uncanny similarity in handwriting characteristics is evident not only in form and proportions, but also particularly significant in writing movement, beginnings, endings, and pen emphasis throughout the writings."[11] None of the experts, however, consider the autopen as the vehicle to provide the copy. If the Ostendorf draft is an autopen copy, it is possible that the copy was made during the period the other legitimate copies were made, 1863. Alternatively, it could be a modern copy. Autopens are readily available to anyone desiring to make copies that match an original. The autopen is in wide use today.[12]

Not all of the experts who examined the draft and judged it authentic had all of the data available at the time of their examination, which may explain their erroneous conclusions. For example, the SAM examination may have been influenced by the chemical treatment performed on the document that resulted in its fluorescence—whatever that treatment was. The technique has given erroneous dates on a few occasions.[13] Only by taking all of the data and subjecting them to analysis *in toto* can one come to the conclusion that the draft is a forgery. Today, the consensus of experts who have examined the Ostendorf draft, and the data resulting from the many tests conducted on it, is that it is a fake, albeit an extremely clever one that has fooled other experts.

As Lincoln once said, or so they say, "You can fool some of the people all of the time."

CHAPTER TEN

THE GAY LINCOLN MYTH
All the President's Men

He often kisses me when I tease him, often to shut me up. He would grab
me up by his long arms and hug and hug.
— From the alleged diary of Joshua Speed

There's some evidence that shows that Speed presented Booth to Lincoln
as a "present" and the young Booth, who was a gorgeous man, was virulently homophobic, . . . if the murder turns out to have had a homophobic
underpinning, that's going to freak everybody out.
— Larry Kramer, *Salon*, May 3, 1999

ABRAHAM LINCOLN HAS BEEN appropriated as the poster boy for
so many different causes, ranging from melancholia (depression) to the National Guard (for his Black Hawk War service), that it
is difficult at times to keep them all straight. Americans of every per-
suasion have wanted to pin their tail on Lincoln's donkey in an effort
to gain status for their personal cause since shortly after his death. I
suppose it is not surprising then to find Lincoln coming out of the
closet to join the ranks of homosexuals in modern America. As with
many of the other tail pinners, those who tried to promote Lincoln as
a homosexual have missed the donkey—this time by a wide margin.
But having tried, it is probably certain that another myth has been
created that may linger for many years to come. Of all the myths and
hoaxes associated with Lincoln, what caused this one to gain public
attention, and where did the homosexual story come from?

Larry Kramer, founding member of the Gay Men's Health Crisis and a writer of screen and stage plays, spent considerable energy
shaking the history tree, hoping to knock a few gay heroes loose
to hold up to the public in defense of homosexuality. In 1999, he

stunned an audience in Madison, Wisconsin, when he claimed to have shaken loose the greatest hero of all, Abraham Lincoln. Kramer backed up his stunning revelation by reading excerpts from the diary he said belonged to Joshua Speed, Lincoln's closest friend and bunkmate in Springfield, Illinois. "He often kisses me when I tease him, often to shut me up. He would grab me in his long arms and hug and hug . . . our Abe is like a school girl."[1]

According to Kramer, the diary was discovered hidden beneath the floorboards of the general store Speed once owned in Springfield.[2] It was in Speed's store in 1837 where the young Lincoln first met the handsome Speed, who invited Lincoln to lodge with him. Having left New Salem in April with little more than a pair of saddle bags and no money, Lincoln accepted Speed's generous offer and the two soon became friends, spending the next four years sharing a bed in a room above the store. Kramer didn't stop with the claim that Lincoln and Speed were lovers. He went on to suggest that John Wilkes Booth murdered Lincoln because Lincoln made homosexual advances toward the handsome actor, who was virulently homophobic.[3]

In the years following his brash claims, Kramer failed to produce the diary or any evidence that the diary ever existed. He also refused to say how he came in possession of excerpts from the diary and who the owner was. Kramer made his claim apparently unaware that the building that housed Speed's store, along with several other buildings in the same block, burned to the ground in 1855, fourteen years after Speed had left Springfield for Kentucky. The block was rebuilt in 1858, and Lincoln and his law partner, William Herndon, had their office above a hardware store in one of the new buildings.

In 2004, five years after Kramer's Madison talk, another claim of Lincoln's homosexuality appeared, this time from a scholar with reasonable credentials, Dr. C. A. Tripp. Tripp, holder of a Ph.D. in clinical psychology from New York University and author of a widely acclaimed book entitled *The Homosexual Matrix,* published a sensational book entitled *The Intimate World of Abraham Lincoln.* In the book, Tripp laid out evidence supporting his claim that Lincoln was gay. In the introduction to Tripp's book, historian Jean Baker writes, "In *The Intimate World of Abraham Lincoln,* C. A. Tripp goes farther than any earlier studies to present the greatest amount of evidence

When Lincoln arrived in Springfield in 1837, Joshua
Speed offered him lodging, which he accepted.
Lincoln spent the next four years sharing Speed's
bed, leading author C. A. Tripp (and others) to
conclude the two men were lovers. (Filson Historical
Society, Louisville, Kentucky)

and the strongest argument currently available that Lincoln's primary
erotic response was that of a homosexual."[4] If Jean Baker is correct,
we need only analyze the evidence Tripp presents to see for ourselves
if he has indeed presented proof of Lincoln's homosexuality.

We might naturally assume that Tripp uncovered some startling
new evidence long hidden, or suppressed by Lincoln scholars, that
reveals Lincoln's homosexuality. Not so. Tripp took what little evidence Lincoln scholars have been aware of for years about Lincoln's
intimate life and massaged it in such a manner as to support his
claim that the Great Emancipator preferred men to woman when it
came to sex. Tripp simply took the known facts of Lincoln's various

relationships and followed them right to where he *wanted* those facts to lead him. Tripp's approach was that of an advocate—not a historian, who follows the facts *wherever* they may lead.

As preposterous as Tripp's claim is, it received national attention in the media. Virtually every major newspaper and magazine in the country ran articles under bold headlines questioning Lincoln's sexuality. Lincoln historians were nearly universal in their response: "Not again." As Lincoln scholar Allen Guelzo pointed out, the moan one could hear from the Lincoln community "was more like the moan of the weary who have seen this sort of thing before, time and again."[5] The moan, Guelzo wrote, is because of the amount of time members of the Lincoln community will have to waste in refuting Tripp's claim. The truth is, however, the claim cannot go unanswered. It must be addressed.

Tripp bases his argument that Lincoln was predominantly homosexual on his relationship with seven individuals, his predilection for telling ribald stories with a homosexual twist, and, perhaps most importantly, his age at puberty. As we will shortly see, the age that a male reaches puberty is accepted by sexologists as a key indicator of that male's sexual behavior and orientation. The seven people who figure in Tripp's argument consist of four males and three females. They are, in the order they first met Lincoln: William Greene, Ann Rutledge, Mary Owens, Joshua Speed, Mary Todd, Elmer Ellsworth, and David Derickson. Greene, Rutledge, and Owens date from Lincoln's New Salem days (1831–1837). Speed, Todd, and Ellsworth date from Lincoln's Springfield days (1837–1861), and Derickson (and Ellsworth again) from when Lincoln was president (1861–1865).

The age Lincoln reached puberty is an important part of Tripp's argument. He draws on famed sexual behaviorist Alfred Kinsey's famous study on male sexuality, thereby giving Tripp a quasi-scientific hook on which to hang his conclusions. Tripp worked as part of Kinsey's research team in the late 1940s and early 1950s, giving him a special familiarity with both Kinsey and his data. Among the many conclusions Kinsey derived from his monumental study on sexual behavior in males is the relationship between age at puberty and sexual activity. Kinsey found that the earlier the male reached puberty, the greater (more intense) the sexual activity. Thus, early bloomers show an increased sex rate along with "a notably erotic mental set—a quick and easy self-starting sexual arousal, with a sex-mindedness widely evident in both their speech and fantasy."[6] The most interesting finding by Kinsey and his researchers dealt with the correlation between the onset of puberty and homosexual incidents among boys. They found the earlier the onset of puberty, the higher the number of homosexual incidents. Boys who reached puberty at or before age eleven showed twice the rate of homosexual incidents as those who began puberty at age fifteen or later. Not only was there a marked increase in sexual behavior in early bloomers, but a marked increase in homosexual incidents whether the males continued to practice homosexuality in later life or not.

Kinsey also noted that a certain amount of homosexual experimenting was normal among adolescent boys. As many as 48 percent of adolescent boys experienced some form of homosexual play during their early years. As Kinsey pointed out, young boys have greater access to other young boys than they do to girls, "A situation that favors same-sex tryouts."[7]

Tripp has taken Kinsey's findings and attempted to apply them to Lincoln. In surveying the literature, Tripp sought evidence of when Lincoln reached puberty and concluded he was an astonishingly young nine years of age. According to Kinsey, most males reach puberty between thirteen and fourteen years of age. Lincoln, Tripp concludes, "was far ahead of the curve, reaching puberty several months *before* he was ten years old—fully four years before average!"[8] If Tripp is right that Lincoln reached puberty at age nine and Kinsey's findings are correct that the earlier the onset of puberty, the more sexual the boy, then Lincoln is off of the charts. Tripp's logic maintains that the earlier the onset of puberty, the higher the incidence of homosexual acts, and the higher the incidents of homosexual acts, the higher the probability of becoming an adult homosexual. The data, according to Tripp, point squarely at Lincoln being predominantly homosexual.

Leaving Tripp's conclusions about early puberty aside for a moment, let's look at how he arrived at Lincoln's age at the onset of puberty, a crucial point in supporting his claim that Lincoln was gay. Tripp turned to the Lincoln literature for clues as to when Lincoln arrived at puberty. He found two accounts that served his purpose. The first is found in William Herndon's *Life of Lincoln*,[9] a book based on Herndon's extensive interviews following Lincoln's death in 1865 with people who knew Lincoln. Chief among these was David Turnham, a neighbor of Lincoln's in Indiana. Turnham wrote Herndon, "I came to Indiana in the year 1819 [March] . . . about 1 M[ile] North East of Thomas Lincoln's [place]. . . . Abe was about ten years of age.—I being 16 ys of age—Abe was a tall dangling award drowl looking boy."[10] And later in the same interview Turnham said, "Abe was a long tall raw boned boy.—odd and gawky—he had hardly attained 6 ft–4 in when he left Indiana [1830, age twenty-one]—weighed about 160—"[11] With Turnham's observations in hand, Tripp next turned to Carl Sandburg. Sandburg wrote in his monumental biography of Lincoln, "When he was eleven years old, Abe Lincoln's young body began to change. The juices and glands began to make a long, tall boy out of him."[12] In quoting Sandberg, Tripp's argument is somewhat circular, however, since Sandburg used the same Herndon interview of David Turnham that Tripp used. These two sources, which are the sole basis for Tripp's conclusion that "Lincoln hit puberty at age nine,"[13] complement one another quite well. Turnham sees Lincoln sprouting at the age of ten (Lincoln is in his eleventh year), and Sandburg accepts that Lincoln's "juices and glands" began working when he was eleven. If the "juices and glands" are already at work when Lincoln is "about ten years of age," they must have begun several months earlier—when Lincoln was nine. This is Tripp's reasoning.

But Turnham never said in his interview that Lincoln's unusual growth occurred when the two boys first met in Indiana. In fact, Turnham's observations could well have fallen at any time within his and Lincoln's stay in Indiana—1819–1830. The shallow evidence for Tripp's conclusion that Lincoln "hit puberty at age nine" rests on shaky ground.

However, even if we accept Tripp's claim that Lincoln reached puberty earlier than the norm, it doesn't mean he became a homosexual. It doesn't even mean he had a predilection toward homosexuality. It doesn't even mean he had any experimental homosexual experiences. The fact that the early onset of puberty shows a marked increase in homosexual incidents among adolescent boys does not mean that homosexuality follows. It only means that early puberty often leads to increased sexual activity, including an increased curiosity and experimentation in homosexuality. And then, according to Kinsey, this occurs only in 48 percent of the cases studied—slightly less than half. Surprisingly, Tripp agrees with this assessment. He negates his own argument when he writes: "Not that such earliness [in puberty] necessarily implies a homosexual result. Note that at its maximum—as with boys who reach puberty at the youngest ages—*the homosexual component still occurs in less than half the subjects* [emphasis added]. This merely means what is already well known: A great variety of factors play into the origins of sexual orientation."[14] With this rather amazing admission, Tripp weakens his own argument.

Tripp next takes up Lincoln's fondness for telling ribald stories and "off-color" jokes as evidence of his sexual predilection. He focuses on a satire Lincoln wrote at the age of twenty entitled *First Chronicles of Reuben*. The little story was aimed at the Grigsby brothers, four boys who lived in the Gentryville area of Indiana where the Lincolns lived. In 1826, Lincoln's older sister Sarah (age nineteen) married Aaron Grigsby. Sarah became pregnant, only to die in childbirth along with the baby in 1828. With her stillborn baby in her arms, she was buried in the small cemetery next to the Little Pigeon Creek Baptist Church, not far from the Lincoln cabin. It was yet another tragedy in young Lincoln's life. Some accounts claim that Lincoln blamed the Grigsbys for not sending for a doctor soon enough, and that Lincoln held a grudge against the Grigsbys for his sister's death.

A year later, in 1829, two of the four Grigsby brothers were married on the same day. While the weddings took place in separate counties, the reception for both couples was held in the father's house in Gentryville. Lincoln penned an anonymous satire of the wedding night in which he said the two men wound up in the wrong bedrooms, causing quite a furor. It was quite a belittling story at the expense of the Grigsby brothers.

Betsy Grigsby, one of the brides, years later told the story in a local paper: "Yes they have a joke on us. They said my man got into the wrong room and Charles [Grigsby] got into my room, but it wasn't so. Lincoln just wrote that for mischief. Natty Grigsby told us it was all written down, all put on record. Abe and my man often laughed about that."[15] At the end of his 713-word satire, Lincoln added a short poem about the marriage of two boys. The poem, like the satire, no longer exists but has been reconstructed from memory by Elizabeth Crawford, another neighbor of the Lincoln family. The poem, as remembered by Mrs. Crawford, reads:

> I will tell you a Joke about Jouel and mary
> It is neither a joke nor a [s]tory
> For rubin and Charles has married two girles
> But biley has married a boy
> The girles he had tried on every Side
> But none could he get to agree
> All was in vain he went home again
> And sens that he is married to natty
>
> So biley and naty agreed very well
> And momas well pleased at the matc[h]
> The egg it is laid but Natys afraid
> The Shell is So Soft that it will never hatc[h]
> But betsy She Said you Cursed ball head
> My Suiter you never can be
> Besides your low Croch proclaimes you a botch
> And that never can answer for me[16]

Tripp accepted Crawford's reconstruction as accurate, seizing upon the poem as "the most explicit literary reference to actual homosexual relations in nineteenth-century America."[17] What Tripp bases that rather extraordinary statement on is hard to say since he gives no reference to support his conclusion. Nonetheless, he believed that Lincoln's basic biology, coupled with "an especially early puberty, and a sex-mindedness that *dominated* [emphasis added] his sense of humor," was evidence of his being gay.

THE HEART OF TRIPP'S ARGUMENT stems from his analysis of Lincoln's relationship with the seven individuals mentioned earlier in this chapter. First among these was eighteen-year-old William "Billy" Greene. Greene first met, or rather first saw Lincoln in the spring of 1831, when a flatboat Lincoln was piloting down the Sangamon River became stuck on a milldam at New Salem. As Lincoln tried to work the boat free, a large crowd gathered on the shore to watch. Heavily laden with cargo, the boat began to take on water. Lincoln made quite a name for himself with the New Salem townspeople when he used an ingenious method to free the stuck boat. The boat hung partly over the dam such that its bow was suspended in air while the stern was taking on water. Lincoln drilled a hole in the suspended bow, allowing the water to run out, lightening the load and eventually freeing the boat. Once over the dam, Lincoln plugged the hole and continued on down the river to the Mississippi and on to New Orleans.

Lincoln had agreed to pilot the flatboat for a merchant named Denton Offutt. Offutt had decided to open a store in New Salem and, impressed with Lincoln, offered him a job as clerk. Offutt also hired Billy Greene to clerk with Lincoln, and for the next eighteen months the two young men wound up sharing a small bed in the back of the store.

In 1865, Greene answered Herndon's request for information about his relationship with Lincoln: "I Saw the boat soon after it landed [on the dam]—on the same hour or day, and then and there for the first time I saw Abraham Lincoln. He had on a pair of mixed blue jeans pants—a hickory shirt and a Common Chip hat. He was at that time well and firmly built: his thig[h]s were as perfect as a human being Could be, and weighed 214: his height was six feet four inches."[18] In his *Life of Lincoln*, Herndon told of the friendship between Lincoln and Greene, writing: "Between the two a lifelong friendship sprang up. They slept in the store, and so strong was the intimacy between them that 'when one turned over the other had to do likewise.'"[19]

Here was Tripp's smoking gun. With no more evidence than Greene's remark about Lincoln's thighs and the close quarters of their shared bed, Tripp concluded that the two friends "promptly fell into an overt homosexual relationship—most probably instigated by Billy."[20] He wrote that Greene's remark "strongly suggests" the two men engaged in one of the most frequently used homosexual techniques "named 'femoral intercourse' (penis between tightly clasped *femora*, Latin for thighs)."[21]

Before we leave the village of New Salem for Lincoln's "Intimate World" of Springfield, it is necessary to deal with two other individuals who played a role in Lincoln's sexuality. They are Ann Rutledge and Mary Owens—two women Lincoln is said to have courted and to whom he even proposed marriage. If Lincoln did propose marriage, it undermines Tripp's argument and requires explanation. Thus Tripp must dispose of these two relationships or seriously weaken his argument.

Ann Rutledge is perhaps as well known to the general public as any woman in Lincoln's life except for his wife, Mary Todd. Mary Owens is less well known, even though her relationship with Lincoln is better documented than Ann's. Lincoln historians accept, with little or no argument, that Lincoln courted and eventually proposed marriage to Mary Owens in New Salem in 1836. The relationship with Ann Rutledge is far more controversial because historians are split over whether or not a love relationship ever existed. Regardless, Tripp must explain Lincoln's relationship with these two women if he is to convince us of Lincoln's homosexuality. Of course, the easy explanation is that Lincoln was bisexual. But Tripp and others who believe Lincoln was gay do not believe he was bisexual. Tripp must come down on the side of the naysayers if his theory of Lincoln's romance with Billy Greene is to hold up.

As discussed in chapter 3 of this book, there are several "witnesses" to the relationship between Lincoln and Ann Rutledge. They are almost evenly divided between those claiming a romance and those denying it occurred. Those who believe a romance existed lean heavily on Herndon's interview of a man named Isaac Cogdal.[22] Cogdal was an old friend of Lincoln's from his New Salem days, and following Lincoln's election to the presidency in 1860, Cogdal visited Lincoln in his temporary office in the Illinois State Capitol. According to Cogdal, Lincoln asked him about several of the old families of New Salem, wanting to know what happened to them and where they were presently. Near the end of their meeting Cogdal turned the tables on Lincoln, asking him, "Abe is it true that you fell in love with and courted Ann Rutledge?" Cogdal told Herndon that Lincoln answered, "It is true—true indeed I did. I have loved the name of Rutledge to this day. I have kept my mind on their movements ever since & love them dearly."[23]

Tripp dismisses the Cogdal interview, concluding the statement by Lincoln does not sound like Lincoln and accusing Cogdal of putting "uncharacteristic words" in Lincoln's mouth. There is some truth

An artist's depiction of Ann Rutledge, believed by many historians to be Lincoln's first love. (From a postcard, ca. 1950)

to this, for Cogdal's recollection of Lincoln's words does not sound like Lincoln. But then why should it? After all, Cogdal is recalling Lincoln's words from memory six years after the fact, and it is the substance of Lincoln's words that matter, not the style.

Tripp calls on the notable Lincoln scholar James G. Randall to support his rejection of the alleged Lincoln-Rutledge love affair. In 1945, Randall wrote an article examining both sides of the question. In the end, Randall dismissed the love affair as fanciful legend, criticizing the informants' memories as too vague and "dim and misty."[24] Tripp adopted Randall's conclusion to shore up his own necessity that Lincoln never loved Ann Rutledge and that the affair was concocted by Herndon because of his hatred for Mary Lincoln. By promoting a love affair between Lincoln and Ann Rutledge, Herndon was getting even with Mary Lincoln, who had come to hate Herndon. His public statements about Ann and Abe only caused Mary to hate him even more deeply. Tripp convinced himself that Lincoln's alleged homosexuality was safe, at least from Ann Rutledge.

Tripp still had to address the two other women Lincoln is believed to have loved, Mary Owens and Mary Todd. Mary Owens was the sister of Elizabeth Abell, wife of Dr. Bennett Abell, two of New Salem's citizens and friends of Lincoln. Lincoln first met Mary Owens in 1833, when she came to New Salem to visit her sister and brother-in-law. She made enough of an impression on Lincoln during her four-week visit that he told Elizabeth Abell that if Mary ever returned to New Salem he would propose marriage to her.[25] Years later Mary Owen's son, Benjamin Vineyard, described her in a letter to Herndon: "She was good looking when a girl, by many esteemed handsome, but growing fleshier as she grew older. She was polished in her Manners, pleasing in her address and attractive in society. She had a little dash of coquetry in her intercourse with that class of young men, who arrogated to themselves claims of superiority. . . . She was a good conversationalist and a splendid reader. . . . She was light-hearted and cheery in her disposition. She was kind and considerate for those, with whom she was thrown in contact."[26]

After an absence of three years, Mary returned in the fall of 1836 (a year after Ann Rutledge's death). Much to Lincoln's surprise, Mary had changed in appearance. She was now stout and had lost some of her prettiness since her first visit. Most historians believe that Lincoln had made a commitment of sorts to wed Mary. Apparently, so did Lincoln. His letters to her after she returned to Kentucky following her second visit deal in an agonizing way with the subject of marriage. They show he was having second thoughts. Unknown to Lincoln, so was Mary. She had come to realize that the two were not only separated by geography, but also by culture and upbringing. In 1866 she wrote to Herndon, explaining, "His training had been different from mine, hence there was not that congeniality which would have otherwise existed."[27] "Mr. Lincoln," she wrote, "was deficient in those little links which make up the great chain of a woman's happiness," adding, "at least it was so in my case."[28] In other words, Lincoln was something of a clod when it came to interacting with Mary Owens.

Lincoln makes every effort in his letters to point out how poor he is and how Mary would have to endure privations as his wife amidst the plenty of the upper classes of Springfield. Lincoln tells her he fears she would not be happy. "I want in all cases to do right, and

Mary Owens, a native Kentuckian, met Lincoln during her first visit to New Salem shortly after Ann's death in 1835. The two contemplated marriage, but Mary broke off the relationship, saying that Lincoln lacked the little links that make up the chain of a woman's happiness. (Courtesy of the Illinois State Historical Library)

most particularly so, in all cases with women. I want, at this particular time, more than any thing else, to do right with you, . . . I now say, that you can drop the subject [of marriage], dismiss your thoughts (if you ever had any) from me forever, and leave this letter unanswered without calling forth one accusing murmur from me. . . . If you feel yourself in any degree bound to me, I am willing to release you."[29]

If Mary Owens ever answered Lincoln's letter, it has not survived. Neither did the relationship. Whatever Lincoln's true feelings for Mary Owens were, he appeared greatly relieved at having ended their relationship. Eight months later he wrote a lengthy letter to Mrs. Orville H. Browning, a close friend, in which he belittles Mary Owens in a cruel way. He describes her as "a fair match for Falstaff," and refers to her "weather-beaten appearance" and "her want of teeth." "Nothing," Lincoln wrote, "could have commenced at the size of infancy, and reached her present bulk in less than thirty-five or forty years."[30]

It is clear that Lincoln and Mary Owens were not two ships simply passing in the night. A relationship clearly existed that was headed toward marriage, at least in Lincoln's mind. Tripp, unable to dismiss the relationship, concludes that Lincoln considered marrying her out of political necessity and not from some romantic or sexual attraction. Tripp writes, "For Lincoln the timing [for marriage] was also right. By 1833, he was headed toward being a 'public man,' and to be in politics virtually demanded that he marry. In fact, his mind was much more on the necessity of marriage than on its actual appeal, as evidenced by his less than ardent words, that he 'saw no good objection to plodding life through hand in hand with her.'"[31]

It is hard to say just what Lincoln's interest in Mary Owens was. Whatever it was, it was not evidence of Lincoln's desire to marry for political purposes and it certainly wasn't evidence of his homosexual nature. Tripp was forced to include the Mary Owens affair because it happened, and is accepted by Lincoln scholars as a romantic interlude in Lincoln's early life, even if a bad interlude. Dismissing it as simply a failed attempt by Lincoln to satisfy his political ambitions is one more example of Tripp's overreaching to shore up his claim that Lincoln was gay.

MARY TODD, LIKE ANN RUTLEDGE, is something of a lightning rod for historians—they either love her or hate her. Love and hate are too strong perhaps to describe her situation, but the fact remains that historians either view Lincoln's marriage as a living hell or believe the couple were deeply in love and compatible in the important things that mattered in their marriage: their children and politics. The literature is filled with snippets of reminiscences to support both arguments. By carefully choosing the words of others, one can build a strong case on either side of the question. The important matter before us is how does Tripp view this marriage and how does he explain the relationship in light of his belief that Lincoln was gay?

In Tripp's eyes Lincoln simply ignored his marriage, spending most of his pre-presidential years on the circuit, staying away as much as he could and silently tolerating Mary's insufferable behavior when he was home. Tripp dismisses the marriage as an uncomfortable arrangement—"This interlocking cooperative mismatch is by itself enough to rank the Lincoln and Mary Todd match as one of the worst marital misfortunes in recorded history."[32] To support his argument, Tripp calls on a host of the Mary Lincoln detractors, and there are many, whose reminiscences leave us wondering why Lincoln ever married her and, having done so, why he remained married.

Mary Todd Lincoln, from a daguerreotype taken around the time of her marriage to Lincoln in 1842. (Courtesy of the Library of Congress)

Tripp cites people such as James Matheny, an early Springfield friend of Lincoln's, who said, "Lincoln often told him directly and indirectly that he was driven into the marriage—said it was concocted & planned by the Edwards family . . . that he was honor bound to marry her."[33]

The one Lincoln scholar who more than any other believes Lincoln's marriage was a woe-filled disaster is Michael Burlingame. Burlingame was asked by Tripp's publisher to write a critique of the book as an afterword. Burlingame wrote: "Insofar as Dr. Tripp's book helps disabuse the reading public of the 'legend of Lincoln's happy marriage' it serves a valuable function, but insofar as it leads people to think that Lincoln was gay, it does a disservice to history, for the evidence Dr. Tripp adduced fails to support the case."[34] To lose Burlingame's support for his analysis of Lincoln's marriage is to lose his whole argument.

Tripp attempts to disparage Mary Lincoln by going into a fair amount of detail describing her unethical behavior in overspending as First Lady—she padded various household budgets and even fabricated false invoices. Of course, Lincoln was furious when he found out, and covered the cost of Mary's profligate ways from his own pocket. All this may be true, but it has nothing to do with Lincoln's sexual orientation. It seems that Tripp believes the more corrosive he can make the marriage, the more inclined we will be to accept his thesis that Lincoln did not marry Mary for love but was coerced into the wedding. The idea is simply preposterous.

TRIPP'S STRONGEST ARGUMENT in support of his theory, aside from Lincoln's alleged early puberty, centers on Lincoln's relationship with two young men, Elmer Ellsworth and David Derickson. Elmer Ephraim Ellsworth was born in Saratoga County, New York, in 1837 and had achieved a certain star quality among his peers by the age of twenty-three. In 1860, he had organized a military unit referred to as the United States Zouave Cadets, which toured twenty cities staging spectacular drill presentations and thrilling audiences. It was at this time that Ellsworth was invited to study law in Lincoln's law office in Springfield. He was soon making speeches on Lincoln's behalf. Following his election to the presidency, Lincoln invited Ellsworth to accompany him to Washington on his inaugural trip and later appointed him inspector general of militia, all this at the young age of twenty-three.

When war came in April 1861, Ellsworth went to New York armed with a letter of recommendation from Lincoln and organized a regiment consisting of New York firemen known as the New York "Fire Zouaves" that was designated the 11th New York Volunteer Infantry. Appointed colonel of the colorful regiment, Ellsworth took his flashy Zouaves to Washington, where on May 24, 1861, he led them across the river to Alexandria, Virginia, to secure the city in Union hands. After removing a Confederate flag from the roof of the Marshall Hotel in that city, Ellsworth was shot and killed by the hotel's proprietor, James W. Jackson. Ellsworth became the first commissioned officer killed in the war. His fame in death soon eclipsed his fame in life.

Ellsworth's death was mourned throughout the North, but nowhere was the sadness greater than in the White House. Lincoln was visibly shaken on hearing of Ellsworth's death. He issued the unusual order that Ellsworth's body lie in state in the East Room of

Lincoln's attraction to the handsome and accomplished Elmer Ellsworth was well known. Lincoln grieved openly when Ellsworth was killed after removing a rebel flag from atop an Alexandria hotel. (Author's collection)

the White House. In a letter of condolence to Ellsworth's parents, Lincoln wrote, "In the untimely loss of your noble son, our affliction here, is scarcely less than your own." Lincoln went on to reveal how personal the loss was: "My acquaintance with him began less than two years ago; yet through the latter half of the intervening period, it was as intimate as the disparity of our ages, and my engrossing engagements would permit."[35]

Lincoln first met Ellsworth in December 1859 when he came to Springfield at the invitation of Colonel John Cook, commander of the Springfield Greys. Cook invited Ellsworth to put on an exhibition for the citizens of Springfield with his dashing Zouaves. Lincoln, according to Tripp, had "a special interest in Ellsworth, and was making every effort to have him settle down in Springfield to study law in his office."[36] Cook, in a series of letters to Ellsworth, told of Lincoln's interest in him and urged him to complete his studies as Lincoln's intern. It appeared to Tripp that Cook was acting more like a "procurer" for Lincoln than a friend trying to help out the young Ellsworth.[37]

Lincoln was impressed with Ellsworth and was heard to remark that he had "a power to command men" and that he was "the best natural talent in that department I ever knew."[38] Tripp seized on the admiration that Lincoln obviously had for Ellsworth. After all, Lincoln himself referred to their relationship as "intimate," causing Tripp to once again overreach the evidence in concluding that Lincoln's affection for the young Ellsworth was homosexual in nature.

Having planted the seed in the reader's mind, Tripp dances around the subject, asking, "Does this mean that the Lincoln-Ellsworth relationship became overtly sexual?" "No," he concludes, "there is no evidence of it."[39] Tripp points out that Ellsworth was "explicitly heterosexual," having fallen deeply in love with nineteen-year-old Carrie Spafford of Rockville, Illinois. It was Lincoln who found Ellsworth "irresistible." It was Lincoln who was in love with Ellsworth. It was Lincoln who was homosexual, not Ellsworth.

Tripp supports his claim that Lincoln's attraction to Ellsworth was sexual by pointing out all the special favors he lavished on Ellsworth. The day after his inaugural, Lincoln wrote to Simon Cameron, his secretary of war, asking him to appoint Ellsworth chief clerk of the War Department.[40] Two weeks later he wrote to Cameron again, instructing him to appoint Ellsworth as adjutant and inspector general of militia, a more significant position than chief clerk.[41] Three days after the firing on Fort Sumter, Lincoln wrote Ellsworth an "open letter" of recommendation to the "older officers of the army," stating, "They would personally oblige me, if they could, and would place you in some position, or in some service, satisfactory to yourself."[42]

To Tripp, this was pretty heady stuff that shows Ellsworth was more than a friend to Lincoln. And yet, Lincoln's requests, and they were requests not orders, are no different in tone than dozens of others that he wrote for other individuals, both family and friends.

"Now that the Ellsworth evidence is in," Tripp boldly writes, "what new images of Lincoln does it offer?"[43] Tripp's reckless treatment of the "evidence" leads him to conclude that Lincoln's love for Ellsworth matched that of his love for Joshua Speed. And what is the "evidence" Tripp refers to? Lincoln's admitted admiration and affection for the young Ellsworth, whose talents drew the admiration of dozens of people who held officious positions. This, coupled with Lincoln's trying to secure positions within the military for Ellsworth that most experts feel he was fully qualified to hold. Tripp ends his discussion of Ellsworth by writing, "What the Ellsworth experience did do to a remarkable degree was to draw back the curtains on the full extent of the shock and the loss Lincoln felt, allowing him to fully state and show these [empathy and sympathy] more clearly than perhaps anywhere else in his life."[44] Indeed, that is precisely what it shows—Lincoln's sensitivity for others. What it does not show is that Lincoln held a homosexual love for the young Ellsworth.

Tripp makes his strongest case for Lincoln's overt homosexuality in his relationship with another young soldier, Captain David V. Derickson. In fairness to Tripp, he begins his book by discussing Derickson, his strongest case. In doing so, Tripp establishes early in his book his strongest evidence, probably hoping to influence our conclusions concerning his other, weaker arguments.

Derickson was a member of Company K of the 150th Pennsylvania Volunteer Infantry, known as the "Bucktails," assigned in the fall of 1862 as Lincoln's "bodyguard." At the time, Lincoln was without any form of personal protection, and the Bucktails were not intended as a personal guard. Their duties were to guard the president indirectly by securing the grounds around the White House and the Soldiers' Home, where Lincoln and his family spent their summer months trying to escape from the heat and humidity of disease-ridden Washington.

Derickson, eleven years Lincoln's junior, was a forty-four-year-old soldier from Meadville, Pennsylvania. Like Ellsworth before him, Derickson became a good friend of Lincoln's, so much so that Lincoln occasionally invited Derickson to accompany him on rides into Washington, and to join him, on occasion, for breakfast or dinner. In 1895, Lieutenant Colonel Thomas Chamberlain, a member of the 150th Pennsylvania, wrote a history of the regiment telling of the regiment's exploits throughout four years of war. Chamberlain served as the commanding officer of the small contingent of troops chosen to guard the White House and Soldiers' Home, and he wrote openly about the relationship between Derickson and Lincoln:

> The President was also not an infrequent visitor in the late afternoon hours, and endeared himself to his guards [Company K] by his genial, kind ways. He was not long in placing the officers in his two companies at their ease in his presence, and Captains Derickson and Crozier were shortly on a footing of such marked friendship with him that they were often summoned to dinner or breakfast at the Presidential board. Captain Derickson, in particular, advanced so far in the President's confidence and esteem that in Mrs. Lincoln's absence he frequently spent the night at his cottage, sleeping in the same bed with him, and—it is said—making use of his Excellency's night-shirt! Thus began an intimacy which continued unbroken until the following spring, when Captain Derickson was appointed provost marshal of the nineteenth Pennsylvania District, with headquarters in Meadville [Derickson's home town].[45]

Here is Tripp's smoking gun. Captain Derickson was invited to sleep with Lincoln in Mary's absence. This is not in the same category as sharing a bed, as Lincoln had done in his youth with Billy Greene and Joshua Speed. It isn't clear just how many times Lincoln invited Derickson to sleep with him, but once was enough for Tripp to conclude the relationship was sexual. Interestingly, neither Derickson nor Chamberlain tried to cover up or in other ways alter the facts of the unusual sleeping arrangement. In their own correspondence, both military men openly wrote of the relationship, in positive terms and never suggesting anything other than a friendship.

The relationship lasted approximately eight months and ended when Derickson requested, and received, a promotion and reassignment to his hometown of Meadville, Pennsylvania, where he was appointed provost marshal for the duration of the war. Derickson later told in his memoir how he learned from Lincoln of his promotion and reassignment: "'Captain, I was over to the war department yesterday, and this little matter of ours is all right.' I thanked him for his kindness when we separated. The next day I received my appointment, and made my arrangements to leave for home. I bid a final farewell to the president and his family, feeling conscious and proud of the fact that I had as a friend and acquaintance one of the kindest and greatest men this country has ever produced."[46]

At the time he left Lincoln for Meadville, Derickson had been married twice and fathered nine children. Following the war he fathered a tenth child. Even more interesting, Derickson had a son who served with him in the 150th Pennsylvania and remained a part of Lincoln's bodyguard after the father returned to Meadville. The son, Charles M. Derickson, also visited Lincoln in his bedroom, but under different circumstances than his father. The son later wrote about his unusual experience, which occurred one night while standing guard duty at Soldiers' Home.

> I remember one night about twelve or one o'clock a cavalryman rode up to the front door and said he had a message to deliver in person to the President. As I was Sergeant of the Guard, I asked him to give it to me; he at first refused but finally complied (having been previously instructed in similar cases). I opened the front door, which was unlocked, walked in, turned up the gas, handed him his spectacles, and the message, which he read and receipted, without leaving his bed. I turned down the gas, closed the door and thought how little he thought of his own safety.[47]

Tripp is puzzled by the fact that Lincoln seemed "oblivious to criticism" about his alleged affair with Derickson. "As was true in other of Lincoln's less lengthy homosexual attachments," Tripp wrote, "he seems never to have felt at all guilty about sex."[48] Of course, Lincoln may have seemed oblivious to criticism because there is none that we know of. There is a diary entry quoted by Tripp that leaves it to the reader to wonder if it reflects an undercurrent of criticism running through official Washington circles. The wife of Assistant Secretary of the Navy Admiral Gustavus V. Fox wrote: "Tish says, 'there is a Bucktail soldier here devoted to the President, drives with him, and when Mrs. L. is not home, sleeps with him.' What stuff!"[49]

Tripp is not puzzled, however, by the fact that both Lincoln and Derickson were married and fathered several children (Lincoln four, Derickson ten). Tripp explains: "Both [Lincoln and Derickson] could be seen as within some huge, undifferentiated 'bisexual' category—

all the more so when it is remembered that nearly all men in that era were married and had children—meaning that virtually every homosexual act or impulse might easily fall into a single, enormous bisexual category."[50] Tripp again cites Alfred Kinsey and his famous study of the human male. Kinsey recognized different degrees of sexual preference, called "mixed sex patterns." To better explain them, he devised a scale of 0 to 6, with 0 being completely heterosexual and 6 being completely homosexual. "By this measure," Tripp wrote, "Lincoln qualifies as a classical 5: predominantly homosexual, but incidentally heterosexual."[51]

SO THERE YOU HAVE IT—the evidence "uncovered" by Tripp leading him to conclude that Lincoln was gay. "Let there be no mistake," Tripp writes. "From any point of view Lincoln was highly peculiar from the start. His homosexual side, while not unusual in itself, was connected with an early puberty of such extremity—fully four years sooner than average—as to make even it extraordinary."[52]

In reaching his conclusion that Lincoln was gay, Tripp places considerable weight on his finding that Lincoln experienced an exceptionally early puberty. Tripp's conclusion that Lincoln reached puberty at an abnormally early age suffers from a more fundamental problem, however. Tripp bases his estimate on a single observation. So sure is Tripp of his timing that he writes, "Thanks to an accident of history, Lincoln's age at puberty happens to be *precisely known*" (emphasis added).[53] Short of a written record by Lincoln or his parents, how could this be? Tripp's reliance on David Turnham's casual observation has too many qualifiers to serve as a scientific basis for Tripp's conclusion. But even if it were true, it falls short of providing proof of Lincoln's sexual orientation.

While Kinsey's data support the link between early puberty and increased homosexual incidents, it still occurs in only 48 percent of males who reach puberty at or before age eleven. But more importantly, there is no evidence from Kinsey's data that those males who show the highest incidents of homosexual contact as adolescents continue to practice homosexual acts later in life. All Kinsey showed was that homosexual experimenting occurs in a significant number of adolescent males, the majority of whom grow up to become heterosexuals.

Tripp's analysis of Lincoln's affairs with Ann Rutledge, Mary Owens, and Mary Todd is on even shakier ground than his early puberty claim. While historians are divided on whether Lincoln and Ann Rutledge were in love and engaged to be married, there is no disagreement that Lincoln had a romantic relationship with Mary Owens and Mary Todd. In both instances, Tripp concludes that Lincoln had doubts about marriage. Perhaps, but Lincoln married Mary and together they had four children over a period of ten years. The evidence is no more favorable to Tripp's claim than it is to Lincoln's love for both women.

Lincoln's bed-sharing evidence is compromised on several points. In the case of Joshua Speed, Lincoln's Springfield friend, during the four years the two men shared a bed, William Herndon shared another bed *in the same room.* With Herndon's passion for telling the truth about his famous law partner, warts and all, it seems unlikely that the biographer was witness to homosexual play only a few feet away for four years and chose to bury any mention of it. The plain fact is that none of Lincoln's bedmates remained silent or refused to comment on their "intimate" connections with Lincoln. Billy Greene, Joshua Speed, and David Derickson spoke and wrote freely about their bed-sharing with the Great Emancipator. It is simply too difficult to accept the notion that Lincoln engaged in sex with these men over a period of twenty-five years and escaped scandal in such Victorian times. Lincoln's relationships with Billy Greene, Joshua Speed, Elmer Ellsworth, and David Derickson were nothing more than they represented themselves to be: warm, friendly admiration for four individuals that Lincoln loved, and not in a romantic way.

The burden of proof rests with Tripp, not with those who oppose his claims. Tripp's efforts to cast America's greatest hero and statesman as a homosexual fall far short of any reasonable requirement. And yet, his book was reviewed in virtually all of the major newspapers in the country and was part of television's evening news on most major networks, including NBC, CBS, ABC, CNN, and Fox. The fact that every major newspaper and magazine ran a review of the book gave it a special push in sales.

And why not? The revelation that Abraham Lincoln might be gay is major news. And herein lies the rub. Tripp's major failing can be found in the afterword of his book, in a piece written by Michael

Lincoln's law partner and close friend William
Herndon. Tripp makes much out of Lincoln and
Speed's sleeping together but fails to mention that
Herndon was sleeping in the same room only a few
feet away during the same period of time. (Courtesy
of the Library of Congress)

Chesson. Chesson enthusiastically supports Tripp's conclusion. In a
somewhat chest-thumping passage, Chesson writes:

As scholars, we are called on to *follow the truth wherever it may lead*
[emphasis added], even if we find that a president had a child by a
slave woman or oral sex with an intern. Yet professional historians, particularly the lords of the Lincoln establishment, have advanced with
less than deliberate speed, and often obfuscation—if not howls of rage
and denial—at the merest suggestion that their hero and mine might
have been anything less than a robust, masculine, "normal," exclusively
heterosexual American male in the mainstream of nineteenth-century

American culture, as found in the northern states, specifically the Indiana and Illinois frontier. Their unspoken credo is "don't ask, don't tell, don't pursue."[54]

This is a strange charge to level at Lincoln scholars. Historians, and a few who try to be, have taken shots at Lincoln from every side imaginable. His honesty has been questioned, his commitment to emancipation has been trashed, his oath to preserve, protect, and defend the Constitution has been severely challenged by historians who chastise him for suspending *habeas corpus* and establishing military tribunals to try civilians. Lincoln scholars have not handled Lincoln with kid gloves as Chesson suggests. Those who attack Tripp's critics have to do better in their defense of Tripp's thesis. It will take more than disparaging those who criticize Tripp's conclusions, accusing them of "obfuscation," to save their hero from embarrassment.

The very problem with Tripp's study is that rather than follow the truth wherever it may lead him, he followed it where he wanted it to go. Tripp was simply an advocate. An admitted homosexual, Tripp attempted to pin his tail on Abraham Lincoln's donkey to add legitimacy to being gay. He certainly did not attempt to foist a hoax on us. Nor did he fabricate data to support his position. He did, however, set out to create a myth that Lincoln was gay. In doing so he laid the groundwork for a myth that may outlive us all.

CHAPTER ELEVEN

NOBLE AMERICAN OR DECEPTIVE DOCTOR?

The Case of Samuel Alexander Mudd

Historical myths fall into two general categories: those that spring up spontaneously and those that are manufactured. All three of the principal myths that grew out of the Lincoln assassination were manufactured.

—James O. Hall

I N THE SEPTEMBER 17, 1979, issue of *Time* magazine, essayist Frank Trippett wrote about the phenomenon of certain people who remain in the public memory and never seem to die.[1] Their cases are never closed, but kept open by a disbelieving public. The mysterious disappearances of aviatrix Amelia Earhart and Judge Joseph Force Crater are two cases in point. Earhart disappeared in 1937 somewhere in the Pacific while attempting to fly around the world. Rumors continue to this day, despite the lack of evidence, of her capture and execution by the Japanese, who believed she was a spy working for the American military. Judge Crater, a justice of the New York Supreme Court, was last seen leaving his favorite restaurant on the night of August 6, 1930, never to be seen again. For the first fifty years after his disappearance the New York police department received as many as three hundred tips a year offering leads as to his whereabouts or reporting sightings.

Among those near the top of Trippett's list of people who keep showing up in the news is Samuel Alexander Mudd, the southern Maryland doctor who treated John Wilkes Booth only hours after he shot President Abraham Lincoln. Mudd was arrested and charged with aiding Booth in his plot to kill Lincoln and helping him to escape. Found guilty by a military tribunal in 1865, Mudd was sentenced to life at hard labor in the army's military prison at Fort Jeffer-

Dr. Samuel Alexander Mudd was the key conspirator in helping Booth assemble his team. (Courtesy of the Surratt House Museum)

son, located in the Dry Tortugas off of the Florida Keys. Mudd was pardoned by President Andrew Johnson a few days before Johnson left the presidency in February 1869. After serving just under four years of a life sentence, Mudd returned home to his wife and four children and picked up his life as a tobacco farmer and part-time physician until his death in 1883 at the age of forty-nine.

From the moment of his arrest until his death, Mudd publically maintained his innocence in Booth's conspiracy. His pleas, and those by his wife and daughter, went unheeded for nearly sixty years. Then, in the late 1920s, Richard Dyer Mudd, Samuel Mudd's grandson, took up his grandfather's cause. For the next seventy years Richard Mudd waged a relentless public relations campaign to overturn his grandfather's conviction, portraying him as an innocent victim of a ruthless federal government that persecuted him for merely carrying out his Hippocratic oath. During the last year of his life, at age 101, Richard Mudd was still actively promoting his grandfather's innocence.[2]

Following Samuel Mudd's death on January 20, 1883, his wife, Frances Mudd, and later his daughter, Nettie Mudd Monroe, took up his cause. In 1906, Nettie Mudd Monroe published *The Life of Dr. Samuel A. Mudd*, based largely on her father's letters from prison and the brief of his attorney, Thomas Ewing, challenging the jurisdiction of the military tribunal.[3] In 1936, Twentieth Century–Fox released the Hollywood film version of Dr. Mudd's plight in a movie entitled *The Prisoner of Shark Island*, starring Warner Baxter and Gloria Stuart. Directed by John Ford and produced by Darryl F. Zanuck, the film had an impressive supporting cast, including John Carradine, Harry Carey, and Frank McGlynn Sr., one of the early film portrayers of Abraham Lincoln.

The movie takes its name from Hollywood's fictional portrayal of Fort Jefferson as a fortress protected by an encircling moat filled with man-eating sharks. The cruel and sadistic Sergeant Rankin (John Carradine) taunts Dr. Mudd by urging him to try to escape so that the guards can watch as the sharks tear him to pieces in a feeding frenzy. The sergeant snarls at a hapless Mudd, telling him that he will welcome swimming with the sharks by the time he gets through torturing him. By the end of the film, Sergeant Rankin experiences a revelation and insists on adding his name to a petition pleading with President Andrew Johnson to free Dr. Mudd for his heroism in overcoming a yellow fever epidemic that nearly wiped out the entire prison population.

A recent compilation of film dramas depicting Abraham Lincoln describes the movie as "accurately depicting the real-life experiences of Samuel Mudd, the doctor who was sentenced to life imprisonment for treating John Wilkes Booth's broken ankle (actually, Booth broke the fibula of his left leg, not the ankle).[4] While *The Prisoner of Shark Island* is wonderful entertainment, virtually nothing in the film is historically accurate other than the name of the leading character, Samuel Mudd. Among the numerous errors were the names of the principal figures. Mrs. Mudd (Sarah Frances Dyer Mudd) is called "Peggy," her father (Thomas Benjamin Dyer) is known as "The Colonel" (he never served in any military organization), Dr. Mudd's daughter (Lillian Augusta Mudd) is known as "Martha," and Dr. Mudd is miraculously allowed to take his faithful ex-slave "Buck" with him to prison.

Despite the movie's gross distortion of history, it is an entertaining film—well-acted and dramatic even by today's standards. The film went far in establishing Samuel Mudd as something of a folk hero in the public's mind. Two years after the film's release, a popular radio show of the 1930s and 1940s, *Lux Radio Theatre*, staged a re-creation of the film. *Lux Radio Theatre* was a regular Monday night radio program that adapted famous movies to the radio, but not always starring the original actors and actresses. The show aired on May 2, 1938, on the Columbia Broadcasting System. Gary Cooper portrayed Dr. Mudd, while Fay Wray (of *King Kong* fame) appeared as Dr. Mudd's wife, "Peggy." The famous film producer and director Cecil B. DeMille hosted the show. As a regular part of every broadcast DeMille interviewed the actors and actresses about their roles. On May 2, however, the radio audience was treated to a special surprise guest, Mrs. Nettie Mudd Monroe, the youngest daughter of Dr. Mudd. Nettie was born in Waldorf, Maryland, on January 1, 1878 (five years before her father died), and died in Baltimore, Maryland on December 31, 1943, one month shy of her sixty-sixth birthday. At the time of her appearance on the *Lux Radio Theatre*, she was sixty years old.

Nettie was introduced during the radio show's intermission by Mr. DeMille and made her statement from the CBS studio in New York City. Hearing Mrs. Nettie Mudd Monroe's voice and listening to her comments about her father provided a special connection to the past and the events surrounding the assassination of Abraham Lincoln. Following are Mr. DeMille's introduction and Nettie Monroe's comments:

Mr. DeMille: During this intermission before Gary Cooper and our all-star cast return for Act 3, a remarkable privilege is ours. The tragic circumstances which gave us the story of tonight's play seem to belong to a dim and distant past. This is a new world and for our reflections on the 1860's we are accustomed to rely on ancient records and books of history, and yet tonight a human link binds us to the time and the hero of our play. With us in the Lux Radio Theatre is the daughter of the prisoner of Shark Island. She is Mrs. Nettie Mudd Monroe of Baltimore, Maryland. Better than any other person she can tell us of that *noble American* who was her father [emphasis added]. I'm honored to introduce the daughter of Dr. Samuel A. Mudd who speaks to us from New York City, Mrs. Nettie Mudd Monroe.

Mrs. Monroe: Thank you Mr. DeMille. I wish to extend to the Lux Radio Theatre both my gratitude and congratulations for devoting this splendid hour to my father's memory. I am amazed by your play, for with [few] exceptions, the *Prisoner of Shark Island* is proven to be a most accurate portrayal. In my possession are many letters which my father wrote to my mother from Fort Jefferson. They tell of how upon his arrival there in 1865 he served for a time upon the wharf piling the bricks. There is one letter I want to read to you that tells more than all others what my father was like. He says: "I endure the severest privations for the most part patiently. I can stand anything my dear wife but the thought of your dependent position, your ills and privations." This thought undoubtedly drove him to attempt his escape. He hoped to reach some spot where he could surrender and get a civil trial.[5] He was certain that a civil court would prove his innocence. But, as the play points out, he was caught, chained hand and foot, and put in a dungeon.

My father had magnificent courage. He survived not only the ordeal of imprisonment, but the ordeal of being free. As far as I know, my father never referred to his four years on the Dry Tortugas, and my mother too was always silent on this subject. The world will never know what she felt. All of these details, I suppose, are best forgotten. For after all, justice did triumph. Furthermore, my father felt no malice for if he had, the events you are about to hear in the next act of your play could never have come to pass. Father's unfortunate life, strangely enough, taught me a very beautiful lesson. It made me realize that out of great suffering can come something glorious. Through injustice the world becomes more just. Through cruelty the world gains kindness. Through his humanity we find mercy. Thank you Mr. DeMille for asking me to be a guest tonight in your Lux Radio Theatre.[6]

Nettie Mudd's remarks, like the movie and radio depiction of her father's tribulations, are distortions of the truth. Her efforts on behalf of her father were only partly effective. While they were able to gain widespread sympathy from the general public, they were unable to garner any political support to overturn Dr. Mudd's conviction and restore the family's good name. That task fell to Nettie's nephew, Richard Mudd.

Born January 24, 1901, in Washington, D.C., Richard Mudd attended Georgetown University, where he earned his bachelor's, master's, and M.D. degrees, graduating in 1926. In 1929, having learned of his grandfather's story, and stimulated by his aunt's book, Richard

Richard Dyer Mudd, grandson of Dr. Samuel Mudd, spent over seventy years attempting to clear his grandfather's name. (Courtesy of Richard D. Mudd)

Mudd began a lifelong effort to overturn his grandfather's conviction by the military tribunal and tell the world his sympathetic story. Over the next seventy years he would write articles, give lectures, petition presidents, and file lawsuits seeking relief for his grandfather posthumously. While he failed in his primary effort to have the military tribunal overturned, he was able to turn his grandfather into an American folk hero, as Cecil B. DeMille said, "that noble American."

Almost fifty years into his quest, Richard Mudd achieved a measure of success. In 1979, President Jimmy Carter wrote a letter to Richard Mudd expressing his opinion that the military tribunal that convicted Samuel Mudd was wrong in his view. Citing President Andrew Johnson's words that appeared in his pardon of Mudd, Carter concluded his letter, writing: "A careful reading of the information provided to me about this case led to my personal agreement with the findings of President Johnson. I am hopeful that these conclusions will be given widespread circulation, which will restore dignity to your grandfather's name and clear the Mudd family name of any negative connotation or implied lack of honor."[7]

President Carter released the letter to the public through CBS newsman Roger Mudd, a distant relative of Samuel Mudd. Roger Mudd included the declaration by the president on the CBS evening newscast. Once again, Samuel Mudd appeared throughout the print and television media, proving *Time* magazine right in its claim that certain figures in American history never die but keep coming back time and again.

The majority of the media misunderstood President Carter's letter. As the news story spread from the broadcast industry to the print media, President Carter's letter was interpreted as having reversed Mudd's 1865 conviction. Some reports even stated that President Carter had granted Mudd a presidential pardon because of his belief that Mudd was wrongly convicted.

The president's letter, however, did not overturn Samuel Mudd's conviction, nor did he pardon Samuel Mudd. In fact, President Carter was careful to point out that Samuel Mudd had already been offered and had accepted a presidential pardon from Andrew Johnson: "All legal authority vested in the president to act in this case was exercised when President Andrew Johnson granted Dr. Mudd a full and unconditional pardon on February 8, 1869."[8] President Carter's letter was more of a personal nature than an official or legal nature. In essence, it said, there is nothing that he, as president, could do legally in Samuel Mudd's case except use the prestige of the presidency to tell everyone that he personally believed that Mudd got a raw deal.

Eight years later, President Ronald Reagan added his support by writing to Richard Mudd:

> I regret to say I've learned that, as President, there is nothing I can do. Presidential power to pardon is all that is in a President's prerogatives and that, of course, was done by President Andrew Johnson.
>
> Believe me, I am truly sorry I can do nothing to help you in your long crusade. In my efforts to help, I came to believe as you do that Dr. Samuel Mudd was indeed innocent of any wrongdoing. But we'll have to accept that "full unconditional pardon" is what we must settle for.[9]

Not satisfied with the response of presidents Carter and Reagan, Richard Mudd pushed on. He next wrote to the Army Board for the Correction of Military Records (ABCMR), asking the board to correct the wrong that the Army committed in trying his grand-father. This board consists of civilian appointees who hear claims from members of the army (or their relatives) who believe that they have been wronged. The board then makes a recommendation to the secretary of the army to assist him in reaching a final determination on those cases brought to his attention. On January 22, 1992, the board granted Richard Mudd a hearing on behalf of his grandfather. Because of its nature, the board hears testimony only from the ag-grieved parties. Opponents of the petition to change the military record are not permitted to testify or present counter evidence. An examiner, representing the judge advocate, presents the facts in the case and answers questions from board members as to relevant military law.

The board did not consider Mudd's innocence or guilt, but only whether the military commission that tried Mudd had legal juris-diction to do so. After hearing the case, the board decided against the military commission 126 years after it ruled. The ABCMR rec-ommended that the secretary of the army set aside the guilty ver-dict and expunge the record in Dr. Mudd's case, in essence, ruling that Mudd was innocent: "The board finds no good reason why Dr. Mudd should not have been tried by a civilian court. It, therefore, unanimously concludes that the military commission did not have jurisdiction to try him, and that in so doing denied him his due pro-cess rights, particularly his right to a trial by a jury of his peers. This denial constituted such a gross infringement of his constitutionally protected rights that his conviction should be set aside."[10]

The board's recommendations were forwarded to William D. Clark, assistant secretary of the army, and the secretary's designee. Clark refused to accept the recommendation of the board, stating in part, "It is not the role of the ABCMR to attempt to settle histori-cal disputes." In his response, Clark went on to write: "Neither is the ABCMR an appellate court. . . . Even if the issue might be decided differently today, it is inappropriate for a non-judicial body, such as the ABCMR, to declare that the law 126 years ago was contrary to what was determined contemporarily by prominent legal authorities."[11]

While the assistant secretary of the army was deliberating over the board's recommendation before his ruling, the University of Rich-mond School of Law, with the enthusiastic approval of Dr. Richard

Mudd, staged a moot court in which a mock trial was held on the question of Mudd's trial by a military tribunal. The school proposed an appellate hearing with experienced jurists trained in military law. This moot court brought the question of Mudd's trial even closer to professional legal scholarship.[12]

Adding a historical touch to the proceedings was the great-great-granddaughter of Mudd's attorney, Brigadier General Thomas Ewing Jr., serving as one of Mudd's lawyers before the moot court. Also representing Mudd was the well-known attorney F. Lee Bailey.

The panel of judges listened to and asked numerous questions of the advocates for each side, after which they deliberated and rendered an opinion. The three judges agreed in their verdict that the military commission lacked legal jurisdiction to try and convict Dr. Mudd. They concluded their opinion with the following statement: "Accordingly, with due respect to the members of the military commission, we would reverse Petitioner's conviction and order him released forthwith from his confinement."[13]

Interestingly, while the panel sat in judgment deliberating only on the question of the legal jurisdiction of the military commission, all three judges could not resist discussing the innocence of the defendant in their findings. Unfortunately, the question of whether the military tribunal that tried Dr. Mudd had legal jurisdiction cannot be separated from the question of his guilt or innocence. Would the panel of judges have ruled otherwise if they were convinced of Mudd's guilt? Presumably, they would still have ruled against the jurisdiction of the military commission, but one wonders.

The denial of Richard Mudd's petition by the assistant secretary of the army did not deter the determined Richard Mudd. He convinced Maryland congressman Steny Hoyer (D., Maryland 5th) to introduce a bill into the Congress of the United States calling for the secretary of the army to "set aside the conviction of Dr. Samuel A. Mudd . . . for aiding, abetting, and assisting the conspirators who assassinated President Abraham Lincoln."

Charles County, the home of Samuel Mudd and his ancestors, was part of Congressman Hoyer's congressional district. One of the cosponsors of the bill was Representative Thomas Ewing of Illinois, representing a part of Lincoln's original congressional district. Ewing was a direct descendant of Samuel Mudd's attorney in 1865. The bill stated in part:

> The conviction of Dr. Mudd was based on evidence of guilt that fell so far short of meeting the prosecution's burden of proof that such conviction amounted to a denial of due process of law which was so extreme as to constitute fundamental unfairness.
>
> Because the conviction of Dr. Mudd was not based on sufficient evidence and resulted in a denial of due process of law, the Secretary of the Army should set aside the conviction.[14]

Hoyer's bill never got out of committee, leaving the legislative remedy to reversing Mudd's conviction in political limbo.

Richard Mudd, determined to press on in his effort to clear his grandfather's name, filed a lawsuit in December 1997 in the federal court for the District of Columbia seeking to force the secretary of the army to accept the recommendation of the ABCMR. Presiding over the hearing was Judge Paul L. Friedman. The suit consisted of three counts aimed at setting aside the original trial record of 1865 and declaring Dr. Samuel Mudd wrongfully convicted.

Count 1 asked the court to rule invalid the secretary of the army's decision to deny the recommendation of the ABCMR because he did not consider all of the evidence in the record. This, the plaintiff claimed, rendered his decision "arbitrary and capricious."

Count 2 asked the court to order the secretary of the army to accept the recommendation of the Army Board for the Correction of Military Records.

Count 3 asked the court to issue a statement that "Dr. Samuel A. Mudd, M.D. was wrongly convicted . . . in violation of Due Process of Law as required by the Fifth Amendment of the United States Constitution."

On October 29, 1998, Judge Friedman issued his ruling. He dismissed Counts 2 and 3 but upheld Count 1. His ruling did not go to innocence or guilt, only to faulty administrative procedure by the secretary of the army. He concluded that the secretary's decision was "arbitrary and capricious" because he did not answer the plaintiff's claim that Samuel Mudd was a citizen of Maryland and therefore must be tried in civil court. This is what Judge Friedman wrote in his opinion, based upon the testimony of the plaintiff's expert witness, Dr. Jan Horbaly, a professor of military law: "The fundamental problem with [the secretary's] decision lies in the fact that [he] never addressed the argument that Dr. Mudd was a citizen of the United States and a citizen of Maryland, a non-secessionist state, and the expert testimony of Dr. Horbaly that the Hunter Commission therefore could not exercise law of war jurisdiction over Dr. Mudd."[15]

The army was forced to go back and respond to the claim that Mudd's citizenship precluded the jurisdiction of the military tribunal. The tribunal, according to Horbaly, would only have had law of war jurisdiction if a state of war existed, and a noncitizen belligerent was charged with violating the law of war.

The army responded to Judge Friedman's ruling arguing that the Supreme Court case known as *Ex Parte Quirin*[16] demonstrated that the military had authority to try Dr. Mudd whether or not he was a citizen of the United States for violations of the law of war. In *Quirin* two of the eight defendants (Nazi saboteurs sent to blow up certain electrical power stations) were U.S. citizens and were tried by a military tribunal. The jurisdiction of the tribunal was challenged before the Supreme Court, and the Court ruled that the tribunal had jurisdiction to try the accused even though two were U.S. citizens. In August of 2000, Judge Friedman was satisfied with the army's response, dismissing Richard Mudd's suit.[17] Richard Mudd had lost again, only this time in a federal court.

Richard Mudd was not through fighting. He decided to appeal Judge Friedman's ruling to the U.S. Court of Appeals for the District of Columbia. In 2003, after hearing all of the arguments by Richard Mudd's attorney and the army's lawyer, the appeals court handed down its ruling. It caught everyone by surprise. The court said: "Since Dr. Mudd was not a member or former member of the armed forces, the grandson's petition is not within the zone of interests regulated by the statute. For this reason, the appeal is denied and the case is dismissed."[18] In other words, the case should never have been allowed in the first place—by the ABCMR or by the federal court in the District of Columbia. Dr. Samuel Mudd, the appeals court ruled, had no standing before either of them.

Battered but not beaten, the Mudd family had one final recourse left to it—appeal the court's ruling to the U.S. Supreme Court. In the interim between the federal court's ruling and the appeals court's decision, Richard Mudd died at the age of 101, leaving the effort to exonerate his grandfather to his descendants—principally to his son, Thomas Mudd, the great-grandson of Samuel Mudd.

Thomas Mudd decided not to challenge the appeals court rul-´ing, bringing an end to the efforts to overturn the jurisdiction of the military tribunal that convicted his great-grandfather. After a century and a quarter, the courts had finally brought an end to the legal efforts to overturn the jurisdiction of the military tribunal that convicted Dr. Mudd and his codefendants.

While the legal jurisdiction of the military tribunal to try Dr. Mudd (and his coconspirators) was finally decided, the question of Dr. Mudd's innocence or guilt was left in limbo. To most Americans, Dr. Mudd remains a folk hero, an innocent victim of an unjust federal government that sought revenge for the murder of Abraham Lincoln. But what was the evidence that led the tribunal to convict Samuel Mudd in the first place, and why do many historians today believe he was guilty of aiding and abetting John Wilkes Booth?

SAMUEL MUDD WAS BORN ON December 20, 1833, at Oak Hill, the farm of his father, Henry Lowe Mudd. The Mudds lived in southern Maryland some thirty miles southeast of Washington. Henry Mudd was a farmer of substantial means, owning several hundred acres of farmland, along with eighty-nine slaves that provided the much-needed labor required for culturing tobacco. The value of the Mudd slaves represented the bulk of the senior Mudd's financial assets, worth $86,000 or the equivalent of nearly $1 million in current purchasing power.[19]

Henry Mudd was a strong advocate of education, and through a combination of public, private, and home tutoring, he provided for his children's schooling. At the age of seven, young Sam began attending public school. Two years later his father hired a tutor to teach his children at home. At fourteen Sam attended St. John's College in Frederick, Maryland, where he received his first formal classical instruction. It was while at St. John's that Sam met his future wife, Sarah Frances Dyer, known affectionately as "Frank" to Sam and his family. Sarah attended a girl's academy in Frederick at the same time Sam was attending St. John's.

Following his course of instruction at St. John's, Sam, now seventeen, enrolled at Georgetown College in the District of Columbia (now Georgetown University). He attended Georgetown from 1850 to 1853. A bright student, Sam had every hope of graduating. In 1853, however, his plans were dashed when he was expelled from the school, accused of being a ringleader in fomenting a riot among his classmates. In what must have been a humiliating moment for Sam's father, he was told to come take young Sam out of the school.

A year after returning home following his expulsion from Georgetown, Sam decided that his real interest was in medicine, not farming, and under the able mentoring of his older cousin, Dr. George Mudd, Sam entered the University of Maryland Medical School. After two years of medical training, Sam graduated in 1856 a doctor.

Having completed his medical education, Mudd returned home and turned his attention to the beautiful Sarah Dyer. The courtship that began during the time they both attended schools in Frederick culminated in their marriage on November 26, 1857. Within the year, Sam and his wife moved onto a tract of 218 acres that adjoined Henry Lowe Mudd's farm, where they began construction on a new house. While Sam and Frank waited for their house to be completed, their first child, Andrew Jerome, was born. In 1859, the three Mudds moved into their new home, and Sam took up the dual role of farmer-doctor. Over the next six years, three more children were born to the couple, Lillian Augusta (June 2, 1860), Thomas Dyer (June 6, 1861), and Samuel Alexander II (January 30, 1864). Sam and Frank would lead a happy normal life in the midst of family and friends in the rural southern community of Charles County, Maryland.

Tobacco proved considerably more profitable than ministering to the ailments of Sam's neighbors, and he devoted most of his time to farming. By the outbreak of the Civil War, the border states of Missouri, Kentucky, and Maryland accounted for half of the nation's production of tobacco, and of that half, Maryland outproduced both Missouri and Kentucky combined. Maryland's wealthiest tobacco plantations were concentrated in southern Maryland, and of the six counties comprising southern Maryland, Charles County was the leading producer of tobacco.

Growing tobacco required many hands and long hours of hard work. In the earliest days of the county, labor was scarce and the de-

The home of Dr. Samuel Mudd in Charles County, Maryland. Booth left provisions here to be picked up on the way to Richmond with Lincoln as his prisoner. Instead, he rested here after having his broken leg set and before continuing his escape to Virginia after killing Lincoln. (Author's collection)

mand for sturdy workers was high. An acre of rich soil could nourish four thousand tobacco seedlings, each seedling requiring a handmade "molehill." Weeding, deworming, removing suckers, and harvesting each plant leaf by leaf could only be done by human labor. A single field slave could plant one and a half acres a day, or six thousand seedlings. A three-hundred-acre farm, the average in the county in the nineteenth century, required ten slaves working twenty days to plant. By the end of the growing season, one thousand pounds of tobacco could be brought to market for each slave that worked the fields. Although undesirable as a part of the culture of Charles County, blacks were crucial to the economy of the region. By 1860, blacks in Charles County accounted for two-thirds of the population.

The institution of slavery, so necessary to the profitable production of tobacco, wed Charles County to her Southern brethren culturally and politically. So important was the institution that even the religious leaders of the region praised it as a blessing reflective of God's benevolence as shown by the apostle Paul in his first epistle to

Timothy—"Let as many servants as are under the yoke count their own masters worthy of all honour, that the name of God and *His* doctrine be not blasphemed."[20]

Samuel Mudd was a strong believer in slavery as a blessing for both the white man and the black man. Abraham Lincoln and the new Republican Party were the antithesis of everything Mudd and his neighbors believed in. Mudd's views on slavery and Lincoln can be gleaned from a letter he wrote to the leading Catholic theologian of the day, Orestes Brownson. Brownson published a journal that was among the more influential writings among Catholics of the period. Shortly into Lincoln's first term, Brownson, a supporter of slavery, had slowly come around to emancipation's being the policy the country and the church should adopt. Mudd, a subscriber to Brownson's journal, wrote to Brownson bitterly admonishing him for supporting Lincoln and his abolitionist policies. In his letter, Mudd scolded the theologian for not accepting the fact that slavery was a favored institution that God himself had created. Mudd wrote: "Christ, our Savior found slavery at his coming and yet made no command against its practice. . . . I think it is a great presumption in man to supply the omissions which God in his infinity thought proper to make." Mudd went on to express his own theory of eugenics and those of many of his neighbors when he pointed out that Northerners and Southerners were "inherently different." "The people of the South," Mudd wrote, "are differently constituted from those of the North—attributable to education and climate . . . they are more sensitive—their sense of honor is much more keen and they would sooner run the risk of death, than live with an injured reputation."[21] Four years later Mudd would change his tune when his life was in jeopardy. Accused of aiding John Wilkes Booth, Mudd would tell his military captors that he had always been "a good Union man" who believed in union and supported the cause.[22]

But 1862 was a different time for Mudd and his neighbors. The ungodly Abraham Lincoln and his Black Republican agents were considered enemies of the institution of slavery and everything it stood for. Lincoln would become a force for change the likes of which the local citizens of southern Maryland never thought possible. The change would ultimately lead to the loss of Charles County's number one investment—slaves. The total value of the slaves living in Charles

County at the outbreak of the war was equal to $12 million in terms of today's economy. Lincoln's policy of emancipation was a devastating blow to the economy of Charles County, wiping out the accumulated assets of many planter families overnight. It resulted in those members of the county who supported the Confederacy welcoming John Wilkes Booth and his plot against Lincoln with open arms.

By the time Lincoln took his oath as president on March 4, 1861, Charles County had raised four militia companies intent on defending Maryland against any coercive move by the Federal government should the state secede from the Union.[23] Among the four militia companies was the Charles County Mounted Volunteers, commanded by Samuel Cox, a prominent plantation owner and good friend of Samuel Mudd. Cox, like Mudd, was a passionate believer in the Confederate cause and would work hard to support her effort at independence. In April 1865, Cox would play a significant role in Booth's attempted escape following his assassination of Lincoln.

Mudd and his older brother James Anthony Mudd were among the several dozen volunteers who joined Cox's militia company. Maryland, however, did not secede, and the local militia companies, rather than disband, went underground and were soon serving the Confederacy as a highly organized network of clandestine secret service agents. It was this network of agents that John Wilkes Booth sought to enlist with the help of Confederate agents in Canada in his plot to kidnap Lincoln and carry him south to Richmond. With the fall of Richmond and the surrender of Lee's army, however, all this changed. Booth came to the conclusion that if there was any chance at all to save his beloved Confederacy, "something decisive & great must be done."[24]

IT WAS GOOD FRIDAY, APRIL 14, 1865. The city of Washington was still in the midst of celebrating the surrender of Robert E. Lee's Army of Northern Virginia. The war was not over by any means, but the end was close, very close. It had been four long and bloody years, and a war-weary nation was ready for peace. Lurking in the shadows in an alley behind Ford's Theatre, John Wilkes Booth was prepared to strike one last blow to save the collapsing Confederacy and secure her independence from the despotic grip of Abraham Lincoln. Booth's original plan to capture Lincoln was no longer possible. Now that Richmond had fallen and Jefferson Davis was on the run, Booth had no safe haven to which he could take his captured prize. He had decided on a better plan. It was designed to decapitate the Federal government, creating enough chaos to give the remaining Confederate forces still in the field time to regroup. If Booth could kill Lincoln; his vice president, Andrew Johnson; and Secretary of State William Seward, along with General Ulysses S. Grant, it just might give Jefferson Davis and his exhausted armies the breathing room they desperately needed. It was a futile plan, but at the time Booth and like-minded people were desperately grasping at anything that might turn defeat into victory.

At approximately 10:20 P.M., Booth entered the theater lobby and climbed the stairs leading up to the dress circle. He then made his way across the rear of the circle to the special box where Lincoln was sitting. With Lincoln were his wife, Mary, and their two guests, Major Henry Rathbone and his fiancée, Clara Harris. Within a matter of seconds Booth entered the box, fired his small derringer point blank into the back of Lincoln's head, and, after a brief struggle with Rathbone, vaulted over the balustrade to the stage below. Booth made his way out the rear of the theater and, mounting his horse, sped off into the night before most people were aware of what had happened. His destination was the Surratt tavern, located thirteen miles south of Washington in Prince George's County, Maryland. After a brief stop at the tavern, where he and his sidekick David Herold picked up some whiskey, a field glass, and a carbine, the two fugitives headed for the home of Samuel Mudd.

When Booth jumped to the stage, he landed awkwardly, fracturing his left fibula a few inches above the ankle. By the time Booth reached the tavern the pain in his leg was becoming unbearable. He needed to see a doctor as soon as possible. Fifteen miles to the south of the tavern was the home of Dr. Mudd, a man Booth had met previously and in whose home he had been a houseguest only a few months before. Digging their spurs into the sides of their mounts, the two men headed south from the Surratt tavern in the direction of Mudd's farm. Arriving around 4 A.M., the two men were invited into Mudd's house. After examining Booth's leg, Mudd set it, forming a splint around the leg to help immobilize the fracture. Mudd then put Booth to bed and told him to rest while he went into the neighboring village of Bryantown to pick up a few supplies. While in Bryantown, Mudd learned from Union soldiers the terrible news that Lincoln had been assassinated and that the killer was a man named "Booth."

When Mudd returned home later that evening he found his two guests about to leave. With the largest manhunt in the nation's history in full swing, Booth could only travel at night under the safe cloak of darkness. Mudd pointed the way toward Piney Church, located due west of Mudd's house. Watching until the men disappeared, Mudd went inside, where his wife had seemed visibly upset. She told her husband that when the injured man came down the stairs from the second floor bedroom she noticed that his chin whiskers were hanging loose from one side of his face. She had become alarmed but had kept her composure until the two men left. Mudd, on hearing his wife's description of the false whiskers, decided he should return to Bryantown and tell the soldiers headquartered there about the two men. His wife, however, pleaded with him not to leave her and the children alone in case the two men should return and do her and the children harm. Mudd decided to wait until the next day, Sunday, when he would see his cousin George Mudd at church and ask him to notify the soldiers.

On Monday morning George Mudd informed the soldiers in Bryantown of the two men that had been at his cousin's house on Saturday. On Tuesday, four military detectives from the provost marshal's office that had arrived in Bryantown earlier in the day visited Dr. Mudd and his wife. As a result of questioning Mudd and his wife, Mudd was taken into custody six days later on Monday, April 24, and placed in the Old Capitol Prison in Washington.

Mudd was charged with conspiring to help Booth kill Lincoln and later helping Booth to escape. He was tried, along with seven other defendants, by a military tribunal composed of nine Union officers. The trial lasted fifty days, and when it was concluded all eight defendants were found guilty. Four were sentenced to death by hanging; three, including Dr. Mudd, received life sentences, and one was sentenced to six years in prison. Mudd and his cohorts were sentenced to serve their prison terms at Fort Jefferson, a military prison located in the desolate Dry Tortugas Islands off of the Florida Keys. After serving three years and eight months of a life sentence,

President Andrew Johnson pardoned Mudd, allowing him to return to his home and family.

The events described above comprise the story that Samuel Mudd told and wanted all that would listen to believe. It was a story deliberately twisted to make a guilty man appear innocent. The story would remain twisted for a century and a half before the truth finally straightened it out. The image of Mudd as a gentle country doctor who unexpectedly became entangled in a tragic murder through no fault of his own belies the facts that continue to mount against him. The details of the time leading up to the assassination and shortly thereafter have been carefully crafted by Mudd and his supporters for over a century. A different, more factual description of the tragic events of that period follows.

THE EARLIEST EVIDENCE OF BOOTH'S PLOT to kidnap Lincoln occurs during the first week of August 1864. Booth was in Baltimore staying at Barnum's City Hotel. He sent invitations to two boyhood chums, Samuel Arnold and Michael O'Laughlen, to join him in his room. He had something to tell them of the utmost importance.

Arnold had attended school with Booth at St. Timothy's Hall in Catonsville, Maryland, in western Baltimore, while the O'Laughlen family lived across the street from the Booth home on Exeter Street. Both Arnold and O'Laughlen had served in the Confederate army before returning to their homes and civilian life in Baltimore. Booth knew this and decided to seek their help. Years later Arnold described his meeting with Booth in a memoir and acknowledged that Booth recruited both himself and O'Laughlen into a plan to capture Lincoln and carry him to Richmond.[25] Hearing Booth's plan, both men agreed to help.

Booth next turned to the logistics of his plan. If he were going to successfully capture Lincoln and carry him south to Richmond, he would need a safe avenue of escape. Southern Maryland was the obvious choice for such a route. The area was filled with Southern sympathizers and Confederate agents who had successfully avoided Union authorities for three years while providing support to Richmond's war effort. In the fall of 1864, these sympathizers had lost much of their wealth to Lincoln's emancipation policies. The area contained a major route, referred to as the "mail line," that ran through Prince George's and Charles counties and over the Potomac River into Virginia and on to Richmond. Confederate agents used the route throughout the war to move people and materiel between various points in the North and Richmond. It was an obvious choice to carry a captured Lincoln south.

But if Booth were to get help from the agents in southern Maryland, he would need an introduction of some sort. In searching for that introduction Booth looked north to Canada, where just such help existed. Montreal was a major site for Confederate agents operating out of neutral Canada. In the spring of 1864, Jefferson Davis had sent two of his closest associates to Canada along with $1 million in gold to establish a spy network to undertake a series of clandestine actions aimed at undermining the morale of the Northern people, thereby preventing Lincoln's reelection in the fall.

On October 18, Booth arrived in Montreal and registered at St. Lawrence Hall, a hotel that served as headquarters to several Confederate agents, including a man by the name of Patrick Charles Martin.[26] Booth was in Montreal a total of ten days, from October 18 to October 27. During those ten days he was seen on several occasions meeting with Patrick Martin and another notorious agent named George Sanders.[27] When Booth left Montreal on October 27, he carried with him a letter of introduction that Patrick Martin prepared for him. The letter was directed to two men living in Charles County, Dr. William Queen and Dr. Samuel Mudd.[28] The letter was Booth's entree to certain key people who could help with his capture plan. It suggests that Samuel Mudd was well known by Patrick Martin and was an important contact for Booth to make.

Returning to Washington after his ten-day stay in Montreal, Booth boarded a stage and headed for Bryantown on November 11. Booth arrived at Bryantown in the early evening and was met by Dr. Queen's son-in-law, John Thompson, and taken back to the Queen residence, where Booth spent the night.[29] The next morning, following services at St. Mary's Catholic Church, Thompson introduced Booth to Dr. Mudd. Booth went to Mudd's house and later that evening returned on the stage to Washington, where he rented a room at the National Hotel.

A month later, on December 17, Booth made a second trip to Bryantown and this time spent the night as Dr. Mudd's houseguest.

St. Lawrence Hall was home to Confederate agents operating out of Montreal, Canada. Booth stayed there from October 18 to October 27, 1864, and met with Confederate agents. (Courtesy of Kieran McAuliffe)

The next day, Sunday, December 18, Mudd and Booth rode into Bryantown, where Mudd introduced Booth to a man named Thomas Harbin.

Harbin had served during the war as a Confederate Secret Service agent involved in undercover operations in Charles County and in King George County, Virginia. He had lived a few miles south of the Mudd farm and served as postmaster at Bryantown before the war. Harbin was well connected throughout the area and knew virtually all of the Confederate operatives working between Washington and Richmond. According to Harbin, he came to Bryantown in December 1864 at Mudd's request and met with him and Booth at

Patrick Charles Martin, a key Confederate agent working out of Montreal, Canada. Martin met with Booth in Montreal on at least two occasions in October 1864. (Courtesy of Kieran McAuliffe)

the Bryantown tavern. Harbin told of being introduced to Booth by Mudd, and although Harbin described Booth as acting rather theatrical, he consented to assist Booth in his plan to capture Lincoln.[30]

Having recruited Harbin into his plot, Booth next went after John Surratt, a young Confederate agent working for Judah P. Benjamin, the Confederate secretary of state. Once again Booth turned to his key connection, Dr. Mudd, for help. This time Mudd came to Washington to meet with Booth. On December 23, Mudd arrived in Washington early in the morning, ostensibly to buy his wife a Christmas present. While in Washington he met with Booth. Mudd agreed to take Booth to the boarding house of Mary Surratt, where he would find John Surratt. While the two men walked along the street toward the Surratt boarding house they ran into John Surratt and Louis Wiechmann, a friend of Surratt's and a boarder at his mother's house. The four men went to Booth's hotel room, where Booth enlisted Surratt into his plot.[31]

St. Mary's Catholic Church, Bryantown, Maryland. Booth met Mudd for the first time at this church on Sunday, November 12, 1864. (Author's collection)

Now, thanks to Dr. Mudd, Harbin and Surratt were on board as members of Booth's capture team. Surratt and Harbin were Confederate agents, both highly competent and trusted, and both well connected throughout the Confederate underground route as it ran from Washington to Richmond. Both men knew all of the intricacies of safe routes and safe houses throughout southern Maryland. Harbin's help was further realized when he and John Surratt recruited George A. Atzerodt into Booth's conspiracy. Atzerodt had worked throughout the war ferrying persons at night across the Potomac River to Virginia. His skill at negotiating the heavily patrolled river was essential. Harbin would later prove invaluable in handling Booth and Herold as they made their escape southward after crossing the Potomac into Virginia following Lincoln's assassination, and Booth had Mudd to thank.

The statement that Booth carried a letter of introduction from a Confederate agent in Montreal introducing him to Samuel Mudd runs counter to everything we have heard about Mudd and his alleged innocence. The letter is a direct link between Booth, Mudd, and Confederate agents in Canada, and ties all three together in the fall of 1864.

Thomas Harbin. Both Surratt and Harbin served as Confederate agents. Booth was introduced to both men by Samuel Mudd in December 1864, following the actor's return from Montreal in October. (Courtesy of James O. Hall)

Without the help of Patrick Martin and Samuel Mudd, Booth could never have put together his team of cohorts or his avenue of escape. Thus, John Surratt, Thomas Harbin, George Atzerodt, Lewis Powell, and David Herold (all conspirators) can be traced to Samuel Mudd, and Booth's introduction to Mudd can be traced to Patrick Martin in Montreal. Mudd was, in fact, the key conspirator in helping Booth assemble his team, and it was Patrick Martin who sent Booth to Mudd.[32]

Mudd's initial claim at the time of his arrest that he had met Booth on only one occasion was just one example of the lies he told. At the time of his imprisonment at Fort Jefferson, Mudd produced an affidavit in which he acknowledged meeting with Booth in Washington and introducing him to John Surratt. In the same affidavit he inadvertently let slip that Booth had been in Charles County a second time and that he met with him then as well. This is the meeting that took place with Thomas Harbin on December 18.[33]

When John Wilkes Booth came to Dr. Mudd's house in the early morning hours of April 15, 1865, seeking medical aid, it was the fourth

Mudd arranged a meeting between Booth and Harbin at the Bryantown tavern on December 18, 1864. As a result of the meeting, Harbin agreed to join Booth's conspiracy. (Courtesy of Robert Cook)

time that the two men had met, and none of the four meetings were accidental. In his three previous meetings with Booth, Mudd played a pivotal role in aiding Booth in his scheme to assemble an "action team" to capture President Lincoln and carry him to Richmond as a prisoner of the Confederacy. Booth not only was an overnight guest at Mudd's house during one of the three meetings, but also had sent provisions to Mudd's house for safekeeping to be used during his planned escape. George Atzerodt, the conspirator recruited by Harbin and Surratt, gave a voluntary statement in which he stated that Booth had sent provisions to Mudd's house to be picked up on the way to Richmond with the captured president.[34]

In his statements given prior to his arrest, Mudd lied about virtually every critical piece of information the authorities were seeking in their effort to capture Booth. Lieutenant Alexander Lovett, the first interrogator of Mudd, and Colonel Henry H. Wells, his second interrogator, both complained of Mudd's evasiveness and apparent untruthfulness during their questioning.[35] This evasiveness led Wells to place Mudd under arrest and send him to Washington under guard.

John Harrison Surratt posing in his Papal Zouave uniform, ca. 1868. (Courtesy of the Surratt House Museum)

Mudd's attempt to convince the military authorities that he only met with Booth on one occasion, and that being accidental, belies all of the facts in his case. Mudd even withheld from his own attorneys the meeting at the National Hotel where he introduced Booth to John Surratt, and the December meeting in Bryantown with Harbin. Mudd's senior attorney, Frederick Stone, was quoted by a reporter in an obituary written about Mudd at the time of his death in 1883: "The court very nearly hanged Dr. Mudd. His prevarications were painful. He had given his whole case away by not trusting even his own counsel or neighbors or kinfolk. It was a terrible thing to extricate him from the toils he had woven about himself. He had denied knowing Booth when he knew him well. He was undoubtedly an accessory to the abduction plot, though he may have supposed it would never come to anything. He denied knowing Booth when he came to his house when that was preposterous. He had been even intimate with Booth."

Nothing could be more damaging to Mudd's claim of innocence than his own attorney's condemnation. In any defense of Dr. Mudd, those advocating his innocence must explain his pattern of lying. An innocent man does not fear the truth. He neither misrepresents it nor withholds it. Dr. Mudd did both.

Today, Dr. Mudd still remains something of a folk hero in the eyes of the public, the underdog who fought against a ruthless government intent on destroying him. Both the print and visual media have found Dr. Mudd an ideal subject, portraying his story to a naive public. Of all the myths surrounding the tragic assassination of Abraham Lincoln, Dr. Mudd's portrayal as an innocent victim heads the list.

CHAPTER TWELVE

THE MISSING PAGES FROM BOOTH'S DIARY

The Great Government Cover-Up

I have a greater desire and almost a mind to return to Washington and in a measure clear my name. Which I feel I can do.

—John Wilkes Booth

We have Booth's diary, and he has recorded a lot in it. . . . It concerns you for we either stick together in this thing or we will all go down the river together.

—Edwin M. Stanton, allegedly quoted in George W. Julian's diary

THE FIRST EPIGRAPH THAT APPEARS above can be found in John Wilkes Booth's little diary or memorandum book that is on display in the museum in Ford's Theatre, where he shot Abraham Lincoln on the night of April 14, 1865. Booth made the entry during his attempted escape while hiding in a pine thicket, waiting until it was safe to cross the Potomac River into Virginia. The entry has spurred conspiracy-minded individuals for over 140 years in their quest to prove that Lincoln's assassination was part of a grand conspiracy between members of Lincoln's own administration and the Confederate government. Beginning in 1865, when Union prosecutors tried to prove that Jefferson Davis was behind Lincoln's murder, to more modern times when several self-professed historians claim Edwin Stanton engineered the president's death, reams of mysterious documents have surfaced, which, if true, would force a rewriting of American history in shocking terms.[1] It all began when the assassin's diary was found on his body after he was killed at the farm of Richard Garrett, near Bowling Green, Virginia.

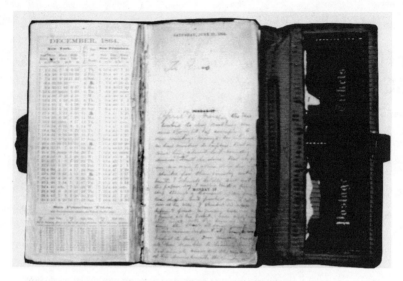

John Wilkes Booth's small memorandum book, which he used as a diary during his attempted escape. It was found on his body and given to Secretary of War Edwin Stanton. (Courtesy of the National Park Service)

On April 25, after Booth safely crossed the Potomac River with his cohort David Herold, three former Confederate soldiers took them to the farm of Richard Garrett, a Virginia tobacco farmer. Garrett, believing the two men were also Confederate soldiers on their way home, offered them food and rest at his home. Booth and Herold bedded down in the Garretts' tobacco barn, content that they were safe for the time being. Around three o'clock in the morning, however, they were suddenly awakened by the sound of horses and men shouting. Stirring from their sleep, the two men peered between the open slats of the barn. In the moonlight they could make out a troop of cavalry gathered in front of the Garrett farmhouse.

After twelve days of searching, Union soldiers finally caught up with Booth and Herold a hundred miles from Washington, deep in Confederate Virginia. Based on a telegram received in the War Department telegraph office on Monday, April 24, Lafayette C. Baker, head of the National Detective Police, had sent two of his detectives and a troop from the 16th New York Cavalry to King George County, Virginia, in pursuit of Booth and Herold. The detectives accompanying the squad of cavalry received a tip that one of the

John Wilkes Booth, from a carte de visite. This image is known as the "wanted poster view." (Courtesy of Kellie and Richard Gutman)

Confederate soldiers who aided the two fugitives could be found in Bowling Green. Rousting the soldier from a dead sleep, the detectives convinced him he should give them up. Realizing he had no choice, the soldier led the troopers to the Garrett farmhouse, where they learned that Booth and Herold were sleeping in the nearby tobacco barn.

Surrounding the barn, the detectives began negotiating with Booth to surrender. After a show of bravado in which Booth tried to convince the soldiers to give him a fair chance to shoot it out with them, the barn was set on fire in an attempt to force Booth into surrendering. Herold had earlier given himself up without a struggle.

As the fire raged through the barn, a shot rang out and Booth fell to the barn floor mortally wounded. The shot came from the pistol of Sergeant Boston Corbett, one of the troopers of the 16th New York. When questioned later, Corbett said he saw Booth raise his carbine as if he were going to shoot at the officers standing outside. Corbett's act would eventually be used by conspiracy theorists who claimed he violated orders not to shoot Booth, but to take him alive. Corbett, the theorists explain, was under secret orders from Secretary of War Stanton to make sure Booth was not taken alive, to prevent him from revealing that Stanton and others were behind Lincoln's murder.

The mortally wounded Booth was dragged from the burning barn and carried to the porch of the Garrett house, where he was laid out on a small mattress. The bullet had passed through his neck, severed part of his spinal cord, and left him paralyzed from the neck down. As Booth lay dying, one of the detectives, Everton Conger, noticed his lips moving as if he were trying to speak. Leaning over and placing his ear close to the dying man's mouth, he heard Booth say in a halting whisper, "Tell . . . my . . . Mother . . . I . . . die . . . for . . . my country."[2]

It was a few minutes past seven o'clock on the morning of April 26, 1865, when Booth died. Before his body was shipped back to Washington, Conger carefully went through the contents of Booth's pockets, making an inventory of each item. He found a small stick pin inscribed "Dan Bryant to J.W.B.," a small boxed compass, a file with a cork stuck on the sharp end for protection, a small pipe, a large handful of shavings to use as a fire starter, a spur, a bank draft made on the Ontario Bank of Canada for 61 pounds, 12 shillings, and 10 pence (the equivalent of $300 in gold or $660 in greenbacks), and the small memorandum book, which Booth used as a diary during his flight. Inside the book were five photographs of women he had known—four actresses and his fiancée, Lucy Hale.

The items were carried back to Washington and turned over to Stanton in his office in the War Department. The bank draft, compass, carbine, Bowie knife, and brace of pistols taken from Booth and Herold were introduced at the conspirators' trial as exhibits.[3] The small memorandum book, or diary, remained in Stanton's safe, seemingly forgotten at the time of the trial. The diary surfaced two years later when it was introduced during the impeachment trial of President Andrew Johnson in the House of Representatives. Although the diary was known to have existed at the time of the Lincoln conspiracy trial, neither the prosecution nor the defense nor the nine military officers serving as judge and jury questioned its absence.

When the diary was finally examined, it was found to have several pages missing. Lafayette C. Baker was called as a witness at Johnson's impeachment trial in 1867 and engaged in the following exchange:

Q. You are still of the opinion that the book [Booth's diary] is not now in the condition it was when you first saw it?

A. That is my opinion.

Q. Did you see the Secretary of War count the leaves at the time you and [Lieutenant Colonel Everton] Conger were together at his house?

A. No, I think not.

Q. Did you count the absent leaves or stubs?

A. No sir; I never saw any stubs until I saw them here.

Q. Do you mean to say that at the time you gave the book to the Secretary of War there were no leaves gone?

A. I do.

Q. That is still your opinion?

A. That is still my opinion.[4]

Conger also appeared as a witness. His testimony went somewhat differently:

Q. To whom did you deliver them [articles taken from Booth's body at the Garrett farm]?

A. To Mr. Stanton.

Q. Did he retain possession of the diary?

A. Yes, sir.

Q. Do you know who has it now?

A. Judge Holt [Judge Advocate General Joseph Holt].

Q. Do you know when he received it?

A. I do not.

Q. Who was present when you delivered the diary to Mr. Stanton?

A. Colonel L. C. Baker.

Q. Have you seen that diary since?

A. Yes, sir; I saw it today.

Q. State whether it is in the same condition as when you delivered it to Mr. Stanton.

A. I think it is.

Q. Have you examined it closely?

A. I have.

Q. Are there any leaves cut or torn out?

A. Yes, sir.

Q. Were they torn out when you first had possession of it?

A. There were some out and I think the same.[5]

The conflict between Baker's and Conger's testimonies was never resolved. What we know for a fact is that several pages were missing from Booth's diary at the time of his capture, and that at least two of the pages were removed by Booth to send notes to Richard Stuart on Monday, April 24. The "missing" pages became one of the first of many controversial questions to come out of the Lincoln assassination. Conspiracy theorists became convinced that they contained the key to who really was behind Lincoln's assassination. The very notion that pages were missing hinted at a cover-up.

JUMPING FORWARD TO 1937, Otto Eisenschiml, a chemist turned historian, published *Why Was Lincoln Murdered?*, a book that caused a seismic upheaval among history buffs and the public in general.[6] Eisenschiml, through clever innuendo and manipulation of facts, framed a series of questions that pointed an incriminating finger at Lincoln's secretary of war, Edwin Stanton, accusing him of masterminding Lincoln's assassination.

One of the entries Booth made in his diary was a statement that caught Eisenschiml's attention: "To night I will once more try the river [Potomac] with the intent to cross; I *have a greater desire and almost a mind to return to Washington and in a measure clear my name. Which I feel I can do*" (emphasis added).[7] Eisenschiml seized on Booth's remark as a launching pad for his bizarre theory that Stanton, along with other powerful figures in the North, wanted Lincoln out of the way so they could deal with a defeated South without his interference. Underlying Eisenschiml's theory of Stanton's involvement was his belief that Stanton had been informed that a plot was afloat and did nothing to stop it from taking place.

Eisenschiml also claimed that Lincoln was refused protection at the same time he wrote that the president's bodyguard was derelict in his duty, thereby allowing Booth access to Lincoln. Both claims are false. Lincoln never requested protection, and his bodyguard that night, John F. Parker, accompanied him to the theater. Once inside, Parker's job was done until it was time for the president to leave. Lincoln's valet and messenger, Charles Forbes, sat outside the box and allowed at least three people to enter at different times during the evening. Unfortunately, Booth was one of the three.

Eisenschiml further claimed that if General Grant had accompanied Lincoln to the theater as originally planned, Booth would never have been able to pass Grant's military guards, thus protecting Lincoln as well as preventing his own assassination. Eisenschiml claimed that Stanton ordered Grant not to go to the theater with Lincoln. Another false claim. Grant frequently moved about Washington unaccompanied by military guards or aides, including those occasions when he attended the theater. Just two months earlier, on February 10, Grant accompanied Lincoln to Ford's Theatre to see John Sleeper Clarke in a comedy entitled *Love in Livery*. As the *Washington Evening Star* reported the next day, no military guards were posted at the president's box, and several people freely entered the box with messages for Lincoln.

While Eisenschiml went to ridiculous extremes in attempting to implicate Stanton in Booth's plot, he did not claim that Stanton withheld the diary to cover up his role in Lincoln's murder. Rather, he believed that Stanton withheld the diary because its contents would have benefited some of the defendants on trial for Lincoln's murder. "Booth's notebook," Eisenschiml writes, "showed plainly that, up to the last day, kidnapping and not murder had been the goal of the conspirators."[8] Here again, Eisenschiml overreaches. Did Eisenschiml really believe Booth and his cohorts could kidnap the president of the United States and transport him 120 miles through enemy-occupied territory without someone getting killed? If Booth and his cohorts had no intention of killing anyone, why were they carrying guns?

While Eisenschiml raises several questions about the assassination, he never questions the missing pages. That was left to later conspiracy advocates who, although lacking Eisenschiml's reputation as a historian, equaled his chutzpah in attempting to rewrite history.

IN NOVEMBER 1975, thirty-eight years after Eisenschiml first accused Stanton of involvement in Lincoln's murder, a rumor spread that these missing pages were in the possession of a Stanton descendant, and that they were filled with incriminating evidence not only resurrecting Otto Eisenschiml's theory of Stanton's role in Lincoln's murder, but also naming dozens of other high-ranking politicians and prominent people as accomplices. Two students of the case, James O. Hall and Richard Sloan, were particularly interested. Hall was the premier scholar on the subject. Over the years he had accumulated a file cabinet filled with hoaxes and confabulations. "Wanting to believe can be a very strong emotion," Hall once said, "and Americans love conspiracy." Sloan was the editor and publisher of a popular Lincoln newsletter, *The Lincoln Log*. If the rumor about the missing pages was true, their exposure could result in the rewriting of American history. Sloan doggedly pursued the rumor and made contact with a man who claimed to have access to the missing pages.

At first, Sloan's informant insisted on anonymity, referring to himself only as "Mr. X."[9] Eventually Sloan gained Mr. X's confidence, and he revealed himself to be Joseph Lynch, a dealer in rare books and Americana, living in Worthington, Massachusetts. Lynch told Sloan that he discovered the missing pages in 1974 in the possession of one of Stanton's great-granddaughters. She had contacted him for an appraisal of some artifacts (she also insisted on anonymity, Lynch claimed). Hall had many questions for Lynch but was sure that if he pressed for an interview, Lynch might be scared away. So Hall fed some of his questions through Sloan, who reported back to him. The whole affair had an air of intrigue. Lynch never gave Sloan his personal telephone number and always placed his calls from a pay phone.[10] It was reminiscent of Bob Woodward and Carl Bernstein's adventures with "Deep Throat" in their investigation of the Watergate cover-up. Sloan kept his newsletter readers informed of the latest news, as it became available to him.[11]

As word of the missing pages spread, a motion picture studio in Salt Lake City, Sunn Classic Pictures, expressed an interest in obtaining the rights to the missing pages for use in a major motion picture about the Lincoln assassination. Lynch, claiming to act as the Stanton heir's intermediary, negotiated with David Balsiger and his partner Charles Sellier Jr. of Sunn Classic Pictures for the use of the missing pages along with other related documents that Lynch claimed were in the heir's possession. Balsiger allegedly paid $39,000 for the right to read the material and take notes.[12] Later, he acquired a full transcript of the missing pages, again through Lynch. They had wanted to see the original pages, but Lynch insisted that the Stanton heir would not permit anyone but him to see them, claiming they were kept in a bank safe-deposit box. In October 1977, Sunn Classic released the movie and a paperback book under the title *The Lincoln Conspiracy*.[13]

Lacking the necessary expertise to evaluate the transcripts, Balsiger and Sellier had hired Ray A. Neff as a consultant. Neff, a professor of health sciences at Indiana State University, was well known in assassination circles for his strange theory that Booth escaped capture at the Garrett farm and eventually made his way to Guwahati, India, where he died in 1883. Similar to the plot outlined in the missing pages, Neff claimed that Stanton and his cronies were behind Lincoln's murder. Neff had amassed a vast collection of documents that spelled out in detail the who and why of Lincoln's death. None of the original documents existed, however; all of the material consisted of typed copies, the originals having been destroyed years earlier. Neff's collection dovetailed neatly with the missing pages.

Sixteen years earlier, Neff had convinced Robert Fowler, the editor of *Civil War Times*, that his unorthodox claims were true. In 1961, the centennial year of the start of the Civil War, Fowler ran a sensational article entitled "Was Stanton behind Lincoln's Murder?"[14] The article, written by Fowler, was based on the "new discoveries" by Neff that he made available to Fowler. Neff claimed to have discovered cipher messages written in the margins of a book originally owned by National Detective Police Chief Lafayette C. Baker. Baker, who was privy to Stanton's treasonous plans, feared for his life because of what he knew. After several scrapes with near death, Baker allegedly succumbed to arsenic poisoning in 1868, presumably to keep him from exposing the other plotters. According to the Baker ciphers, Stanton headed a group of over fifty prominent people in the North who sought to remove Lincoln.

Neff's treasure trove included "secret service documents, congressmen's diaries, old letters, book manuscripts, deathbed confessions, secret cipher-coded messages, rare photographs, and correspondence secretly intercepted by Secretary of War Edwin Stanton."[15] The discovery of such a wealth of previously unknown material was unprecedented in the annals of historical research. It was this "gold mine" that consultant Neff brought to Balsiger and Sellier and which, together with the missing pages from Booth's diary, they used as the basis for their movie and book.

There was a problem, however. In the years following the 1961 article in *Civil War Times*, several historians presented evidence that Neff's claims were based on faulty research and fabricated documents (one historian referred to them as "ingenuine").[16] They were found to contain wrong names, wrong dates, wrong places, and wrong relationships, which seriously challenged their authenticity. Most disturbing of all, Neff's documents were merely typescript copies of originals that no longer existed.[17]

Between 1977 and 1981, the revamped *Civil War Times Illustrated*, under its new editor, William C. Davis, ran a series of editorials retracting the 1961 article.[18] Davis wrote, "Rarely does a magazine print a retraction or refutation of one of its own articles, but this is precisely what we do now. It is a debt we owe to the cause of history."[19] Davis wrote that if they are not "outright forgeries, [they] are so highly suspect as to make them inadmissible as evidence in any serious investigation."[20]

Davis, however, was referring only to the documents in Neff's collection, not the missing pages of Booth's diary. What about these pages? Unlike the Neff material, the originals of the missing pages allegedly still existed, although they too were unavailable for historians to examine. When pressed to produce the original pages, Lynch claimed the owner was reluctant to release them because of her concern that the documents might legally belong to the federal government, and she did not want to become embroiled in a messy legal battle.[21]

One of the caveats that raised doubts over the authenticity of the missing pages was Lynch's claim that they had faint blue lines printed on them, while the diary displayed in Ford's Theatre was believed to contain pages without lines. Lynch received permission from Michael Harman, custodian of the relics in the Ford's Theatre collection, to examine the diary. To his delight, he found that the diary had the same faint blue lines as the missing pages. Lynch further reported that he found "suspicious erasures . . . and evidence of invisible ink that was beginning to show up" on several of the pages. But his most shocking conclusion was that the writing in the diary was forged![22] It wasn't, Lynch said, Booth's writing.

The forgery claim made no sense at all. When Balsiger learned of Lynch's "findings," he sent Ray Neff, now working for Balsiger, to Washington in hopes of having him examine the diary and photograph the pages using ultraviolet and infrared illumination in an effort to confirm Lynch's claims. As incredible as it sounds, Harman granted Neff permission!

James O. Hall, on learning that Neff had photographed the diary on behalf of a commercial movie studio, became concerned that the pictures would become the property of Neff and Balsiger and that other researchers would not have access to them. Any claims made about secret writing or evidence of tampering or forgery could not be independently verified. Hall was concerned because of Neff's involvement in the earlier controversy about Lafayette Baker's alleged secret cipher markings that William Davis had termed "ingenuine."[23] Hall's concern was that Neff was working as a consultant for a private, profit-making company. The National Park Service had no way of protecting itself should a controversy later arise. Hall suggested that the National Archives or the FBI carry out a thorough analysis of the diary, including Booth's handwriting. Hall had recently uncovered two important letters written by Booth shortly before the assassination that had been misfiled in the National Archives. Their provenance was solid. They could be considered authentic samples of Booth's handwriting in determining the legitimacy of the handwriting in the diary.

To everyone's surprise, the Park Service rejected Hall's suggestion. The principal reason given was that the diary was fragile, and any further handling might damage it. Faced with the Park Service's decision to deny further access to the diary, Hall sought the help of influential friends, who contacted several political leaders, including Vice President Walter Mondale and Senator Hubert Humphrey. The Park Service suddenly had a change of heart and announced they would turn the diary over to the FBI's forensic laboratory for analysis. Hall, in writing to FBI Director Clarence Kelly, said, "It is our hope that you will use the most sophisticated means to photograph each and every page of this diary, to bring up whatever is there or to demonstrate that nothing is there."[24] Hall went on to point out that a claim had been made that the writing in the diary was not that of John Wilkes Booth and that the forgery was committed to aid in a government cover-up. The analysis of the handwriting by FBI experts would settle the question once and for all.

The FBI's report states that "no invisible writing, unusual obliterations or alterations or any characteristics of a questionable nature were found," and that "the handwriting in the diary was prepared by the writer of the specimens furnished by the National Archives[25] known to be in the handwriting of John Wilkes Booth."[26] No invisible writing, no secret (encoded) writing, no altered writing, and no erasures were found. Several of the stubs left behind when pages were removed showed signs of handwriting. There were faint blue lines printed on each of the dated pages, just as Lynch claimed. In all, the FBI report noted that a total of forty-three sheets (eighty-six pages) were missing from the diary.[27]

Now that the FBI had put to rest any questions concerning the diary's condition, attention turned to what was written on those alleged missing pages that Joseph Lynch had uncovered. Richard Sloan suggested Lynch meet with Hall. He pointed out that sooner or later, Lynch or Sunn Classic Pictures would have to produce proof that the pages existed. Hall, after all, was the leading authority on the assassination and if anyone could authenticate the missing pages, it was him. Lynch appeared nervous at Sloan's suggestion. He told Sloan he didn't trust historians. Lynch felt they would take advantage of him or misquote him.[28] After considerable cajoling and prodding by Sloan, Lynch agreed to meet with them both, in a hotel room in White Plains, New York. Once the two men met, Lynch overcame his distrust of Hall and gave him a copy of the full typescript of the pages. In return, he asked Hall for his evaluation of their authenticity. Hall agreed. From Lynch's perspective, Hall's approval would blunt any criticism.

Following are excerpts from the missing diary pages, interspersed with explanations of the people and events mentioned in the excerpts:[29]

I [Booth] have finally decided to take the step which I hoped would not be necessary. Sent a message by a friend to Jefferson Davis and await summons from him.

I received instructions to proceed to Montreal and wait upon Clement Clay and Jacob Thompson. I am to proceed at once.

Clement C. Clay and Jacob Thompson, two Confederate politicians, were sent to Montreal in April 1864 to establish a clandestine operation working out of Canada. Jefferson Davis gave Thompson $1 million in gold to finance a series of attacks against the North in an effort to demoralize its citizens, resulting in Lincoln's defeat in the fall elections.

Clay and Thompson finally arrive and inform me if I were willing to undertake a mission for the Confederacy, they could use my services.

I ran into John Surratt the other day and by a conversation, he told me that he was now serving the Confederacy as a courier between Washington, Richmond, and Canada.

John Surratt, Mary Surratt's son and a cohort of Booth's, worked as an agent for the Confederate State Department, reporting directly to Judah P. Benjamin, the Confederate secretary of state.

He comes tonight bringing with him four trusted friends he swears by. We are to meet at Ella Washington's boarding house in Washington.

Surratt brought to me this morning Thomas Jones, Dr. Mudd, and Col. Cox.

Jones said that he had a brother-in-law who could also be enlisted [Thomas Harbin] but that the brother-in-law had to support his family and would require $100 a month. When I go South, he will introduce me to him.

Thomas Jones served during the war as the Confederate Signal Service's chief agent in Charles County, Maryland. Jones lived in a house on a high bluff overlooking the Potomac River with a clear view of the Confederate signal camp on the Virginia side. Following Lincoln's assassination, Jones hid Booth and Herold in a pine thicket for five days before putting them safely across the Potomac River. Jones's brother-in-law was Thomas Harbin, also a Confederate agent. Harbin had served as postmaster in Charles County before the war. Several years after the war Harbin was interviewed by George Alfred Townsend, a highly respected newspaper reporter and author. Harbin told Townsend that Dr. Mudd introduced him to Booth at a prearranged meeting at the Bryantown tavern on December 18, 1864. As a result of the meeting Harbin agreed to join Booth's kidnap plot. Once Booth and Herold crossed the Potomac River following Lincoln's murder, Harbin arranged for them to be taken to the summer home of Dr. Richard Stuart, where they hoped to receive food and rest. Stuart refused Booth lodging and sent him to the cabin of William Lucas, a free black, where the two fugitives spent the night.

In Richmond, I saw Judah Benjamin first. He brought me to Vice-President Stevens and the two of them and I went to see Jefferson Davis.

I received instructions in all detail and an order for $70,000 drawn on a friendly bank.

In Philadelphia today I met with Jay Cooke. After waiting for an hour and a half, he entered the room with great apology citing as his reason for the delay—press of business.

Cooke was a prominent banker and financier who used his own bank and influence with other bankers to raise large sums of money for the government by selling government bonds. By January 1864, Cooke had raised over $600 million to help Lincoln finance the war and keep it going.

The discussions that we had concerning the project he was very concerned with being compromised, but said that he would arrange for me to meet a number of people who have interests in the plans, in New York on Friday next at the Astor House.

Cooke brought his brother Henry—greeted me warmly and said he thought most highly of Judah Benjamin and anyone who that wily fox, Benjamin, would send would be the best man available.

Henry Cooke was a journalist who in 1856 used his paper, the *Ohio State Journal*, to get Salmon P. Chase elected governor of Ohio. In 1861 he became head of his brother's bank in Washington, and in 1862 he became president of his brother's street railway system that ran between Washington and Georgetown.

> We had lunch, then went to a room where the people present were a number of speculators in cotton and gold.

> Present were Thurlow Weed, a person by the name of Noble, a man by the name of Chandler, a Mr. Bell—who said he was a friend of John Conness.

Weed was the political "boss" of the Whig and, later, Republican parties in New York. He supported William Seward for the Republican nomination for president in 1860. Isaac Bell was a cotton merchant. Zachariah Chandler was a Radical Republican senator from Michigan (1857–1875) and a constant thorn in Lincoln's side. He was also a business associate of John Conness, senator from California.

> Answering a knock on my door this morning, I found Lafayette Baker on my doorstep. I thought the end had come.

Baker was head of the War Department's National Detective Police (NDP), which after the war became the Secret Service. Baker had a shady reputation for bending the law in carrying out his investigations, but he was very effective at dealing with corrupt government and military individuals.

> But instead, he handed me letters from Jefferson Davis, and Judah Benjamin, and from Clement Clay. I gave him the money and sent a message to Richmond. I don't trust him. I wait for answer. I receive reply, my orders—trust him! I do not!

Davis was president of the Confederate States. Benjamin was the Confederate secretary of state at the time of Lincoln's assassination, and Clay was a Confederate diplomat who became one of two commissioners Davis sent to Canada to carry out undercover actions against the North.

He [Senator John Conness] also said Montgomery Blair was with us, but that Blair had to be careful. He was watched constantly.

Montgomery Blair served as Lincoln's postmaster general. He resigned in 1864, forced out of Lincoln's cabinet by the Radical Republicans.

Baker comes and brings with him Col. Conger. I told Baker to have him leave because I did not know him and talking to too many people can be dangerous.

Lieutenant Colonel Everton J. Conger was a detective in Lafayette Baker's NDP. He was the ranking officer in charge of the troop of cavalry that captured Booth and Herold at the Garrett farm. Conger removed the diary from Booth's body and turned it over to Stanton. One conspiracy theory has Conger shooting Booth under orders from Stanton to prevent Booth from implicating Stanton and others should he be taken alive.

[Judah] Benjamin says that the Jacobeans [word missing] received their promises and their money.

Jacobean is a social club of the Republican Party.

I purchased a carbine entirely covered in leather. I darken it with lamp black.

Booth purchased a Jenks carbine on March 20.

I took Paine and Surratt with me and we waited on the road near the garden. In the late hours of the morning we heard a horse approaching. It was him. It was dark and I waited until he was 25 or 30 yards from me. I fired! I saw his hat fall.
    Paine fired twice. He stayed in the saddle and galloped away. Within minutes they pursued us. Within two miles, we eluded them. Another failure!

Paine was an alias used by Lewis Powell. This excerpt apparently refers to the incident in which Lincoln had his hat shot off of his head while approaching the main gate to the Soldiers' Home, where Lincoln and his family stayed during the summer months. Lincoln later made light of the incident, saying it was an accidental stray shot. Ward Hill Lamon, Washington marshal and a close friend of Lincoln's, believed it was an assassination attempt. Lincoln's hat was later recovered by a sentry who said it had a bullet hole through it.

> I met Conger at the Herndon House. He was in mufti and warned no new attempts until we have a new plan.

The Herndon House was a boarding house located one block from Ford's Theatre. Booth paid for a room for Lewis Powell. Booth, Powell, Atzerodt, and Herold met in Powell's room around seven o'clock on the evening of April 14 to go over Booth's assassination plans.

> If I try again without orders they will find me in the Potomac along with my friends.

> Paine said he would kill the tin soldier if I wished. I told him not to.

The "tin soldier" presumably refers to Lafayette Baker.

> A new plan—other arrangements to be made. I am to have charge.

The "new plan" is presumably an assassination plan.

> I believe that Baker and Eckert and the Secretary are controlling our activities and this frightens me.

Thomas T. Eckert was assistant secretary of war and head of the war department's telegraph office.

> I have found the additional men needed. The routes are arranged. It is too late to withdraw.

> By the almighty God, I swear that I shall lay the body of this tyrant upon the altar of Mars. And if by this act I am slain, they too shall be cast into Hell for I have given information to a friend who will have the nation know who the traitors are.
> Pax Vale[30]

Mars is a reference to Secretary of War Stanton. *Pax Vale* means "Peace and Farewell."

IN ANALYZING THE TRANSCRIPT, there are several things to consider. First is the alleged "Stanton heir," whom Lynch claimed owned the missing pages. When Hall contacted the known descendants of Edwin Stanton, none of them were aware of the missing pages, or any other documents relating to Lincoln's assassination. When confronted with this finding, Lynch claimed that the great-granddaughter was descended from an illegitimate child of one of Stanton's sons. This claim, however, is difficult to believe without some sort of documentary proof.

The second consideration is the internal evidence of the transcript. Even the best of fabricators make mistakes. One need only read the first two sentences to see that the transcript is problematic. The entry reads: "They say that Jubal Early has attack[ed] Rockville and even though one can see the flames and hear the gunfire, no one knows how the battle goes. At lunch someone said that Lincoln and Stanton had almost been killed when a shell burst within five feet of them on the parapet of Fort Stevens."

In early July 1864, Confederate general Jubal Early marched out of the Shenandoah Valley with orders to attack Washington and sack parts of the city. The objective was to force Grant to send part of his army facing Lee to Washington, thus relieving pressure on Lee. On July 9, Early pushed aside a delaying force under Union major general Lew Wallace near Frederick, Maryland, and marched south toward the capital. Early's forces reached the outlying environs of Washington near Silver Spring on July 11, where his troops were stopped at Fort Stevens. A Federal force from the 6th Army Corps arrived just in time to repel the Confederate attack.

Fort Stevens was located a short distance from Soldiers' Home, where Lincoln was staying with his family at the time of Early's attack. On July 12, Lincoln visited the fort and climbed atop the parapet to watch the action. His recognizable form drew Confederate fire, and an army surgeon standing next to Lincoln was shot in the hip, knocking him from the parapet.

The entry clearly indicates that Booth was in Washington at the time of Early's attack on July 11 and 12. In reality, he was several hundred miles away in Franklin, Pennsylvania, tending to his oil investments. On June 7, 1864, Booth wrote to Isabel Sumner, a beautiful sixteen-year-old girl he was courting at the time, "I start tomorrow for the mountains of Penn. Where I remain about three weeks."[31] The correspondence continued through the end of August. On July 14, Booth wrote to Isabel from New York City, "I have just returned from the mountains of Penn—God bless you."[32] Booth's trip to Pennsylvania is corroborated by his brother Junius, who wrote in his diary for June 9, "John & Joe Simonds left for Oil City."[33] Clearly, whoever fabricated the missing pages was unaware of these letters that were in the possession of a descendant of Isabel Sumner.

The next questionable entry reads, "At a party given by Eva's parents, I met Senator John Conness. Conness says Eddie and he are friends from the days in California in '55 and '56."

Conness was a senator from California (from March 3, 1863, to March 3, 1869) who switched from the Democratic Party to the Republican Party in 1864. The transcript supplied with the Sunn Classic Pictures promotional material identifies "Eddie" as John Wilkes Booth's older brother, Edwin Booth. Of the known letters written by Booth, three mention his brother Edwin by name. The first is a letter to Edwin with the salutation, "Dear Ted."[34] The remaining two letters are to friends, in which Booth calls his brother "Ned" ("I am glad Ned is doing well,"[35] and "When did you see Ned?").[36] The name "Eddie" is absent from any known writing of John Wilkes Booth or, for that matter, any of the other members of the Booth family.

The fifth entry in the diary reads: "John Morgan is dead. Another brave spirit has paid the ultimate price for his patriotism. I met him years ago at a soiree in New Orleans. He was a gentleman and we will miss him."

John Hunt Morgan was a brigadier general in the Confederate army who mostly operated behind enemy lines as a guerilla raider. Morgan was engaged in several small operations that gained him fame as a dashing cavalier. He was killed on September 4, 1864, in Greeneville, Tennessee, while attempting to escape from Union cavalry that had surrounded his headquarters. The only time that Booth was in New Orleans was the period from March 6 through April 3, 1864, five months prior to Morgan's death. Booth was fulfilling an acting engagement at the time, while Morgan was carrying out raids in Kentucky, including Mt. Sterling (March 22) and Danville (March 24). At the time of Booth's engagement, New Orleans was occupied by Union troops, making it doubtful if not impossible for Morgan to attend a soiree where he allegedly met Booth.

The next entry notes that Grant has advanced to within seven miles of Richmond. This occurred on September 28, 1864. It reads: "I have finally decided to take the step which I hoped would not be necessary. Sent a message to Jefferson Davis and await summons from him." The timing is off in this entry. We know that Booth made his decision to kidnap Lincoln in late July, not October. During the first week of August, Booth summoned two old friends from his Baltimore boyhood days, Samuel Arnold and Michael O'Laughlen, to meet with him in his room at the Barnum Hotel in Baltimore. It was during this meeting that Booth went over his kidnapping plan with Arnold and O'Laughlen.

The next troublesome entry claims that Booth, along with Lewis Paine (Powell) and John Surratt, lay in wait for Lincoln, and as he approached, Booth fired once and Paine fired twice. Booth writes, "I saw his hat fall." In the companion book version of *The Lincoln Conspiracy,* the date given in the missing pages for this failed attempt on Lincoln's life is March 22. Apparently the person who wrote the diary was unaware that Booth was in New York City on March 22. The records of the National Hotel, where Booth stayed when in Washington, show he checked out on March 21 and took the 7:30 P.M. train to New York. There is a record of Booth sending a telegram from the St. Nicholas Hotel in New York to Louis Weichmann at the Surratt boarding house on March 23. Booth did not return to the National Hotel until the evening of March 25.

These errors, Booth's presence in Washington at the time of Early's attack, the use of the name "Eddie" when referring to Edwin Booth, the alleged meeting between Booth and Morgan in New Orleans, the timing of Booth's decision to kidnap Lincoln, and his attempt to shoot Lincoln on March 22, 1864, when he was actually in New York City, are careless mistakes that point to the missing pages as being fabrications. The disposition of the real missing pages is unclear. We know Booth used two of the sheets (four pages) to write notes to Dr. Stuart. The other forty-one sheets (eighty-two pages) were more than likely also used by Booth as note paper. One thing seems clear, however: they were not used by Booth to record the bogus writings that appear in the typescript Lynch claimed came from Booth's diary and which David Balsiger and Charles E. Sellier Jr. relied on.

There are other documents that Sunn Classic Pictures and David Balsiger relied on that also appear to be fabricated. The principal one is a supposedly unpublished entry from the journal of George Washington Julian, a Radical Republican congressman from Indiana. The passage was used by Sunn Pictures in an attempt to authenticate the missing pages. It shows that Booth's diary was intact when it was turned over to Stanton, just as Lafayette Baker had claimed. It relates that the diary turned up in Stanton's office on April 24, two days before Booth was cornered and killed at the Garrett farm. Just how the diary turned up in Stanton's office beforehand is an amazing story that *The Lincoln Conspiracy* tries to explain.

According to Balsiger's scenario, Booth's diary was not found on his body on April 26, as most history books claim. It was found by one of Lafayette Baker's Indian scouts, Whippet Nalgai,[37] lying in the tall grass along the banks of a creek where Booth left it by mistake. Working separately from the Union search party that cornered Booth, Nalgai found the diary with several other items belonging to Booth at the spot where Booth and Herold landed after crossing the Potomac River on the night of April 23–24. Booth had rested along the bank of the creek while Herold sought the help of Mrs. Elizabeth Quesenberry, a Confederate agent who lived nearby. After listening to Herold's story, Quesenberry sent for Thomas Harbin, the agent Booth had enlisted in December 1864 with the aid of Dr. Samuel Mudd. Harbin arranged for horses and a guide to take Booth and Herold to the summer home of Richard Stuart in King George County, Virginia. According to *The Lincoln Conspiracy*, Booth mistakenly left the diary and several other items in the grass when he went to Stuart's home. Later that same day, while searching for Booth, Whippet Nalgai discovered the diary. Nalgai rushed the diary back to Washington and delivered it to Lafayette Baker, who gave it to Stanton on April 24.[38] After examining the diary, Stanton summoned three Radical Republicans to his office: George Julian, Senator Zachariah Chandler of Michigan, and Senator John Conness of California.

The scene in Stanton's office is described in the April 24 unpublished entry from Julian's journal. Julian wrote that on entering Stanton's office he "sensed something was amiss." Stanton told him, "We have Booth's diary, and he has recorded a lot in it." Senator Conness, who was scanning the pages when Julian arrived, was "moaning repeatedly, 'Oh, my God. I am ruined if this ever gets out.'"[39] Stanton took the diary from Conness and asked Julian to look at it. Julian demurred. "I was better off not reading it," he later wrote in his journal. Stanton pressed him in threatening language: "It concerns you for we either stick together in this thing or we will all go down the river together." Stanton gave the diary to Thomas Eckert, his assistant, and told him to secure it in his iron safe, warning those in the room, "We cannot let it out."[40] The excerpt is sensational to say the least, and it confirms the claims made in the missing pages.[41]

Following his death in 1899, Julian's journals passed to his daughter, Grace Julian Clarke. In 1926 she loaned them to Indiana historian Claude Bowers, who was working on his anti-Radical book, *The Tragic Era.*[42] According to an explanatory statement in the Neff-Guttridge Collection at Indiana State University, Bowers "photographed the journal pages without Grace Clarke's knowledge."[43] At some point before his death, Bowers transcribed the photographic copies in the presence of an Indianapolis businessman by the name of Hugh Smith. Smith then had Bowers's transcriptions verified by a notary public. According to Smith, Bowers for some strange reason then destroyed the photographs. Smith, thinking ahead, "took one [of Bowers's transcribed copies] back to Indianapolis to have proof of the journal entries should Bowers ever need support in the future."[44] Why do you suppose Bowers needed to substantiate his writings? And why did he rely on Hugh Smith to provide that support? Why didn't he simply keep the photographic copies in his own files? Bowers never made any claims or statements in his writings that referred to the alleged Julian excerpts. None of his writings refer to Booth's diary, or its missing pages. If Bowers was seriously concerned about having support for his writing, why did he destroy the photographs of Julian's journal? None of it makes any sense.

In 1974, Neff was fortunate enough to meet with Smith in Muncie, Indiana. Using the first person plural, Neff wrote: "During our interview with Hugh Smith he showed us the Photostats and said he had decided to destroy them. He did, however, permit us to have them transcribed in the presence of a notary public."[45] Smith, emulating Bowers before him, then destroyed his copies, leaving Neff with the only surviving copy of Julian's "unpublished" excerpt. The only source still alive who can verify this strange story is Neff himself; everyone else is dead. Neff's "copy" of the "excerpt," now part of the Neff-Guttridge Collection at ISU, is the sole evidence for the strange meeting that Neff and Balsiger claim took place in Stanton's office.

But once again, the devil is in the details. Unbeknownst to the authors of *The Lincoln Conspiracy* at the time of publication, authentic excerpts from Julian's diary had appeared in a 1915 issue of the *Indiana Magazine of History*. Even more fortuitous, the key entry for April 24, the very date on which Stanton allegedly revealed the contents of the missing pages to Conness and Julian, is among the published entries. It reads:

Monday, [April] 24th
     On Saturday last we had General Rosecrans before our committee, and his account of the campaign of Western Virginia makes McClellan look meaner than ever. On last Friday went with Indianans to call on President Johnson. Governor Morton transgressed the proprieties by reading a carefully prepared essay on the subject of reconstruction. Johnson entered upon the same theme, indulging in bad grammar, bad pronunciation and much incoherency of thought. In common with many I was mortified.[46]

There is no mention of a meeting in Stanton's office, of Booth's diary, or of Stanton's warning that everybody will go down the river together if they don't stick together. Did the editor of the *Indiana Magazine of History* decide to delete such an important entry, leaving out the incredible story of what took place in Stanton's office? It seems unreasonable. If the editor had such sensational material proving treason within Lincoln's own cabinet, why would he withhold it from the public? Even more puzzling, why would Claude Bowers, a man so virulently anti-Radical Republican, withhold such anti-Radical information from his book about the Radicals? He could have driven a stake through the very heart of the Radical Republicans by exposing this treasonous plot involving Stanton.[47]

In an attempt to locate the alleged "unpublished" portion of Julian's journal, historian James O. Hall sought the help of curators at the Indiana State Library where Julian's papers reside, and at the Lilly Library at the University of Indiana, where the Claude Bowers papers are housed. Their efforts came up empty. There were no "unpublished" portions of the journal; no correspondence pertaining to the "unpublished" version; no notes by Bowers or anyone else; no photographs, photostats, or photocopies; and no typescripts. There was nothing in the Claude Bowers papers to indicate that he made copies before returning the journals to Grace Clarke.[48]

Once again, fortune smiled on the seekers of truth. It turns out that Bowers was not the only historian to be allowed to use the journals for research. Mabel Engstrom, a graduate student at the University of Chicago, was allowed to use them in researching her master's thesis on George Julian (which she submitted in 1929). In 1977, Mabel Engstrom, now Mabel Herbert, wrote to the managing editor of *Civil War Times Illustrated*, who was investigating the question of Booth's diary and the alleged missing pages. She wrote: "I just cannot remember reading anything in the journal which stated that Julian was aware of any plot relating to the assassination of Lincoln. Of course, it has been fifty years or so since I read the journal. However, I think I would have remembered such an important statement if it had been in the journal."[49] Again, it is highly unreasonable to believe that Mrs. Herbert would not remember such a dramatic entry. Her recollections only cast further doubt on the authenticity of the "unpublished excerpt" from the journal.

No one in Stanton's office that day bothered to ask how Booth's diary got there while he was still at-large. It is an important point because all of the evidence places the diary on his body at the time of his death. Indeed, at least four eyewitnesses reported seeing Booth and his diary south of the Potomac River *after the date* that the diary was allegedly found in the tall grass where Booth rested.

The first of these witnesses was Dr. Richard Stuart. On the night of April 23, Booth and Herold arrived at his summer home in King George County, Virginia, ten miles south of the Potomac River. After crossing the river, Thomas Harbin arranged to have the men taken to Stuart's house. The doctor allowed the two men into his home long enough to eat, but he refused them shelter. Instead, he sent them a short distance away to the cabin of William Lucas, where they spent the night. The next morning Lucas's son, Charlie, took Booth and Herold to the Rappahannock River crossing at Port Conway, where they ran into three Confederate soldiers.

While at the Lucas cabin, Booth, angered by Stuart's lack of hospitality in refusing shelter to him, decided to insult Stuart by offering to pay for the small amount of food they received. Booth tore a leaf from his diary and wrote a note offering Stuart $5.00. Deciding that was too much, Booth slipped the note back in his diary, tore another page from it, and wrote a second note offering $2.50. In his sworn statement to authorities, Stuart described it as "a leaf from a memorandum book rolled around and the money rolled up in it."[50] Booth sent the note to Stuart via Lucas on the very day Julian's purported journal entry said the diary was in Stanton's possession. Detectives found the first note, offering $5.00, tucked in Booth's diary when it was recovered.[51]

The second witness to Booth's having the diary in his possession after April 24 was William Garrett, the oldest son of Richard Garrett. Booth and Herold arrived at the Garrett farm on the evening of April 24. William Garrett later told detectives that on April 25 he saw Booth seated on the porch, where "he had *a small memorandum book* in his hand and was writing in it" (emphasis added).[52]

The third and fourth witnesses are the two detectives who cornered Booth at the Garrett farm, Everton Conger and Luther B. Baker. Both testified to removing Booth's diary from his body on April 26. During the conspirators' trial in 1865, Luther Baker gave the following testimony: "We took all the papers from his pocket—as soon as we removed him from the barn, and delivered them to Colonel Conger. . . . They were *a diary*, three drafts or checks, and forty-five dollars in greenbacks" (emphasis added).[53]

At the 1868 impeachment trial of Andrew Johnson, Baker testified a second time and was asked: "Who took the memorandum book from his [Booth's] pocket?" Baker replied, "Colonel Conger. He looked at it and handed it to me. I looked at it, and then we put it in a handkerchief with other things."[54]

There can be no doubt that Booth had the diary on him when he was killed. The missing pages and the excerpt from Julian's journal are pure fabrications in support of the myth that Stanton engineered Lincoln's assassination.

Just who was responsible for creating the missing pages and the other fabricated documents remains a mystery. It isn't even clear when they were written, although it seems likely that they are modern fabrications. But whoever it was went to considerable lengths to see to it that their hoax would rewrite the true history of the Lincoln assassination. Clearly, the hoaxer was not a Stanton descendant. Hall and Sloan were never absolutely sure that it was Lynch. Sunn Classic Pictures was careful to call them the "purported" missing pages. Like the other myths associated with Abraham Lincoln, the myth of the missing pages and Stanton's complicity in Lincoln's death will continue to live on, finding new believers in future generations.

CHAPTER THIRTEEN

PEANUT JOHN
The Man Who Held Booth's Horse

Stepping into the alley we came upon a colored boy who we
questioned sharply.
                    —Almarin C. Richards, Police Superintendent,
                                        Washington, D.C.

WHEN I FIRST BECAME A MEMBER of the Lincoln Group of
the District of Columbia in 1976, I became friends with Elmer Stein, one of the many old-time Washingtonians who belonged
to that group. Elmer came up to me at the first meeting I attended
and extended his hand in a friendly gesture. "Hello," he said. "I'm
Elmer Stein." "Hello, I'm Ed Steers," I said, and we shook hands.
Elmer then said something rather odd: "Now you can tell all your
friends that you shook the hand of the man who shook the hand of
the man that held John Wilkes Booth's horse." "Well," I said with a
laugh. "Tell me how that came about." "I will," Elmer said, obviously
delighted I'd asked. He then told me the story.

It was during a particularly hot July night in 1930 when I was working
the night shift as a fireman at Engine House Number 14 on 8th Street
between Kahn's and Lansburg's department stores. It was hotter than
blue blazes. Around 11 P.M. this old colored fellow came into the station
and asked me if he could have a drink of water. I said he could, and he
went over to the bucket sitting beneath the water tap we used for washing the trucks. He lifted the ladle that was in the bucket and took a long
drink of cool water. When he was finished he came over and thanked
me again for the drink. We started to chat and I asked him his name,
and he said he was called "Peanut." He was quite short, with white,
kinky hair. I asked him how old he was because he seemed very old. He

said he didn't know, but he suspected he was pretty old. Then he told me he used to work in the stables across the street. As a young boy he worked mostly in stables around the city. Then he shocked me when he said he held John Wilkes Booth's horse the night Lincoln was killed. He bent over and with a crooked finger pointed to the top of his head. There beneath the thinning hair was a scar plain as it could be. "See dis scar?" he said. "Dat's war ole John Wilkes Booth knocked me down wid de butt of his knife." He went on to describe how he was in the alley behind the theater (known as Baptist Alley from when the theater was a Baptist Church) when Mr. Spangler told him to hold a horse. A little while later Booth came running out the door and yelled for him to give him the horse. He hesitated, he said, because he thought the man was trying to steal Mr. Booth's horse. That was when Booth hit him on top of his head with the butt of his knife, knocking him to the ground. Booth grabbed the reins from his hands and mounted the horse and galloped down the alley, leaving poor old Peanut on the ground holding his bleeding head.

Was the "old colored fellow" the real "Peanut" John Burroughs? Was Peanut John really black? Historians have no doubt that Peanut was at the theater and held Booth's horse. Some historians assume Peanut was black, probably because he worked around the theater as a "gofer" doing all sorts of odd jobs and selling peanuts to theater patrons—and because Almarin C. Richards, superintendent of Metropolitan Police, told the story of how he was in the theater that night and chased Booth out the back door into the alley. In one report Richards said: "Stepping into the alley [behind the theater] we came upon a colored boy who we questioned sharply."[1] Richards's remark seems to make it clear that Peanut John was black. The problem historians have with the remark is that over the next forty years Richards gave as many as six different versions of his role on that tragic night.[2]

Burroughs testified at the conspiracy trial in May 1865 to the events that took place in the alley before and after Booth shot Lincoln. In all, there were just over 360 witnesses that testified at the trial, twenty-nine being black. Each black witness is identified in the court record as "Colored." Burroughs, however, has no such designation next to his name, which leads one to conclude that he was white.

Baptist Alley in the rear of Ford's Theatre. On the
night of April 14, 1865, Booth left his horse here
while he entered the theater through the rear door,
shown here. He then made his way to the box where
President Lincoln was enjoying a rollicking comedy
titled *Our American Cousin*. (Author's collection)

The recording of the trial testimony was carried out by Benn Pitman,
a professional recorder who used a form of shorthand developed by
his brother Isaac Pitman. Benn was a fastidious recorder who insisted
on accuracy. It is not likely that the absence of the word "Colored"
next to John Burroughs's name was an oversight on Pitman's part.
Most historians accept Pitman's recording as accurate, meaning that
Peanut John was white. If true, and we believe it is, the man Elmer
Stein befriended on the hot July evening was an imposter.

What of the man called Peanut John? When Booth arrived at the
theater sometime between 9 and 10 P.M., he handed Edman Spangler

the reins to his horse. Spangler worked as a carpenter and scene-shifter at the theater. When Booth turned his horse over to Spangler for safekeeping, Spangler was already busy shifting scene sets during the play. Spangler protested, telling Booth he should simply tie his horse reins to a post. Booth said the horse was finicky and did not like being left alone tied to a rail. Spangler reluctantly agreed to watch the horse.

Spangler waited until Booth disappeared inside the theater and then called for Burroughs. When Burroughs asked Spangler what he wanted, Spangler turned the reins over to him, telling him to be sure and take good care of Mr. Booth's horse. He would only be gone a few minutes. When Burroughs objected, saying he had to keep a watch on the side stage door, Spangler told him not to worry—if anything happened Burroughs was "to lay the blame on him."[3]

Peanut wasn't sure he should leave his post near the stage door, but he knew Mr. Booth was a very important man in the eyes of Mr. Ford. Holding the reins in one hand, Peanut took advantage of the break to stretch out on a small bench that sat next to the building. Five minutes passed, then ten, and still no Booth. Half an hour passed, and by now Peanut lost track of the time. Resting on the bench, he started to fall asleep when suddenly the rear door flew open with a loud bang, startling the young boy. A man rushed through the door toward the bench where Peanut was sitting, the reins still in his hand. The man grabbed for the reins, but Peanut pulled away, thinking the man was intent on stealing the horse. Grabbing again for the reins, the man raised his arm high over his head and brought it down, striking Peanut on top of his head with the butt of a large Bowie knife, knocking Peanut to the ground.

As Peanut lay on the ground stunned, Booth swung himself into the saddle and, wheeling his horse around, galloped down the alley, disappearing into the darkness. Suddenly several men came running through the door shouting, "Stop that man." It was too late. The rider had spurred his horse to a fast gallop and was soon beyond reach. Peanut, holding his bruised and bleeding head, heard one of the men yell out, "He has shot the President! He has shot the President!"

Not a great deal is known about Burroughs, but what is known derives from his being a prosecution witness at the time of the conspirators' trial in 1865.[4] Peanut explained that around three o'clock on the afternoon of April 14, he helped Edman Spangler remove the partition separating boxes 7 and 8, converting them into a single box to be used by the presidential party that night. Burroughs told prosecutors that sometime around five or six o'clock, Booth rode up Baptist Alley and stabled his horse in a small shed behind the theater.[5] The prosecution questioned Burroughs at length about what he and Spangler talked about earlier in the day when they were removing the partition from the presidential box. Burroughs said Spangler said to him, "Damn the President and General Grant." Burroughs asked Spangler why he damned the president since he had never done any harm to Spangler? "He ought to be cursed when he got so many men killed,"[6] Spangler answered. The testimony did not bode well for Spangler.

When cross-examined by Thomas Ewing, Spangler's lawyer, Burroughs admitted that Spangler often took care of Booth's horse when he came to the theater. Ewing also got Burroughs to admit that Booth sometimes entered the theater through the rear door. Thus, it was not unusual for Booth to ask Spangler to watch his horse, nor for Booth to use the rear door. Even so, Spangler began to appear as if he was a party to Lincoln's assassination. August Kautz, one of the nine officers sitting in judgement, observed that "an accomplice [in the theater] seemed absolutely necessary to enable Booth to accomplish his purpose."[7] Spangler was the logical choice to be that accomplice. He was found guilty by the tribunal and sentenced to six years in prison.

Peanut Burroughs disappears from the standard records that vouch for a person's existence. Since that fateful time in the spring and summer of 1865, no trace has been found of him in city directories or the U.S. Census reports. There is one story that, if true, says that Peanut lived to a ripe old age and frequented the haunts around downtown Washington. Wherever Peanut went in later life, one thing seems assured; his name will live on in immortality thanks to John Wilkes Booth and Abraham Lincoln.

DESPITE THE EVIDENCE supporting Peanut Burroughs's being the young man who held Booth's horse that tragic night in April, others have stepped up to claim that dubious distinction. It seems associating with Abraham Lincoln guarantees certain immortality to those who grab hold of his coattails, even if the association is bad.

As the years passed, storytellers regaled anyone who would listen of their personal association with the great man. Dozens of people said they had been sitting in the box not more than a few feet from the president when he was shot that terrible night. Another dozen claimed to have carried his body across the street from Ford's Theatre to the Petersen House. Over a hundred people said they had visited the death room where the president lay motionless. There are literally hundreds of tombstones scattered across the American landscape with epitaphs that tie the deceased in one way or another to the tragic death of Abraham Lincoln. It is a testament to the power of Lincoln that even those who had no connection with him in life chose to be remembered in death as having touched some part of this great man's story.

Even the act of unknowingly aiding the country's most hated man in some small way drew its share of fame seekers. And as Peanut Burroughs slipped from American memory, others would eventually replace him.

The first of such persons to emerge was a former slave named Nathan Simms. Simms, anonymous in life, gained recognition in death by claiming to have held Booth's horse on the night of the murder. Located in the town cemetery of Bradford, Pennsylvania, near the community of Chester is one of the hundreds of tombstones that proudly display an epitaph linking the deceased with Abraham Lincoln. It reads:

Nathan Simms
1851–1934.
    The slave boy who helped Booth escape the night of Lincoln's assassination, but told the Union soldiers the next day the direction Booth took, thus aiding in his capture.

The tombstone was a special project of Boy Scout Troop 52, located in nearby Marshalton, Pennsylvania. In 1960, the troop spearheaded the raising of funds to purchase a stone and have it engraved with the epitaph. It was a worthwhile community project that the scout troop cheerfully undertook as one of its many good deeds.

Nathan Simms. (Photograph
by Chris Sanderson, courtesy of
Kenneth Trimble)

Little is known about Simms other than his claim that he held
the reins of Booth's horse on the night of the assassination. Simms's
claim has become garbled over time. One version of the story has
come down over the years claiming that Simms held Booth's horse
in the alley behind Ford's Theatre, while another version claims that
Simms held Booth's horse when he stopped at the Surratt tavern,
in Surrattville, Maryland, later that night. In this second version,
Simms claimed that he helped Booth from his horse and watched as
Booth limped into the tavern accompanied by David Herold. Simms
went on to claim that Mary Surratt greeted the two men at the door
and after a brief exchange said, "I'm glad the old rebel is dead."[8] According to the story, the two men emerged from the tavern carrying
rifles and whisky, and Simms helped Booth mount his horse and
watched as he and Herold rode off down the country road toward
Beantown and the home of Dr. Mudd.

NATHAN SIMMS
1851 — 1934
THE SLAVE BOY WHO HELPED BOOTH ESCAPE
THE NIGHT OF LINCOLN'S ASSASSINATION, BUT
TOLD THE UNION SOLDIERS THE NEXT DAY
THE DIRECTION BOOTH TOOK, THUS AIDING
IN HIS CAPTURE

Gravestone of Nathan Simms in the Bradford Cemetery, Marshallton,
Pennsylvania. The gravestone was a project of Boy Scout Troop 52 and their
leader, Kenneth Trimble. (Courtesy of Catharine Quillman)

Of course, it is known that Mary Surratt was in her boarding
house at the time Booth arrived at her tavern thirteen miles to the
south and could not have greeted him. Simms later said that he told
investigators that "Mr. Booth had been a frequent visitor at Surratts-
ville for some months, he and Mrs. Surratt's son John, being regular buddies."[9] While Booth and John Surratt were indeed "buddies,"
there is no evidence that Booth ever visited the Surratt tavern before
that fateful night. He did visit Mary Surratt and her son John on
several occasions at her boarding house on H Street in the District
of Columbia.

Simms regaled his listeners with all sorts of juicy tidbits about
Mary Surratt and her dealings. "Not long ago I went with her into
Washington to purchase nine or twelve pistols," Simms said. "The
pistols were put into a small coffin, furnished by an undertaker, who
placed it in a hearse. Of course, the soldier guards at the bridge [lead-
ing out of Washington] thought it was a genuine funeral and did not
make any attempt at searching."[10]

Simms made his way to Annapolis, Maryland, where he found
employment. Sometime after 1870, no one is sure just when, Simms
migrated to Chester County, Pennsylvania, where he lived out his

uneventful years working at odd jobs.[11] On his death in 1934 the local newspapers carried Simm's story, telling how he claimed to have held Booth's horse the night of the assassination.

Whether Simms actually held Booth's horse at the time Booth stopped at the Surratt tavern isn't clear, but what is clear is that Simms's story of Booth dismounting and going into the tavern and conversing with Mary Surratt is clearly the product of a faded memory—or that of an imposter wanting to grab a piece of immortality by hitching onto the coattails of America's greatest president. The poet Vergil coined a phrase that accurately describes the situation: *sic itur ad astra,* or "thus is the way to the stars." In any event, rest in peace Nathan Simms. You are remembered.

AMONG THE MORE COLORFUL PRETENDERS as Booth's horseholder was a man with the interesting nickname of "Coughdrop Joey" Ratto. Coughdrop Joey's real name was Giuseppe Ratto [also Ratti].[12] Born in Genoa, Italy, in 1854, Joey immigrated to the United States as a young boy before the Civil War and landed in Washington, D.C., in 1861. He grew up around 10th and E Streets, in the same neighborhood where Ford's Theatre sits. Joey was described by those who knew him as "mentally slow," a condition that made him a favorite target in his adult years for the taunts of the local kids who lived in the neighborhood.

Joey was an unusually small person. At maturity, he barely stood five feet tall. He sported a large handlebar moustache and wore the same clothes every day, regardless of the season: an oversized pair of pants, a sport jacket, a top coat, and a black hat that he kept pulled down over his ears. Ratto lived in a small room over a furniture store located at 416 10th Street, across the street from Ford's Theatre.[13] He became a creature of the streets and back alleys around the theater.

Despite his lack of a regular job and limited mental state, Joey supported himself by his wits. He earned his nickname from selling the strong licorice-flavored Lewis Brothers' cough drops to the clientele that frequented the downtown Washington saloon district. These particular cough drops gave off an especially potent aroma on the breath of an imbiber. Coughdrop Joey was a valuable asset to the noonday drinking crowd who didn't want to return to work smelling like a cheap saloon. Joey showed a particularly keen ability to adapt

"Coughdrop Joey" Ratto (1854–1946). Ratto was known for his alleged connection with John Wilkes Booth. (Courtesy of Bert Sheldon)

to harsh economic conditions, somehow finding a way to survive. When prohibition took away his cough drop business, Joey turned to collecting newspapers, which he sold to the local produce and fish merchants for wrapping their fish. Despite the hard times, Joey always managed to find income from other peoples' trash.

Joey had acquired an old hand wagon that he pushed around the city filled with his daily finds. The wagon became a favorite target for the neighborhood kids, who would steal it and hide it. The local policemen in Joey's neighborhood were always helping track down the pushcart. It was one of the rituals that Joey had to endure. It was no wonder that he behaved like a recluse, seldom talking or even recognizing people who tried to speak to him. He had a strange habit of crossing a street whenever he felt like it, oblivious to traffic, much to the consternation of drivers.

No one knows just when Joey became known as the man who held Booth's horse on that tragic night. Bert Sheldon, for years a D.C. policeman and later a lieutenant on the Capitol Hill police force, became one of the leading scholars on Abraham Lincoln and one of the founders of the Lincoln Group of the District of Columbia. Several years ago, Bert told me that he jokingly accused Joey of holding Booth's horse. Before Bert or Joey knew it, the rumor spread, and Joey soon became the object of kids' taunts. All they needed to do to set Joey off was ask him if he held Booth's horse. Joey would fly into a rage, waving his arms and jumping up and down, all the while yelling at his tormentors in broken English. Then he would take off after them, chasing them down the street. On other occasions, when taunted, Joey would simply yell, "They can't prove it. Nobody can prove nothing."

Joey lived out his years as a kind of celebrity to the people who worked in the area around Ford's Theatre. He became known as "the man who held Booth's horse." In the final years of his life he was befriended by Father Nicholas De Carlo of the Holy Rosary Church located on 3rd Street, N.W., in Washington. With father De Carlo's help, Joey lived the final years of his life at the Sacred Heart Home in Hyattsville, Maryland, where he died in 1946 at the age of ninety-two. Relatives living in the area provided for his funeral. He lies buried in an unmarked grave in a family plot in St. Mary's cemetery, not far from Soldiers' Home in northeast Washington.

Joey was eleven years old at the time of Lincoln's assassination and a habitue of the alleys around Ford's Theatre. He may well have held Booth's horse on one occasion or another, but not on the night of April 14, 1865. That distinction, if it be such, goes to "Peanut John" Burroughs—not "Coughdrop Joey" Ratto. Like Nathan Simms before him, however, Coughdrop Joey will be remembered in the Lincoln literature because of his alleged association with Abraham Lincoln.

CHAPTER FOURTEEN

THE MAN WHO NEVER WAS

Andrew Potter and the Traitors Who Ordered Lincoln's Death

If we let the country believe Booth is dead, well . . . Booth will be dead.
—Attributed to Edwin M. Stanton,
in *The Lincoln Conspiracy*

T HE CIVIL WAR IS OFTEN DESCRIBED as the first modern war. Modern in its use of railroads, the telegraph, rifled cannon and muskets, breech-loading weapons, anti-personnel and water mines (called torpedoes), field hospitals, and trench warfare. The Civil War even saw the first use of a submarine that successfully sank an enemy vessel, albeit at its own destruction.[1] And it saw the first well-organized secret service in clandestine operations behind enemy lines.

The use of spies is as old as warfare. What was new during the Civil War was the organization of secret services, designed as special agencies within the respective state and war departments of both the Union and the Confederacy. The Confederacy outnumbered the Union in operations. Included were separate units within the War Department, State Department, Army's Signal Service, as well as a Torpedo Bureau in the War Department and a Navy Battery Bureau. The North, much like the South, never created a single centralized agency. Initially, intelligence gathering was left up to individual commanders. In 1863, an agency was created under Major General Joseph Hooker known as the Bureau of Military Information. A year earlier, in the fall of 1862, Secretary of War Edwin Stanton created a special unit within the War Department reporting directly to him and appointed Colonel Lafayette C. Baker as its head. This unit adopted the official name of National Detective Police (NDP), which became the U.S. Secret Service shortly after the war.

Lafayette Curry Baker, head of the National Detective Police (NDP). The NDP performed the role of a secret service during his tenure as its chief. Baker assigned two of his own detectives to accompany a troop of twenty-six men from the 16th New York Cavalry in pursuit of Booth and Herold. (Courtesy of the Library of Congress)

The designation "National" of the NDP is somewhat of a misnomer. The organization spent most of its time and resources within the environs of Washington, investigating corruption stemming from government contracts, bribery, graft, and the activities of Confederate agents and Southern sympathizers operating within the nation's capital. Washington was by tradition a Southern city, with its commerce closely linked with that of the South. The loyalty, as well as competence, of the local metropolitan police was suspect, and many of the daily responsibilities of the local police were taken over by the military. Under Baker, the NDP became the investigative arm of the War Department.

Lafayette Baker had spent the opening months of the war working as an undercover agent for General Winfield Scott, the commanding general of the U.S. Army. In March of 1862, Stanton appointed Baker a "special agent," and in September appointed him "special provost marshal" with the rank of colonel and made him head of the newly formed NDP. Baker assumed his new role with zealous enthusiasm. He soon developed an unsavory reputation because he blurred the lines separating his official duties from private transactions that often involved bribery and kickbacks. Despite this, Baker and his organization became an effective force during the war, exposing corruption both within and outside the Federal government.

Following Abraham Lincoln's assassination on April 14, 1865, Baker was instrumental in the capture of John Wilkes Booth and his accomplice, David Herold. As Booth and Herold made their way through southern Maryland and across the Potomac River into Virginia, several law enforcement agencies were hard at work trying to capture them, without success. For ten days Booth and Herold had managed to elude the hundreds of detectives and law enforcement officers searching for them. Then, on Monday, April 24, the government received a lucky break. Baker was in the War Department telegraph office when a telegram arrived from the military station at Chapel Point in southern Maryland stating that two unidentified men had crossed the Potomac River on Sunday, April 16. The men were later identified as Thomas Harbin and Joseph Baden, two Confederate agents. Erroneously believing the men to be Booth and Herold, Baker received permission from Stanton to send a cavalry troop in pursuit. Baker chose Lieutenant Colonel Everton Conger and his cousin Luther B. Baker, both agents working for Baker, and requested the commanding officer of the 16th New York Cavalry to provide twenty-five men under the command of a reliable and discreet officer.[2] Two days later the cavalry troop caught up with Booth and Herold at the farm of Richard Garrett near Bowling Green, Virginia, killing Booth and capturing Herold.

Sharing in the reward and the glory, Baker retired from his post as head of the National Detective Police and returned to his home in Philadelphia, were he died in 1868 at the age of forty-two. The NDP detectives working under Baker either left the service, returning to civilian life, or became part of the new Secret Service agency created on July 2, 1865, as part of the U.S. Treasury Department.

The story of Lincoln's assassination, the subsequent killing of Booth, and the trial of his conspirators remained little more than a footnote to the overall story of Abraham Lincoln. The country, having suffered through the bloodiest crisis in its history, put the war and Lincoln's tragic death behind it and looked to the bright future. The assassination of Lincoln came to be viewed as a great tragedy brought about by an insane actor whose lust for fame drove him to commit his mad act. Booth's death at the Garrett farm and the subsequent punishment of those that helped him brought an end to that tragic period in our history.

Then, in 1907, a Memphis, Tennessee, attorney named Finis Bates published a book claiming that Booth was not killed at the Garrett farm, as everyone believed. Booth, Bates claimed, had escaped his pursuers, leaving a surrogate in his place. After knocking about for several years, Booth eventually made his way to Enid, Oklahoma, where he committed suicide in 1903. The story generated a brief flurry of attention but soon fell by the wayside. Serious historians and history buffs ignored the story, concluding it was nothing more than conspiratorial nonsense. Then, in 1937, an amateur historian named Otto Eisenschiml published the first of two popular books that pointed an accusing finger at Lincoln's own secretary of war, Edwin Stanton.[3] Unlike Bates before him, Eisenschiml was successful in convincing a large number of people that Stanton, with the knowledge and help of Lafayette Baker, engineered Lincoln's death. Over the years, assassination historians demolished Eisenschiml's claims, pointing out that his theories consisted almost entirely of innuendo and manipulated facts, not hard evidence. Even so, Eisenschiml's theory continued to find acceptance by a small group of conspiracy-minded people, especially in the media.

Then, in 1957, a startling discovery was made that allegedly uncovered the evidence needed to prove that Stanton and others were involved in Lincoln's murder. Ray Neff, who believes that Booth escaped capture in 1865 and made his way to Guwahati, India, where he died in 1883, purchased an 1864 volume of *Colburn's United Service Magazine* from a Philadelphia bookstore. A few weeks later, while Neff was browsing through the volume, he found strange markings in the inner margins of several of the book's pages. Suspecting the markings were some sort of code, Neff sought the help of a code expert. When it was deciphered, it told a story of high treason, including Stanton and over fifty prominent people in the North. Baker, who was privy to Stanton's treasonous plans, feared for his life because of what he knew.[4] Baker's early death in 1868, Neff concluded, was the result of arsenic poisoning.

Neff began experimenting with the pages of the Colburn book and was able to develop "invisible writing" that yielded the signature "L C Baker," along with an encrypted passage that ended with: "I fear for my life. LCB." The volume and the cipher messages allegedly belonged to Lafayette C. Baker. This discovery spurred Neff to examine every page and to decipher every code he found in it. One entry in particular piqued Neff's interest. It read: "Address Earl Potter, Ladoga, Indiana." After a ten-year search, Neff claimed to have found evidence that Earl Potter, and his younger brother, Andrew, worked as detectives in Baker's NDP unit.[5] According to Neff, Earl Potter was the "Administrative Director," and Andrew served as the "Director of the Secret Service," officially known as the National Detective Police.[6]

The Potter brothers appear for the first time in the assassination literature in 1977 in a paperback book entitled *The Lincoln Conspiracy* by David Balsiger and Charles E. Sellier Jr.[7] Earl and Andrew Potter were completely unknown to historians until Neff found them in the 1960s. It was amazing that these two important Civil War figures escaped detection by every historian who had conducted research in the Civil War field since records of that terrible conflict became available. In writing their book, Balsiger and Sellier hired Neff as a "special consultant" and based their final work on the files that Neff had acquired over a twenty-year period (1957–1977).[8] Here is how the Potter scenario unfolds.

After sending his trusted colleagues Everton Conger and Luther Baker after Booth and Herold (along with members of the 16th New York Cavalry), Lafayette Baker secretly sends Earl and Andrew Potter to Fredericksburg, Virginia, to find Booth. It is a two-pronged approach, and Baker is confident that between the two prongs he will eventually capture Booth. The Potter brothers are nearing Fredericksburg when they receive word that Booth has been shot and killed

Andrew Giles Potter (1840–1932), the man who never was. According to information accompanying this photograph, it was taken following Potter's retirement. (Courtesy of the Neff-Guttridge Collection, Special Collections Department, Cunningham Memorial Library, Indiana State University, Terre Haute, Indiana)

at the Garrett farm near the small village of Port Royal several miles to the east. Heading for Port Royal, the Potter brothers meet up with Luther Baker and Booth's body at Belle Plaine on the Potomac River. The body, now in Luther Baker's care, is loaded on board the *John S. Ide*, a steamer waiting to pick up Baker and his precious cargo and take them back to the Washington Arsenal.

Once on board the *Ide*, Luther Baker leads Earl and Andrew Potter to where two soldiers stand guard over the body, now covered with an old army blanket. Baker pulls back the blanket, exposing the face. The two brothers lean forward to get a close look. The corpse has a long, bushy moustache that is reddish in color, matching its "reddish-sandy hair." The brothers look at Baker as Andrew says that Booth "sure grew a moustache in a hurry. Red, too."[9] It was known that Booth's hair was black and that he shaved off his moustache when he rested at Dr. Mudd's house on Saturday, April 15. "My God!" Luther Baker exclaims. "We got the wrong man!"[10]

Earl and Andrew return to Washington and head straight for Lafayette Baker's office, where they tell him the startling news. Baker is incredulous. He immediately goes to Stanton and tells him the man shot in the tobacco barn is not Booth, but someone else. After a long pause, Stanton makes a fateful decision: he decides to announce to the world that Booth has indeed been shot and killed. "If we let the country believe Booth is dead, well . . . Booth will be dead."[11] Thus begins one of the greatest cover-ups in U.S. history.

Booth escapes and the country is fooled into believing that Lincoln's killer is dead. Earl and Andrew Potter are sent after Booth, hoping to run him down, so that he never lives to tell his tale. The Potters return to the Garrett farm, where they pick up his trail and head west to Orange County, Virginia. Here they receive reports that a man fitting the fugitive's description had been there a few days before, accompanied by David Herold and a black man. They head further west, only to lose the trail. Forced to return home empty-handed, the brothers soon put the assassination and John Wilkes Booth behind them. Lafayette Baker, who knows the truth of Stanton's involvement in the original plan to kidnap Lincoln, will become a target because of what he knows. Three years later, in 1868, Baker will die under mysterious circumstances.[12] Earl and Andrew leave government service for a private detective agency, but not before smuggling out their secret papers telling of the mysterious murder at the Garrett farm and Stanton's cover-up. The files with their damaging evidence would serve to protect the Potter brothers from possible harm. As long as they live, the papers will remain sealed and in their sole possession.

The story of the Potter brothers does not end here, however. The two men return to civilian life and continue in their profession, joining the United States Detective Service, a private firm unaffiliated with the government. In 1872 they are called back into service by President Ulysses S. Grant to undertake a secret mission on his behalf. Concerned over a series of deaths involving several important people in the government, including Baker (1868) and Stanton (1869), Grant authorizes an undercover investigation "to ascertain whether any of these deaths were from other than natural causes."[13] The man Grant asks to take charge of the investigation is former Union general Lew Wallace, one of the commissioners who sat in judgement of the Lincoln conspirators during their trial by a military tribunal. Wallace agrees and hires the Potter brothers to carry out the fieldwork.

Earl and Andrew set about the country interviewing persons believed to have pertinent information relating to the assassination of
President Lincoln and the deaths of select government officials. According to Neff, the Potters "logged more than two hundred interviews, over a four-year period."[14] Their escapades became the basis
for a book coauthored by Neff entitled *Dark Union: The Secret Web
of Profiteers, Politicians, and Booth Conspirators That Led to Lincoln's
Death.*[15] Repeating much of what appears in Balsiger and Sellier's
book, *Dark Union* picks up the story of Booth's escape and the sin-
ister government cover-up, thanks to the discoveries of the Potter
brothers.

At the end of their investigation the Potter brothers turn their
files over to Lew Wallace and return home; their work is done. Wallace, after evaluating the information, concludes that the risk of pro-
ceeding with the prosecution of those implicated with Lincoln's assassination is too great. Too many important people have blood on
their hands. Wallace writes Grant a warning letter: "Who knows
what direction testimony might take and just what previously un-
disclosed secrets might be dislodged by an astute defense." Wallace
recommends "the report be sequestered."[16] Grant thereupon agrees,
becoming part of the cover-up.[17] With the results of the investigation silenced, Wallace stores his report along with the Potter papers
in the carriage house on his estate in Crawfordsville, Indiana. Here
they remain until sometime in the 1920s, when Andrew Potter, now
in his eighties, decides to write a book based on his life experiences.
He forms a collaboration with an Indiana schoolteacher by the name
of Edwin Stokes. However, in order to proceed with the project he
needs his old files as source material. Potter will supply the information, and Stokes will do the writing. When Potter goes to access his
papers that are still stored in Lew Wallace's carriage house, he finds
them in a deplorable condition. According to Neff, "There had been
a fire in the carriage house and the roof leaked, making the records
soggy, and pigeons had roosted over the records and a layer of pigeon
manure covered them. Everything had to be mover [*sic*] to a farmhouse near Ladoga and the records washed and then transcribed."[18]

Andrew hires a local woman named Susan Wade to transcribe
the records, after which all of the badly damaged originals are destroyed, leaving only Andrew Potter's nice, clean typescripts. Potter,

unfortunately, is never able to complete his project with Stokes. Having lost his considerable savings in the depression, he turns the papers over to an old friend, Gaylord McCluer. Potter heads west to Colorado, where, in 1932 at the age of ninety-two, he dies in a car accident. During a winter snowstorm his car runs off the road into a snow bank and he suffers a fatal head injury. Six years later, in 1938, Stokes, now in possession of Andrew's manuscript, dies. The manuscript passes to Edwin's cousin, Wallace Stokes, who arranges with the New Hoosier Press of Terre Haute, Indiana, to print a two-volume limited edition of Potter's memoirs. In 1964 the New Hoosier Press solicits orders before printing the volumes. Unable to sell enough prepublication copies to cover the printing costs, the project is canceled. In 1968, Neff purchases the surviving Potter papers from an antique dealer who had acquired part of the collection.[19]

It was the information garnered in his interviews that led Andrew Potter to the conclusion that another man, James W. Boyd, was killed in Booth's place at the Garrett farm, and that Booth escaped, not to Enid, Oklahoma, as Finis Bates had claimed, but to Guwahati, India.[20] Witness after witness provided Potter with enough scurrilous accusations to indict dozens of former Federal officials for complicity in a plot to kidnap Lincoln and then cover up his murder. General Lew Wallace and President Ulysses S. Grant were clearly implicated in obstruction of justice when they decided to "sequester" Potter's report. But the president and general had nothing to fear, for Andrew took his knowledge to his grave. It wasn't until Andrew's papers turned up in 1968 that the "true story" of what really happened in the assassination of Abraham Lincoln supposedly came to full light.

With the publication of *Dark Union* in 2003, Neff's vast collection of materials, including the Potter Papers, were turned over to Indiana State University in Terre Haute. They currently reside in the Special Collections Department of the University's Cunningham Memorial Library. Known as the Neff-Guttridge Collection,[21] the files contain thousands of pages of typed copies of documents (but only a handful of original documents, of no consequence to Lincoln's assassination) and fifteen hundred photographs.

The proof that Stanton and other Northern figures engineered Lincoln's death lies with the documents that make up the bulk of the Neff-Guttridge Collection. These documents form the sole ba-

A photograph in the Neff-Guttridge Collection claimed to be that of James W. Boyd. It bears little resemblance to the description of the real Boyd written on the oath of allegiance he signed (gray hair, blue eyes, six feet-two inches tall). At no time did Boyd serve in the Union army. Boyd was killed on January 1, 1866. (Author's collection)

sis for the revisionist history put forward in *The Lincoln Conspiracy* and in *Dark Union*. There are no documents in public or private archives outside of Indiana State University that corroborate any of the claims made in the two books—not in the Library of Congress, the National Archives, or in the James O. Hall Research Center of the Surratt House Museum, located in Clinton, Maryland.

Of the documents examined, all are merely typed copies of purported originals that were destroyed after they were copied. According to the description found in the collection at Indiana State University, a series of physical calamities seriously damaged or destroyed all of the original holographic documents in the original files. In other instances, the originals from which typed copies were made simply disappeared without a trace, thus leaving only the typed copies as proof of their existence. This happened not only to the Potter Papers but to virtually all of the other documents in the Neff-Guttridge Collection.

Given that none of the original documents exist, what can we learn by examining the copies now at ISU? Prior to their being deposited there, copies of the typescripts of some of the interviews Potter allegedly conducted were acquired by historian James O. Hall. Hall examined the documents and prepared a report of his findings that now resides in the collection housed in the Surratt Society's James O. Hall Research Center in Clinton, Maryland. Much of what follows is gleaned from Hall's analysis.

Among the interviews made by Andrew Potter is one of Mary A. Nelson, a sister of David Herold.[22] The interview allegedly took place in Denver, Colorado, on August 22, 1873. It begins:

Q. Mrs. Nelson, you were the sister of the late David Herold were you not?
A. Yes.
Q. And your husband *was* [emphasis added] Edward W. Nelson?
A. That is true.

The facts stated in the interview tumble from the very beginning. Mary Nelson's husband's full name was Frederick Massena Nelson, not Edward W. Nelson. A District of Columbia marriage record shows the couple married on July 23, 1860. In the interview, Mary Nelson refers to her husband in the past tense, but Nelson was alive and living with his wife in Charles County, Maryland, not Denver, Colorado, at the time the alleged interview took place. Census records for Charles County, Maryland, for 1870 show F. M. Nelson, m/w, aged 42, farmer, and M. A. Nelson, f/w, aged 32, keeping house. The 1880 and 1890 census reports show them both still living in Charles County. Frederick M. Nelson died on May 11, 1909, in Charles County and is buried in the Bumpy Oak Cemetery, not far from his home. His tombstone bears the name Frederick Massena Nelson. Mary Nelson died eight years later, on July 1, 1917, and is buried in the Herold family plot in Congressional Cemetery in Washington, D. C. Moreover, two surviving nieces of Mary A. Nelson,

James O. Hall. (Courtesy of Kieran McAuliffe)

still living in 1974, stated in correspondence with James O. Hall, "She [Mary Nelson] never lived in Denver nor even went [visited] there. . . . We doubt that she ever went outside the District of Columbia or the state of Maryland." A check of the Denver City directories for 1873 through 1875 failed to find any person named Edward W. Nelson (or Frederick M. Nelson) or Mary A. Nelson.

At one point in the interview, Mrs. Nelson was asked if she knew William A. Browning, Andrew Johnson's secretary and a principal figure in *Dark Union*'s alleged pork for cotton deals. Mrs. Nelson answered: "I've known him for many years and his brothers and sisters."

Again, the documentary record is at variance with Potter's interview. William Browning had no sisters. He was one of nine boys born to Peregrine W. Browning and his wife, Margaret Browning, both residents of the District of Columbia.

In response to another question, Mrs. Nelson relates that William Browning was married to a girl from Maryland by the name of Priscilla Russell: "He got married just before the war. . . . She and Bill hit it off and they got married." Mrs. Nelson even talked of visiting with Browning's wife and called her "Penny."

There is no record of William A. Browning's marriage among the District of Columbia marriage records. The 1860 census returns for the District of Columbia list a Wm. *W.* Browning, age twenty-seven, born in 1833 in Maryland, married to a Priscilla Browning, age twenty-five, born in Maryland. William A. Browning was born in the District of Columbia in 1835, not Maryland in 1833, and his middle initial was "A.," not "W." According to Browning family genealogist Peregrine Browning, William A. Browning, Andrew Johnson's secretary, died a *bachelor*, having never married.[23] It appears that whoever constructed the interview located a William W. Browning in the census records for the District of Columbia and mistakenly confused him with William A. Browning.

In another part of the interview, Mrs. Nelson is asked to tell what she knew about William Browning's death (Browning died on March 2, 1866). Mrs. Nelson answers: "Only what was told to me by his sister Kathleen. . . . Kathy told me that he was completely paralyzed and couldn't talk or move before he died." As stated above, Browning did not have a sister. The 1840 and 1850 census records show no daughter in the Peregrine Browning family, nor does Peregrine Browning's will, probated in 1909, list a daughter. The only authenticated photograph of William A. Browning is a family picture taken in 1858. It shows mother, father, and nine boys—no girls.[24] The interview in Neff's files contains too many substantive errors to be authentic.

In a separate document in the Neff-Guttridge Collection, Assistant Judge Advocate John A. Bingham is alleged to have interviewed conspirator Michael O'Laughlen. The interview is dated April 27, thirteen days after Lincoln's assassination and one day after Booth was killed. The interview takes place aboard the monitor USS *Montauk*. At one point in the interview, Bingham questions O'Laughlen about a trip he made to New York and who he remembers seeing there. Bingham asks, "Who else did you see in New York? Did you see Lewis Powell there?" At the time of the alleged interview, the government only knew Lewis Powell by his alias, "Paine," or "Payne," the name that appeared on his oath of allegiance.[25] Bingham did not know his real name was "Powell" until the third week of May, during his trial. The fact that Bingham used the name "Powell" on April 27 supports the conclusion that the interview is a fabrication.

As fantastic as the claim that Stanton engineered Lincoln's murder and that John Wilkes Booth made good his escape is, the story of Andrew Potter and the Potter Papers runs a close second. The files that Potter amassed while working as a secret agent during the war and later as a detective hired by President Ulysses S. Grant are now safely ensconced in Indiana State University, where anyone can study them and learn this incredible story behind Lincoln's murder. There is only one problem with them —they are the work of a man who never existed!

In an attempt to learn more about Andrew Potter, the author made a systematic search of the usual public records that normally exist for any person who was born, lived, and died in the United States and worked for the federal government. Since Potter worked for the NDP during the Civil War and was allegedly given a commission as an officer in the Indiana State Militia, a search was made of several record groups in the National Archives, where papers pertaining to the persons and activities associated with the NDP and military records are preserved. These files include all record groups that might be expected to contain documents pertaining to Lafayette Baker's day-to-day operation, such as the index of the Turner-Baker papers (records of associate Judge Advocate Levi C. Turner, Record Group 94), Lafayette C. Baker's Secret Service Accounts (Record Group 110, entry 95, seven boxes), the L. C. Baker Papers (Record Group 110, entry 105, four boxes), the yearly index to letters received by the secretary of war, 1865 (Record Group 107, M-495), the Union Provost Marshal's File of Papers Relating to Individual Civilians (M-345, and index M-416), correspondence and accounts relating to scouts, guides, spies, and detectives (Record Group 110, entry 31 and entry 36), unbound telegrams of the secretary of war (Record Group 107, M-504), Union Volunteer Records, and Military Records in the Indiana State Archives.

The next step was to search the U.S. Census reports for Virginia (1840, 1850, and 1860), Indiana (1870), and Colorado (1930). These were the states where Potter allegedly was born, lived, and died. As a control test, the records were also searched for known individuals, such as Lafayette Baker and NDP detectives Luther B. Baker and John F. Baker (no relation to L. C. Baker or Luther B. Baker).[26]

Each search proved negative, except for the control searches, which produced numerous references to Lafayette, Luther, and John Baker. Not one reference to Andrew Potter (or Earl Potter) was found. While Potter may have "spirited" his files away when he left government service, he could not take the files of other federal offices and agencies. And yet, no record could be found of this important man, who presumably ran Lafayette Baker's operation for three years.

As part of his cover during the war, Potter allegedly received a commission from Indiana's governor, Oliver P. Morton.[27] A search for his commission was made of the military records in the National Archives and of the Indiana State Archives.[28] Once again, no record was found for an Andrew Baker.

Other documents examined were five separate payroll disbursement records for the years 1862–1863. These were found loosely filed among various NDP papers in file boxes in Record Group 110, entry 95, Secret Service Accounts. These payroll accounts list the name of each employee of Baker's unit along with his position, pay, and signatures. The number of detectives ranged from a low of twenty-one to a high of twenty-five. The name "Potter" was not among them, whereas the names of Lafayette C., Luther B., and John F. Baker do appear in each of the records.

In Potter's alleged autobiography, located in the Potter Papers at ISU, he lists twenty-four men who served in the "Detective Division" under his supervision.[29] Not one of the twenty-four names appear on

Opposite Top: A page from the payroll ledger for Lafayette C. Baker's National Detective Police (NDP) for May 1863. Of the thirty-seven employees of the NDP, none are named Potter. (Courtesy of the National Archives and Records Administration)

Opposite Bottom: Three signatures of Lafayette C. Baker, head of the National Detective Police. The first is a signature from a Secret Service payroll ledger (Author's collection). The second is from a letter in the Neff-Guttridge Collection (Courtesy of the Neff-Guttridge Collection, Special Collections Department, Cunningham Memorial Library, Indiana State University, Terre Haute, Indiana). And the third signature is from a book owned by Baker (Courtesy of the Surratt House Museum). The middle signature appears to be a clumsy forgery.

WE, the Subscribers, acknowledge to have received from _John Potts_, Disbursing Clerk, War Department, the sums opposite our respective names, in full of our salaries in the _Provost Marshals Office_ _War Department_ for the _Month ending May 31st 1863._

NAMES.	CAPACITY.	AMOUNT.		AMOUNT TAXABLE.	AMOUNT OF TAX. 3 per cent.	NET AMOUNT.	SIGNATURES.
		ANNUAL SALARY.	MONTH. Dollars. Cents.				
L. C. Baker	Provost Marshal	3600	300 00	250 00	7 50	292 50	L. C. Baker
Ira Brown	Deputy	1500	125	75	2 25	122 75	Ira Brown
H. C. Redfield	Clerk	1800	150	100	3 00	147 00	H. C. Redfield
Henry W. Finch	"	1500	125	75	2 25	122 75	Henry W. Finch
A. F. Rofsetter	"	1500	125	75	2 25	122 75	A. F. Rofetter
John F. Baker	"	1200	100	50	1 50	98 50	John F. Baker
John Lee	Detective	1200	100	50	1 50	98 50	John Lee
I. I. Camp	"	1200	100	50	1 50	98 50	I. I. Camp
M. Trail	"	1200	100	50	1 50	98 50	M. Trail
S. M. Brant	"	1200	100	50	1 50	98 50	S. M. Brant
I. A. Baker	"	1200	100	50	1 50	98 50	I. A. Baker
Wm. H. Steens	"	1200	100	50	1 50	98 50	Wm Steens
T. T. Johnson	"	1200	100	50	1 50	98 50	T. T. Johnson
John Odell	"	1200	100	50	1 50	98 50	John Odell
Thos. Bowles	"	1200	100	50	1 50	98 50	Thos Bowles
Thos. C. Steens	"	1200	100	50	1 50	98 50	Thos C. Steens
Ira Wright	"	1200	100	50	1 50	98 50	J. Wright
S. K. Murdock	"	1200	100	50	1 50	98 50	S. K. Murdock
Wm. F. Wilder	"	1200	100	50	1 50	98 50	W. F. Wilder
Daniel Prayer	"	1200	100	50	1 50	98 50	Daniel Prayer
L. B. Baker	"	1200	100	50	1 50	98 50	L. B. Baker
Henry Phillips	"	1200	100	50	1 50	98 50	Henry Phillips
I. B. Turhille	"	1200	100	50	1 50	98 50	I. B. Turhille
Jacob Emrick	"	1200	100	50	1 50	98 50	Jacob Emrick
A. Birmingham	"	1200	100	50	1 50	98 50	A. Birmingham
Wm. H. Raynor	"	1200	100	50	1 50	98 50	Wm H. Raynor
							Baker
A. F. Palmer	"	1200	100	50	1 50	98 50	A. F. Palmer
I. Bakeoven	Captain	720	145 16	20 19	72	144 43	I. Bakeoven
Chs. Peacock	Engineer	720	120	20	60	119 00	Charles Peacock
Thomas Brant	Pilot	600	55 33			55 00	Thomas H. Brant
Corwin Wilder	Deckhand	600	50			50 00	Corwin Wilder
Fred. Moor	Messenger	240	20			20 00	Fredrick Moor
Col. Wilson	Cold & Cook	300	60 48			60 48	Col. Wilson HW Finch
Jos. Allen	Oster	300	25			25 00	Jos. Allen HW Finch
Barney Allen	"	300	25			25 00	Barney Allen HW Finch
Den Williams	"	300	25			25 00	Den Williams HW Finch
Jos. Jackson	Deckhand	300	25			25 00	Jos. Jackson HW Finch
			3510 97	1719 19	9 50	3502 39	

Approved to be paid from Contingency of the Army.
By order of the Secretary of War
Edwin M. Stanton

W. Holt

L. C. Baker
A. F. Sumner

L. C. Baker

L. C. Baker.

the payroll disbursement, and no reference was found to any of the twenty-four in the official L. C. Baker Papers in Record Group 110, entry 105. In a separate document in the Neff-Guttridge Collection, William P. Earle, a National Detective Police agent, is described as James W. Boyd's "control" officer.[30] As with the other individuals mentioned throughout the Potter Papers, William B. Earle's name is also missing from Baker's payroll records and other NDP papers.

We can only conclude that the Andrew Potter who was so critical to the conspiracy theories involving Stanton and others in Lincoln's assassination does not exist outside of the Neff-Guttridge Collection at Indiana State University. He is unique among even the most secret of secret service agents in the nation's history. Throughout his entire life (of ninety-two years) he left no record in any public file from his birth to his death. It is simply beyond belief that so important an individual would go through life without leaving a trace of his existence outside of a private collection.

If there is no Andrew Potter, who is responsible for the Potter Papers? Like Andrew Potter, it remains a mystery. The trail is twisted with many forks and dead ends. There are many possibilities, dating as far back as the post–Civil War period, an era filled with scoundrels who made a living defrauding the government and the public.[31] As we have seen in the case of Otto Eisenschiml, bogus research and fraudulent claims are not restricted to the nineteenth century. The twentieth century abounds with hoaxes and fabrications, from Piltdown man to the Hitler diaries to the love letters of Lincoln and Ann Rutledge. And like those tender writings between Lincoln and Rutledge, Andrew Potter and the Potter Papers are nothing more than a clever hoax.

NOTES

Introduction

1. William M. Thayer, *The Pioneer Boy, and How He Became President* (Boston: Walker, Wise, 1863), 20.

2. Lincoln to Jesse W. Fell, enclosing an autobiographical sketch, December 20, 1859, in Roy P. Basler, ed., *The Collected Works of Abraham Lincoln*, 9 vols. (New Brunswick, N.J.: Rutgers Univ. Press, 1953–1955), 3:511.

3. Robert S. Harper, *Lincoln and the Press* (New York: McGraw-Hill, 1951), 49.

4. Lincoln's remarks at the Decatur Convention, in Basler, ed., *The Collected Works of Abraham Lincoln*, 4:48.

5. Don E. Fehrenbacher and Virginia Fehrenbacher, eds., *Recollected Words of Abraham Lincoln* (Stanford, Calif.: Stanford Univ. Press, 1996), 198.

6. Ibid., liii.

7. Don E. Fehrenbacher, *Lincoln in Text and Context: Collected Essays* (Stanford: Stanford Univ. Press, 1987), 181.

8. This and previous quotes from Lincoln's speech to the New Jersey state senate, Trenton, New Jersey, on February 21, 1861, in Basler, ed., *The Collected Works of Abraham Lincoln*, 4:236.

9. William H. Herndon, *Herndon's Lincoln: The True Story of a Great Life* (1889; reprint, Springfield, Ill.: Herndon's Lincoln Publishing Co., n.d.), 400. Supposedly, Lincoln made the remarks near local supporters, who thought his "House Divided" address radically impolitic.

10. All these recollections are published in Douglas L. Wilson and Rodney O. Davis, eds., *Herndon's Informants: Letters, Interviews, and Statements about Abraham Lincoln* (Urbana: Univ. of Illinois Press, 1998), 578, 541, 9, 108.

11. Mary Lincoln to Abram Wakeman, September 23, [1864], in *Mary Todd Lincoln: Her Life and Letters,* ed. Justin G. Turner and Linda Levitt Turner (New York: Knopf, 1972), 180.

12. W[illiam]. D[ean]. Howells, *Life of Abraham Lincoln* (1860; reprint, Bloomington: Indiana Univ. Press, 1960), 41.

13. Lincoln to Edwin M. Stanton, April 15, 1862, in Basler, ed., *The Collected Works of Abraham Lincoln*, 5:537.

14. Wilson and Davis, eds., *Herndon's Informants*, 660–61.

15. A. H. Chapman, quoted in Wilson and Davis, eds., *Herndon's Informants*, 101.

16. Roy P. Basler, *The Lincoln Legend: A Study in Changing Conceptions* (New York: Octagon Books, 1969), 104, vii.

CHAPTER ONE. The Birthplace Cabin

1. Dwight T. Pitcaithley, "Abraham Lincoln's Birthplace Cabin: The Making of an American Icon," in *Myth, Memory, and the Making of the American Landscape*, ed. Paul A. Shackel (Gainesville: Univ. Press of Florida, 2001), 250. The article contains an excellent summary of the cabin's provenance.

2. Ibid., 240–54.

3. Roy P. Basler, ed., *The Collected Works of Abraham Lincoln*, 9 vols. (New Brunswick, N.J.: Rutgers Univ. Press, 1953), 4:56.

4. Ibid., 4:70.

5. Roy Hays, "Is the Lincoln Birthplace Cabin Authentic?," *Abraham Lincoln Quarterly*, 5, no. 3 (September 1948): 129.

6. Ibid.

7. For example, Louis A. Warren. See the epitaph at the beginning of the chapter.

8. Paul M. Angle to Newton B. Drury, May 26, 1949, Box 3, "Correspondence Re Abraham Lincoln Birthplace Cabin," History Division Files, National Park Service, Washington, D.C., quoted in Pitcaithley, "Abraham Lincoln's Birthplace Cabin," 246.

9. Hays, "Is the Lincoln Birthplace Cabin Authentic?," 131.

10. Pitcaithley, "Abraham Lincoln's Birthplace Cabin," 242–43.

11. Hays, "Is the Lincoln Birthplace Cabin Authentic?," 158.

12. Ibid., 145.

13. Ibid., 150.

14. Ibid.

15. Ibid., 153. Dennett was declared insane in 1904 and committed to an asylum, ending any challenge he might make to recover the cabin logs.

16. Ibid., 159–60.

17. Ibid., 161.

18. Ibid.

19. Quoted in Pitcaithley, "Abraham Lincoln's Birthplace Cabin," 246 (emphasis added).

20. Hays, "Is the Lincoln Birthplace Cabin Authentic?," 163.

21. Ibid., 127–63.

22. Louis A. Warren, "The Authenticity of Lincoln's Birthplace Cabin: The Jacob Brother's Tradition," *Lincoln Lore*, no. 1016 (September 27, 1948): 1.

23. Ibid.

24. Joseph H. Barrett, *Life of Lincoln* (New York: Moore, Wilstach and Barrett, 1865).

25. Douglas L. Wilson and Rodney O. Davis, eds., *Herndon's Informants: Letters, Interviews, and Statements about Abraham Lincoln* (Urbana: Univ. of Illinois Press, 1998), 55–56.

26. Warren, "The Authenticity of Lincoln's Birthplace Cabin: The Jacob Brother's Tradition," 1; Louis A. Warren, "The Authenticity of Lincoln's Birth-

place Cabin: The John A. Davenport Tradition," *Lincoln Lore,* no. 1019 (October 18, 1948): 1; Louis A. Warren, "Early Visitors at Lincoln's Birthplace Cabin," *Lincoln Lore,* no. 1244 (February 9, 1953): 1.

27. The presence of a window in 1861 is at variance with the statement of the soldier from the 19th Illinois. It is always possible that the Harvey account refers to the Knob Creek place.

28. Quoted in Pitcaithley, "Abraham Lincoln's Birthplace Cabin," 243.

29. Pitcaithley, "Abraham Lincoln's Birthplace Cabin," 252.

CHAPTER TWO. Lincoln's Father

1. R. Vincent Enlow, *The Abraham Lincoln Genesis Cover-Up: The Censored Origins of an Illustrious Ancestor* (New Providence, N.J.: Genealogy Today Publications, 2001), 2.

2. Roy P. Basler, ed., *The Collected Works of Abraham Lincoln,* 9 vols. (New Brunswick, N.J.: Rutgers Univ. Press, 1953–1955), 4:56.

3. In 1869, Haycraft wrote a history of Elizabethtown, Kentucky, and its environs, which took in the birthplace and the boyhood homes of Lincoln: Samuel Haycraft, *A History of Elizabethtown, Kentucky and its Surroundings* (1869; reprint, Elizabethtown, Ky.: Hardin County Historical Society, 1975).

4. Basler, ed., *The Collected Works of Abraham Lincoln,* 4:56.

5. Scripps solicited and received from Lincoln a lengthy autobiographical sketch that became the basis for a thirty-two-page pamphlet published by Horace Greely's *New York Tribune.*

6. Basler, ed., *The Collected Works of Abraham Lincoln,* 4:60.

7. Paul H. Verduin, "Brief Outline of the Joseph Hanks Family," in *Herndon's Informants: Letters, Interviews, and Statements about Abraham Lincoln,* ed. Douglas L. Wilson and Rodney O. Davis (Urbana: Univ. of Illinois Press, 1998), 281.

8. Louis A. Warren, ed., "The Paternity Myth," *The Lincoln Kinsman,* no. 31 (January 1941): 1.

9. Louis A. Warren, *Lincoln's Parentage and Childhood* (New York: Century, 1926), 50–51.

10. William E. Barton, *The Life of Abraham Lincoln,* 2 vols. (Indianapolis: Bobbs-Merrill, 1925), 1:16–17.

11. Douglas L. Wilson and Rodney O. Davis, eds., *Herndon's Informants: Letters, Interviews, and Statements about Abraham Lincoln* (Urbana: Univ. of Illinois Press, 1998), 250.

12. Ibid., 240. Erastus R. Burba (1815–1893) moved to Kentucky from New York in 1843, settling in Hodgenville. In 1862 he was elected county clerk of LaRue County. (That part of Hardin County where Lincoln was born became LaRue County.)

13. Wilson and Davis, eds., *Herndon's Informants,* 674.

14. William E. Barton, *The Soul of Abraham Lincoln* (New York: George H. Doran, 1920).

15. Quoted in Mark E. Neely Jr., *The Abraham Lincoln Encyclopedia* (New York: McGraw-Hill, 1982), 20, and Benjamin P. Thomas, *Portrait for Posterity: Lincoln and His Biographers* (New Brunswick, N.J.: Rutgers Univ. Press, 1947), 89.

16. William E. Barton, *The Paternity of Abraham Lincoln: Was He the Son of Thomas Lincoln?* (New York: George H. Doran, 1920).

17. Ibid., 316.

18. J. Henry Lea and J. R. Hutchinson, *The Ancestry of Abraham Lincoln* (Boston: Houghton Mifflin, 1909), 65.

19. Ibid., 65.

20. Barton, *The Paternity of Lincoln*, 315–17.

21. Ibid., 318.

22. Enlow, *The Abraham Lincoln Genesis Cover-Up*, 2.

23. James H. Cathy, *The Genesis of Lincoln* (1899; reprint, Wiggins, Miss.: Crown Rights, 1999), 21.

24. Ibid., 42–79.

25. James C. Coggins, *The Eugenics of President Abraham Lincoln: His German-Scotch Ancestry Irrefutably Established from Recently Discovered Documents* (1940; reprint, Dahlonega, Ga.: Crown Rights, 2001), 128.

26. William E. Barton, *The Lineage of Lincoln* (Indianapolis, Ind.: Bobbs-Merrill, 1929).

27. Coggins, *The Eugenics of President Abraham Lincoln*.

28. Ibid., 43.

29. Here, she is in error. She presumably meant 1700s, because the two brothers came to Virginia in 1750.

30. Coggins, *The Eugenics of President Abraham Lincoln*, 114.

31. Ibid., 115.

32. Ibid., 205.

33. Ibid., 208.

34. Ibid.

35. Ibid., 210.

36. Ibid., 210–11.

37. Carl Sandburg, *Lincoln Collector: The Story of Oliver R. Barrett's Great Private Collection* (New York: Bonanza Books, 1960), 107.

38. Barton, *The Lineage of Lincoln*, 186.

39. Ibid.

40. Ibid.

41. Edward Steers Jr., "Nancy Hanks, West Virginian? A Review of the Current Status of Research into the Birthplace of Nancy Hanks Lincoln," *Lincoln Herald* 100, no. 2 (summer 1998), 69.

42. Barton, *The Lineage of Lincoln*, 341.

43. Louis A. Warren, ed., "Nominated for Lincoln's Paternity," *The Lincoln Kinsman*, no. 53 (November 1942): 6.

44. Wilson and Davis, eds., *Herndon's Informants*, 38 (emphasis added).

CHAPTER THREE. Abe and Ann

1. Carl Sandburg, *Abraham Lincoln: The Prairie Years*, 2 vols. (1926; reprint, New York: Charles Scribner's Sons, 1944).

2. Carl Sandburg, *Abraham Lincoln: The War Years*, 4 vols. (1939; reprint, New York: Charles Scribner's Sons, 1944).

3. Jay Monaghan, *Lincoln Bibliography, 1839–1939*, 2 vols. (Springfield: Illinois State Historical Library, 1945), 2:209.

4. Sandburg, *The Prairie Years*, 1:186.

5. Ibid., 1:189.

6. John Ford, dir., *Young Mr. Lincoln*, with Henry Fonda, Marjorie Weaver, and Pauline Moore, Twentieth Century–Fox, 1939.

7. John Cromwell, dir., Robert Sherwood, screenwriter, *Abe Lincoln in Illinois*, with Raymond Massey, Ruth Gordon, and Mary Howard, RKO Radio Pictures, 1940.

8. Benjamin P. Thomas, *Lincoln's New Salem* (Springfield, Ill.: Abraham Lincoln Association, 1934), 81.

9. John Evangelist Walsh, *The Shadows Rise: Abraham Lincoln and the Ann Rutledge Legend* (Urbana: Univ. of Illinois Press, 1993): 27–28.

10. Ibid.

11. Ibid., 28, 29.

12. Thomas, *Lincoln's New Salem*, 82.

13. John Y. Simon, "Abraham Lincoln and Ann Rutledge," *Journal of the Abraham Lincoln Association* 11 (1990): 14–16.

14. The lecture is published in its entirety as *Lincoln and Ann Rutledge and the Pioneers of New Salem: A Lecture by William H. Herndon* (Herrin, Ill.: Trovillion Private Press, 1945).

15. Simon, "Abraham Lincoln and Ann Rutledge," 15.

16. Ibid.

17. Wilma Frances Minor, "Lincoln the Lover: I. The Setting—New Salem," *Atlantic Monthly*, December 1928, 838–64.

18. Edward Weeks, *My Green Age* (Boston: Little, Brown, 1973), 251.

19. Ibid.

20. Ibid.

21. Don E. Fehrenbacher, *The Minor Affair: An Adventure in Forgery and Detection*. The Second R. Gerald McMurtry Lecture Delivered at Fort Wayne, Indiana (Fort Wayne, Ind.: Louis A. Warren Lincoln Library and Museum, 1979), 8.

22. Weeks, *My Green Age*, 251.

23. Barton's books included William E. Barton, *The Paternity of Lincoln: Was He the Son of Thomas Lincoln?* (New York: George H. Doran, 1920); William E. Barton, *The Life of Abraham Lincoln*, 2 vols. (Indianapolis: Bobbs-Merrill, 1925); William E. Barton, *The Women Lincoln Loved* (Indianapolis: Bobbs-Merrill, 1927); William E. Barton, *The Lineage of Lincoln* (Indianapolis: Bobbs-

Merrill, 1929); William E. Barton, *Lincoln at Gettysburg* (Indianapolis: Bobbs-Merrill, 1930); William E. Barton, *President Lincoln*, 2 vols. (Indianapolis: Bobbs-Merrill, 1933), published posthumously.

24. Fehrenbacher, *The Minor Affair*, 13.

25. Quoted in ibid.

26. Ida M. Tarbell, *The Early Life of Abraham Lincoln* (New York: S. S. McClure, 1896); Ida M. Tarbell, *The Life of Abraham Lincoln*, 4 vols. (New York: Lincoln History Society, 1900); Ida M. Tarbell, *He Knew Lincoln* (New York: McClure, Phillips, 1907); Ida M. Tarbell, *Father Abraham* (New York: Moffat, Yard, 1909).

27. Quoted in Fehrenbacher, *The Minor Affair*, 14.

28. Albert J. Beveridge, *Abraham Lincoln, 1809–1858*, 2 vols. (Boston: Houghton Mifflin, 1928).

29. Weeks, *My Green Age*, 255.

30. Fehrenbacher, *The Minor Affair*, 13–14.

31. Ibid.

32. Ellery Sedgwick, "The Discovery. A New Storehouse of Lincoln Material," *Atlantic Monthly*, December 1928, 834.

33. Minor's writing was not up to Sedgwick's standard, so Sedgwick had his editorial assistant, Theodore Morrison, rewrite the entire manuscript (Fehrenbacher, *The Minor Affair*, 13).

34. Minor, "Lincoln the Lover: I. The Setting—New Salem," 838.

35. Ibid., 842.

36. Ibid., 844.

37. Ibid., 848.

38. Wilma Frances Minor, "Lincoln the Lover: II. The Courtship," *Atlantic Monthly*, January 1929, 1.

39. Ibid., 7.

40. Ibid., 8.

41. Ibid., 14.

42. Wilma Frances Minor, "Lincoln the Lover: III. The Tragedy," *Atlantic Monthly*, February 1929, 215–25.

43. Ibid., 216.

44. Ibid.

45. Ibid.

46. Ibid.

47. Ibid.

48. Ibid., 218.

49. Ibid., 219.

50. Walsh, *The Shadows Rise*, 14.

51. Minor, "Lincoln the Lover: III. The Tragedy," 222.

52. Ibid., 225.

53. Fehrenbacher, *The Minor Affair*, 23.

54. Paul Angle, "The Minor Collection: A Criticism," *Atlantic Monthly*, April 1929, 522.

55. Fehrenbacher, *The Minor Affair*, 23.

56. Adin Baber, *A. Lincoln with Compass and Chain* (Kansas, Ill.: privately printed by the author, 1968).

57. Minor, "Lincoln the Lover: II. The Courtship," 11.

58. R. Gerald McMurtry, "The *Atlantic Monthly* Fiasco," *Lincoln Lore*, no. 1583 (January 1970): 2.

59. Fehrenbacher, *The Minor Affair*, 26–27.

60. Ibid., 11–12.

61. Ibid., 27.

62. Ibid., 25.

63. Ibid., 28–29.

64. Ibid., 20.

65. Ibid.

66. [Ellery Sedgwick], "The Contributors' Column," *Atlantic Monthly*, February 1929, 283.

67. Fehrenbacher, *The Minor Affair*, 29–30.

68. Weeks, *My Green Age*, 257.

69. Fehrenbacher, *The Minor Affair*, 29.

70. Weeks, *My Green Age*, 258.

71. Angle, "The Minor Collection: A Criticism," 525.

CHAPTER FOUR. Ann Rutledge's Resting Place

1. There is in the Rare Book Division of the Library of Congress a copy of a small textbook entitled *Kirkham's Grammar* that was used by both Abraham Lincoln and Ann Rutledge. The book has pasted inside the front cover a receipt in Lincoln's hand signed by him and dated "March 8th 1832." On the title page is the inscription "Ann M. Rutledge is now learning Grammar." This book links the two during their New Salem period. See John Evangelist Walsh, *The Shadows Rise: Abraham Lincoln and the Ann Rutledge Legend* (Urbana: Univ. of Illinois Press, 1993): 141–44.

2. Douglas L. Wilson and Rodney O. Davis, eds., *Herndon's Informants: Letters, Interviews, and Statements about Abraham Lincoln* (Urbana: Univ. of Illinois Press, 1998), 253.

3. Wilson and Davis, eds., *Herndon's Informants*, 383.

4. Ibid., 21.

5. Lincoln biographer David Herbert Donald in *Lincoln's Herndon* (New York: Knopf, 1948), in *Lincoln* (New York: Simon and Schuster, 1995), and in *"We Are Lincoln Men": Abraham Lincoln and His Friends* (New York: Simon and Schuster, 2003).

6. William H. Herndon, *Lincoln and Ann Rutledge and the Pioneers of New Salem: A Lecture by William H. Herndon* (Herrin, Ill.: Trovillion Private Press, 1945), 40.

7. For a history of the village and Lincoln's days there, see Benjamin P. Thomas, *Lincoln's New Salem* (Chicago: Lincoln's New Salem Enterprises, 1934).

8. Herndon, *Lincoln and Ann Rutledge*, 40.

9. Ibid., 40–41.

10. Gary Erickson, "The Graves of Ann Rutledge and the Old Concord Burial Ground," *Lincoln Herald* 71, no. 3 (fall 1969): 94.

11. Herbert Sartorious quoted in Erickson, "The Graves of Ann Rutledge," 93.

12. Affidavit of James Hollis, April 27, 1958, quoted in Erickson, "The Graves of Ann Rutledge," 98.

13. Ibid., 90–107.

14. Ibid., 97.

15. Walsh, *The Shadows Rise*, 171–72.

CHAPTER FIVE. Was Lincoln Baptized?

1. Wayne C. Temple, *Abraham Lincoln: From Skeptic to Prophet* (Mahomet, Ill.: Mayhaven Publishing, 1995), 140.

2. Lyon G. Tyler, "Confederate Leaders and Other Citizens Request the House of Delegates to Repeal the Resolution of Respect to Abraham Lincoln, the Barbarian" (Matthews Courthouse, Va.: privately printed, 1928).

3. Jean H. Baker, *Mary Todd Lincoln* (New York: Norton, 1987), 267–68; Paul M. Angle, "Editor's Preface," in William H. Herndon and Jesse W. Weik, *Herndon's Life of Lincoln: The History and Personal Recollections of Abraham Lincoln* (New York: Da Capo Press, 1983), xxviii–xxix.

4. Merrill D. Peterson, *Lincoln in American Memory* (New York: Oxford Univ. Press, 1994), 134.

5. Allen Guelzo, *Abraham Lincoln: Redeemer President* (Grand Rapids, Mich.: Eerdmans, 1999), 116–17.

6. Roy P. Basler, ed., *The Collected Works of Abraham Lincoln*, 9 vols. (New Brunswick, N.J.: Rutgers Univ. Press, 1953), 1:382.

7. *The Illuminated Bible* (Chicago, Ill.: Columbia Educational Books, 1941).

8. An example of writing in defense of Lincoln's religious beliefs can be read in a pamphlet published in 1919 by B. F. Irwin, "Lincoln's Religious Beliefs" (Springfield, Ill.: privately printed by H. E. Barker, 1919).

9. Basler, *The Collected Works of Abraham Lincoln*, 8:332–33.

10. Snakeroot is the common name of the plant whose scientific name is *Eupatorium rugosum*. The plant is the source of a neurological toxin known as tremetol. When ingested by lactating animals the chemical is transmitted to the milk, and when the milk is consumed the toxin causes what was commonly known as "milk sickness." Because the disease affected none of the young children, it is possible that Lincoln's mother died of a bacterial disease transmitted by milk, brucellosis, and tremetol.

11. Lloyd Ostendorf and Walter Oleksy, eds., *Lincoln's Unknown Private Life: An Oral History by His Black Housekeeper Mariah Vance, 1850–1860* (Mamaroneck, N.Y.: Hastings House Book Publishing, 1995), 29.

12. Ibid., 264.

13. Ibid., 265.

14. Ibid.

15. Ibid., 266.

16. Ibid., 270–71.

17. Douglas L. Wilson and Rodney O. Davis, eds., *Herndon's Informants: Letters, Interviews, and Statements about Abraham Lincoln* (Urbana: Univ. of Illinois Press, 1998), 97. A. H. Chapman married the daughter of Dennis Hanks and Elizabeth Johnson, Lincoln's second cousin and stepsister, respectively. Chapman wrote to William Herndon in 1865 concerning Thomas Lincoln's church affiliations: "Joined the Free will Baptist Church in Hardin Co Ky in 1816 was immersed by a preacher named William Downs, in Knob Creek H Co [Hardin County] Ky on his removal to Ind united with the Old Predestinarian Baptist & on his removal to Coles Co Ills united with the same church but afterwards left them & joined the Christian Church in Charleston Ills & lived a member of that church in Good Standing until his death" (Wilson and Davis, eds., *Herndon's Informants,* 97). There is no similar account of Sarah Bush Lincoln's baptism, although she joined the Little Pigeon Creek Baptist Church on June 7, 1823, and presumably was baptized as a condition of her membership.

18. Ostendorf and Oleksy, eds., *Lincoln's Unknown Private Life,* 267.

19. Ibid., 267–68.

20. Ibid., 266.

21. Freeman Ankrum, *Maryland and Pennsylvania Historical Sketches* (West Newton, Pa.: Times-Sun, 1947).

22. Ibid., 37.

23. Ostendorf and Oleksy, eds., *Lincoln's Unknown Private Life,* 269.

24. Ibid., 272–73.

25. Ibid., 273.

26. Quoted in Louis A. Warren, "Abraham Lincoln and the Disciples," *Lincoln Lore,* no. 675 (March 1942): 1.

27. Theodore Calvin Pease and James G. Randle, eds., *The Diary of Orville Hickman Browning,* 2 vols. (Springfield: Illinois State Historical Library, 1925), 2:439, 443, notes the weather as "cold and raw," and "Roofs all covered with snow. Frost on the ground for some time now," respectively.

28. Quoted in Wayne C. Temple, "Lincoln As Seen by T. D. Jones," *Illinois Libraries* (June 1976): 447.

29. William E. Barton, *The Life of Abraham Lincoln,* 2 vols. (Indianapolis: Bobbs-Merrill, 1925), 2:117. Elkins is buried in the Connely Cemetery in Bryantsville, Indiana, a short distance from U.S. Highway 50 southwest of Bedford, Indiana. See Claude Parsons, "Men Who Knew Lincoln," *Times-Mail,* February 10, 1997, C1.

30. Warren, "Abraham Lincoln and the Disciples," 1.

31. Ibid.

32. James L. McMillan, *Addresses of Henry Russell Pritchard with Biographical Sketch* (Cincinnati: Standard, 1898), 1–22.

33. G. M. Weimer to Clyde O. Summers, Chicago, October 5, 1942, quoted in Jim R. Martin, "The Secret Baptism of Abraham Lincoln," paper presented at the Illinois History Symposium, Springfield, Illinois, December 4, 1987.

34. Ibid.

35. Ibid.

36. Edward Steers Jr., "Was Mistah Abe Babsized?" *Lincoln Herald* 101, no. 4 (winter 1999), 170.

37. Ostendorf and Oleksy, eds., *Lincoln's Unknown Private Life,* 267.

38. *Danville Republican,* July 26, 1860, 3. We can eliminate the 9:50 P.M. train from Danville, since it arrived in Springfield around 3:20 A.M.

39. See James O. Hall, "Review Essay," in *Journal of the Abraham Lincoln Association,* 19, no. 1 (winter 1998): 73–95.

40. Guelzo, *Abraham Lincoln: Redeemer President,* 446.

CHAPTER SIX. The Mole in the White House

1. Mark E. Neely Jr., *The Abraham Lincoln Encyclopedia* (New York: Mc-Graw-Hill, 1982), 66.

2. Howard K. Beale, ed., *The Diary of Edward Bates, 1859–1866,* vol. 4 of the *Annual Report of the American Historical Association,* 1930 (Washington, D.C.: Government Printing Office, 1933).

3. Mark E. Neely Jr., ed., "Abraham Lincoln Did NOT Defend His Wife before the Committee on the Conduct of the War," *Lincoln Lore,* no. 1643 (January 1975): 1.

4. Harold Holzer, ed., *Dear Mr. Lincoln: Letters to the President* (Reading, Mass.: Addison-Wesley, 1993), 21.

5. Lincoln had at least two of his Shenandoah Valley distant cousins serving in the Confederate army: Benjamin Franklin Lincoln and Albert Curtis Lincoln. See John W. Wayland, *The Lincolns in Virginia* (1946; reprint, Harrisonburg, Va.: C. J. Carrier, 1987), 209.

6. Jean H. Baker, *Mary Todd Lincoln* (New York: Norton, 1987), 225.

7. Ibid., 222; Stephen B. Oates, *With Malice Toward None: The Life of Abraham Lincoln* (New York: Harper and Row, 1977), 375–77.

8. Carl Sandburg, *The War Years,* 4 vols. (New York: Charles Scribner's Sons, 1944), 4:199.

9. Margaret Leech, *Reveille in Washington, 1860–1865* (New York: Harper and Brothers, 1941), 293.

10. Sandburg, *The War Years,* 4:200; Neely, ed., "Abraham Lincoln Did NOT Defend His Wife before the Committee on the Conduct of the War," 1.

11. Quoted in Neely, ed., "Abraham Lincoln Did NOT Defend His Wife before the Committee on the Conduct of the War," 1.

12. Neely, ed., "Abraham Lincoln Did NOT Defend His Wife before the Committee on the Conduct of the War," 2. The break-in occurred on June 17, 1972, impeachment proceedings began in July 1973, and President Nixon resigned the following year, on August 9, 1974.

13. Ibid., 1.

14. E. J. Edwards, "The Solitude of Abraham Lincoln" (Putnam, Conn.: Privately printed by Gilbert A. Tracy, by Permission of the Author, 1916), 6–7.

15. Ibid., 6–7.

16. Neely, ed., "Abraham Lincoln Did NOT Defend His Wife before the Committee on the Conduct of the War," 2.

17. George Schaefer, prod. and dir., *Sandburg's Lincoln*, 6 parts, NBC, New York, 1974–1976, part 3.

18. Sandburg, *The War Years*, 2:199.

19. Neely, ed., "Abraham Lincoln Did NOT Defend His Wife before the Committee on the Conduct of the War," 2–4.

20. Ibid., 2.

CHAPTER SEVEN. You Can Fool All of the People Some of the Time . . .

1. Wayne C. Temple, ed., *The Taste Is in My Mouth a Little: Lincoln's Victuals and Potables* (Mahomet, Ill.: Mayhaven, 2004); C. A. Tripp, *The Intimate World of Abraham Lincoln* (New York: Free Press, 2005).

2. Harry E. Pratt, *The Personal Finances of Abraham Lincoln* (Springfield, Ill.: Abraham Lincoln Association, 1943); Joshua Wolf Shenk, *Lincoln's Melancholy: How Depression Challenged a President and Fueled His Greatness* (Boston: Houghton Mifflin, 2005); Mark S. Reinhart, *Abraham Lincoln on Screen: A Filmography, 1903–1998* (Jefferson, N.C.: McFarland, 1999); P. M. Zaul, ed., *Abe Lincoln Laughing: Humorous Anecdotes from Original Sources by and about Abraham Lincoln* (Berkeley: Univ. of California Press, 1982).

3. Louis A. Warren, *Lincoln's Gettysburg Declaration: "A New Birth of Freedom"* (Fort Wayne, Ind.: Lincoln National Life Foundation, 1964); Philip B. Kunhardt Jr., *A New Birth of Freedom: Lincoln at Gettysburg* (Boston: Little, Brown, 1983); Garry Wills, *Lincoln at Gettysburg: The Words That Remade America* (New York: Simon and Schuster, 1992).

4. Harold Holzer, *Lincoln at Cooper Union: The Speech That Made Abraham Lincoln President* (New York: Simon and Schuster, 2004).

5. F. Lauristan Bullard, *Abraham Lincoln and the Widow Bixby* (New Brunswick, N.J.: Rutgers Univ. Press, 1946).

6. Ronald C. White Jr., *Lincoln's Greatest Speech: The Second Inaugural* (New York: Simon and Schuster, 2002).

7. Roy P. Basler, ed., *The Collected Works of Abraham Lincoln*, 9 vols. (New Brunswick, N.J.: Rutgers Univ. Press, 1953). Since publication in 1953, two supplemental volumes have been added.

8. Don E. Fehrenbacher and Virginia Fehrenbacher, eds., *Recollected Words of Abraham Lincoln* (Stanford, Calif.: Stanford Univ. Press, 1996).

9. Ibid., lii–liii.

10. Ibid., liii.

11. Archer H. Shaw, ed., *The Lincoln Encyclopedia: The Spoken and Written Words of A. Lincoln Arranged for Ready Reference* (New York: Macmillan, 1950); Caroline Thomas Harnsberger, ed., *The Lincoln Treasury* (Chicago: Wilcox and Follett, 1950).

12. Louis A. Warren, "Axioms Credited to Lincoln, Unauthentic," *Lincoln Lore*, no. 1085 (January 23, 1959): 1.

13. Carl Sandburg, *Abraham Lincoln: The Prairie Years—II*, 2 vols. (1926; reprint, New York: Charles Scribner's Sons, 1944), 2:142.

14. John G. Nicolay and John Hay, eds., *The Complete Works of Abraham Lincoln*, 10 vols. (New York: Francis D. Tandy, 1905), 3:349.

15. Fehrenbacher and Fehrenbacher, eds., *Recollected Words*, 1.

16. Alexander K. McClure, *Lincoln's Yarns and Stories: A Complete Collection of the Funny and Witty Anecdotes That Made Abraham Lincoln Famous as America's Greatest Story Teller* (Chicago: John C. Winston, 1901), 124.

17. Fehrenbacher and Fehrenbacher, eds., *Recollected Words*, liii.

18. Thomas F. Schwartz, "'You Can Fool All of the People': Lincoln Never Said That," *For the People: Newsletter of the Abraham Lincoln Association* 5, no. 4 (winter 2003): 1.

19. Kate Louise Roberts, *Hoyt's New Cyclopedia of Practical Quotations* (New York: Funk and Wagnalls, 1922).

20. Schwartz, "'You Can Fool All of the People': Lincoln Never Said That," 6.

21. Michael Burlingame, "New Light on the Bixby Letter," *Journal of the Abraham Lincoln Association* 16, no. 1 (winter 1995): 59–71.

22. Nicolay and Hay, eds., *The Complete Works of Abraham Lincoln*.

23. Burlingame, "New Light on the Bixby Letter," 60.

24. Bullard, *Abraham Lincoln and the Widow Bixby*, 54.

25. Douglas L. Wilson and Rodney O. Davis, eds., *Herndon's Informants: Letters, Interviews, and Statements about Abraham Lincoln* (Urbana: Univ. of Illinois Press, 1998), 331.

26. This "photograph" copy was undoubtedly the lithograph produced by Michael Tobin.

27. Quoted in Roy P. Basler, "Who Wrote the Letter to Mrs. Bixby?" *Lincoln Herald* 45, no. 1 (February 1943): 9–14

28. Burlingame, "New Light on the Bixby Letter," 62.

29. A similar scrapbook belonging to Hay is among his papers in the Library of Congress. This scrapbook also contains a clipping of the Bixby letter.

30. Burlingame, "New Light on the Bixby Letter," 71.

31. James Emerson, "America's Most Famous Letter," *American Heritage*, February/March 2006, 41–49.

CHAPTER EIGHT. The World Will Little Note . . .

1. The eBook of *The Perfect Tribute* is for the use of anyone anywhere at no cost and with almost no restrictions whatsoever. You may copy it, give it away, or reuse it under the terms of the Project Gutenberg License included with the eBook or online at www.gutenberg.net.

2. Mary Raymond Shipman Andrews, *The Perfect Tribute* (New York: Charles Scribner's Sons, 1907), 3.

3. Andrews, *The Perfect Tribute*, 7.

4. Ibid., 8–9.

5. Joseph G. E. Hopkins, managing editor, *Concise Dictionary of American Biography* (New York: Charles Scribner's Sons, 1964), 279.

6. Andrews, *The Perfect Tribute*, 12.

7. Ibid., 13.

8. Ibid., 13–14.

9. This is the Second Draft. Roy P. Basler, ed., *The Collected Works of Abraham Lincoln*, 9 vols. (New Brunswick, N.J.: Rutgers Univ. Press, 1953), 7:18–19.

10. Andrews, *The Perfect Tribute*, 18.

11. Ibid., 21.

12. Ibid., 22.

13. Ibid., 40.

14. E. B. Long and Barbara Long, eds., *The Civil War Day by Day: An Almanac, 1861–1865* (New York: Doubleday, 1971), 377.

15. Ibid., 378.

16. Louis A. Warren, *Lincoln's Gettysburg Declaration: "A New Birth of Freedom"* (Fort Wayne, Ind.: Lincoln National Life Foundation, 1964), 29.

17. Ibid., 38.

18. Ibid., 37.

19. Ibid., 45.

20. Wills signed his letter to Lincoln, "Agent for A. G. Curtin, Gov. of Penna. And acting for all the states" (Ibid., 46).

21. Don E. Fehrenbacher and Virginia Fehrenbacher, eds., *Recollected Words of Abraham Lincoln* (Stanford, Calif.: Stanford Univ. Press, 1996), 46.

22. Ibid., 412.

23. David C. Mearns and Lloyd A. Dunlap, *Long Remembered: Facsimiles of the Five Versions of the Gettysburg Address in the Handwriting of Abraham Lincoln* (Washington, D.C.: Library of Congress, 1963), 3.

CHAPTER NINE. The "Lost" Draft of the Gettysburg Address

1. David C. Mearns and Lloyd A. Dunlap, *Long Remembered: Facsimiles of the Five Versions of the Gettysburg Address in the Handwriting of Abraham Lincoln* (Washington, D.C.: Library of Congress, 1963), 14.

2. The words "under God" do not appear in either the first or second drafts but are in the third draft. Newspaper reports include the words, indicating that Lincoln said them in delivering his speech.

3. Frank L. Klement, *The Gettysburg Soldiers' Cemetery and Lincoln's Address* (Shippensburg, Pa.: White Mane, 1993), 154.

4. Roderick J. McNeil, "Scanning Auger Microscopy for Dating Two Copies of the 'Oath of a Freeman,'" in *The Judgement of Experts*, ed. James Gilreath, 115–29 (Worcester, Mass.: American Antiquarian Society, 1991).

5. Klement, *The Gettysburg Soldiers' Cemetery and Lincoln's Address*, 163.

6. The newsletter is no longer published, but during the years of publication it dealt with several of the controversies having to do with the alleged missing pages from Booth's diary and the claim that Booth was not killed in the Garretts' barn but escaped (see chapter 12).

7. Richard Sloan, "Sloan: A Forgery, a Tracing, Overlaying of Two Drafts Shows," *The Lincolnian* 10, no. 5 (May–June 1992): 4.

8. Ibid., 5.

9. James Gilreath, "Ostendorf's Gettysburg Address Claim Supported Only By Improbable Conjectures, Manuscript Expert Says," *The Lincolnian* 10, no. 4 (March–April 1992): 4–5.

10. Joe Nickell, *Detecting Forgery: Forensic Investigation of Documents* (Lexington: Univ. Press of Kentucky, 1996).

11. Ibid., 193.

12. President John F. Kennedy was said to have used an autopen in the White House.

13. Nickell, *Detecting Forgery*, 193–94.

CHAPTER TEN. The Gay Lincoln Myth

1. Carol Lloyd, "Larry Kramer Claims to Have Discovered a Diary Proving Lincoln Was Gay," *Salon* (May 3, 1999): 1.

2. Stephanie Simon, "Lincoln Country Aghast as Local Paper Prints Gay Allegation," *Los Angeles Times*, June 6, 1999, 1.

3. Jefferson Robbins, "Writer Asserts Proof Lincoln Was Gay," *Sunday State Journal Register* [Illinois], May 16, 1999, 1.

4. Jean Baker in C. A. Tripp, *The Intimate World of Abraham Lincoln* (New York: Free Press, 2005), xii.

5. Allen C. Guelzo, "The Lincoln Bedroom," *Claremont Review of Books* 5, no. 3 (summer 2005): 52.

6. Tripp, *The Intimate World of Abraham Lincoln*, 34.

7. Ibid., 34.

8. Ibid., 32.

9. William H. Herndon and Jesse W. Weik, *Herndon's Life of Lincoln: The History and Personal Recollections of Abraham Lincoln* (New York: Da Capo Press, 1983), 25.

10. Douglas L. Wilson and Rodney O. Davis, eds., *Herndon's Informants: Letters, Interviews, and Statements about Abraham Lincoln* (Urbana: Univ. of Illinois Press, 1998), 120.

11. Ibid., 121.

12. Carl Sandburg, *Abraham Lincoln: The Prairie Years*, 2 vols. (1926; reprint, New York: Charles Scribner's Sons, 1944), 1:43.

13. Tripp, *The Intimate World of Abraham Lincoln*, 31.

14. Ibid., 36.

15. *Rockport* (Ill.) *Journal*, February 12, 1897, quoted in Louis A. Warren, *Lincoln's Youth: Indiana Years, Seven to Twenty-One, 1816–1830* (New York: Appleton Century Crofts, 1959), 195.

16. Wilson and Davis, eds., *Herndon's Informants*, 152.

17. Tripp, *The Intimate World of Abraham Lincoln*, 41.

18. Wilson and Davis, eds., *Herndon's Informants*, 17.

19. Herndon and Weik, *Herndon's Life of Lincoln*, 68.

20. Tripp, *The Intimate World of Abraham Lincoln*, 47.

21. Ibid., 48.

22. Wilson and Davis, eds., *Herndon's Informants*, 440.

23. Ibid. Don and Virginia Fehrenbacher, the editors of *Recollected Words of Abraham Lincoln* (Stanford, Calif.: Stanford Univ. Press, 1996), rank the authenticity of this quotation as a "D," "a quotation about whose authenticity there is more than average doubt." They give no explanation of why they believe this to be true.

24. James G. Randall, "Sifting the Ann Rutledge Experience," in the appendix of his *Lincoln, the President: Springfield to Gettysburg*, 2 vols. (New York: Dodd, Mead, 1945), 2:321–42.

25. Herndon and Weik, *Herndon's Life of Lincoln*, 116.

26. Wilson and Davis, eds., *Herndon's Informants*, 610.

27. Ibid., 256.

28. Ibid.

29. Roy P. Basler, ed., *The Collected Works of Abraham Lincoln*, 9 vols. (New Brunswick, N.J.: Rutgers Univ. Press, 1953), 1:94.

30. Ibid., 1:118.

31. Tripp, *The Intimate World of Abraham Lincoln*, 91.

32. Ibid., 180.

33. Ibid., 157.

34. Michael Burlingame, "A Respectful Dissent," in Tripp, *The Intimate World of Abraham Lincoln*, 225.

35. Basler, *The Collected Works of Abraham Lincoln*, 4:385.

36. Tripp, *The Intimate World of Abraham Lincoln*, 113.

37. Ibid., 113.

38. Ruth Painter Randall, *Colonel Elmer Ellsworth* (Boston: Little, Brown, 1960), 210.

39. Tripp, *The Intimate World of Abraham Lincoln*, 116.

40. Basler, ed., *The Collected Works of Abraham Lincoln*, 4:273.

41. Ibid., 4:291.

42. Ibid., 4:333.

43. Tripp, *The Intimate World of Abraham Lincoln*, 123.

44. Ibid., 124.

45. Thomas Chamberlain,, *History of the One Hundred and Fiftieth Regiment, Pennsylvania Volunteers, Second Regiment, Bucktail Brigade* (Philadelphia: McManus, 1905), 41–42, quoted in Tripp, *The Intimate World of Abraham Lincoln*, 3–4.

46. Tripp, *The Intimate World of Abraham Lincoln*, 15.

47. Ibid., 16–17.

48. Ibid., 19.

49. Ibid., 1; Virginia L. Woodbury Fox, 1860–78, box 1, reel 1, Levi Woodbury Family Papers, Manuscript Division, Library of Congress, Washington, D.C.

50. Tripp, *The Intimate World of Abraham Lincoln*, 19.

51. Ibid., 20.

52. Ibid., 209.

53. Ibid., 31.

54. Ibid., 239.

CHAPTER ELEVEN. Noble American or Deceptive Doctor?

1. Frank Trippett, "Some Cases Never Die, or Even Fade," *Time*, September 17, 1979, 63.

2. In the last year and a half of his life, Richard Mudd spoke with me by telephone on five occasions to discuss his grandfather's case. Richard Mudd died on May 21, 2001, at the age of 101.

3. Nettie Mudd, ed., *The Life of Dr. Samuel A. Mudd* (New York: Neale, 1906).

4. Mark S. Reinhart, *Abraham Lincoln on Screen: A Filmography, 1903–1998* (Jefferson, N.C.: McFarland, 1999), 222–23.

5. For Dr. Mudd's own explanation of why he attempted to escape, see Edward Steers Jr., "Rewriting History: Reader Beware," *Surratt Courier* 21, no. 3 (March 1996): 8–9.

6. Edward Steers Jr., "A Remarkable Voice from the Past: Mrs. Nettie Mudd Monroe Speaks of Her Father as 'The Prisoner of Shark Island,'" *Surratt Courier* 26, no. 11 (November 2001): 3–4.

7. Edward Steers Jr., *His Name Is Still Mudd* (Gettysburg, Pa: Thomas Publications, 1997), 118–19.

8. Ibid., 77.

9. Ibid., 120.

10. Ibid., 78.

11. Ibid., 79.

12. The entire case, along with commentaries by legal scholars, both pro and con, is presented in John Paul Jones, ed., *Dr. Mudd and the Lincoln Assassination: The Case Reopened* (Conshohocken, Pa.: Combined Books, 1995).

13. Ibid., 112.

14. Steers, *His Name Is Still Mudd*, 80.

15. *Richard D. Mudd v. Togo West*, case no. 1:97 CVO2946 (U.S. District Court for the District of Columbia, December 9, 1997).

16. *Ex Parte Quirin*, 317 U.S. 1 (1942).

17. *Mudd II*, 134 F. Supp. 2d 147–48.

18. *Mudd v. White*, No. 01–5103 (D.C. Circ. November 8, 2002).

19. The Mudd family owned eighty-nine slaves at the outbreak of the war: fifty males and thirty-nine females. The values used for the Mudd slaves are: $800 for slaves age 0–12; $1,200 for slaves age 13–50; and $600 for slaves over 50. These valuations are based on Jeffrey Rogers Hummel, *Emancipating Slaves, Enslaving Free Men* (Chicago: Open Court, 1996), and Hugh J. Aitkin, *Did Slavery Pay?* (Boston: Houghton Mifflin, 1971).

20. *Port Tobacco Times*, January 17, 1861, page 1, col. 1. See 1 Timothy 6:1–2.

21. Nettie Mudd, *The Life of Dr. Samuel A. Mudd* (1906; reprint, LaPlata, Md.: Dick Wildes Printing, 1983), 352–53, 355.

22. Statement of Samuel A. Mudd, National Archives and Records Administration (NARA), RG 153, M-599, reel 5, frames 0226–0239.

23. *Port Tobacco Times*, January 3, 1861. The four companies were the Mounted Volunteers of Charles County, the Smallwood Riflemen, the Bryantown Minutemen, and the Nanjemoy Rifle Company.

24. John Rhodehamel and Louise Taper, eds., *"Right or Wrong, God Judge Me": The Writings of John Wilkes Booth* (Urbana: Univ. of Illinois Press, 1997), 154.

25. Samuel Bland Arnold, *Memoirs of a Lincoln Conspirator*, edited by Michael W. Kauffman (Bowie, Md.: Heritage Books, 1995).

26. William A. Tidwell, James O. Hall, and David W. Gaddy, *Come Retribution: The Confederate Secret Service and the Assassination of Abraham Lincoln* (Jackson: Univ. Press of Mississippi, 1989), 265.

27. Testimony of Robert Anson Campbell in Ben: Perley Poore, *The Conspiracy Trial for the Murder of the President, and the Attempt to Overthrow the Government by the Assassination of its Principal Officers*, 3 vols. (New York: Arno Press, 1972), 2:83–89.

28. Edward Steers Jr., *Blood on the Moon: The Assassination of Abraham Lincoln* (Lexington: Univ. Press of Kentucky, 2001), 73. See testimony of Eaton Horner in Poore, ed., *The Conspiracy Trial*, 1:430.

29. Testimony of John C. Thompson in Poore, ed., *The Conspiracy Trial*, 2:269.

30. In an interview with noted journalist George Alfred Townsend, Harbin told of the meeting he was asked to attend where Mudd introduced him to Booth. The interview appeared in the *Cincinnati Enquirer*, April 18, 1892, 2.

31. Affidavit of Samuel Mudd, in Clara E. Laughlin, *The Death of Lincoln* (New York: Doubleday, Page, 1909), 215–20. See also Steers, *Blood on the Moon,* 77–78.

32. Steers, *Blood on the Moon,* 78–79.

33. Affidavit of Samuel Mudd, in Laughlin, *The Death of Lincoln,* 215–20.

34. Atzerodt's confession appears in Steers, *His Name Is Still Mudd,* 121–24.

35. Steers, *Blood on the Moon,* 153.

CHAPTER TWELVE. The Missing Pages From Booth's Diary

1. In the past four years alone, three books have appeared claiming that Lincoln's murder was the result of conspiracies involving members of Lincoln's own cabinet and prominent northern politicians and businessmen in league with their Confederate counterparts: Leonard F. Guttridge and Ray A. Neff, *Dark Union: The Secret Web of Profiteers, Politicians, and Booth Conspirators That Led to Lincoln's Death* (Hoboken, N.J.: John Wiley and Sons, 2003); Charles Higham, *Murdering Mr. Lincoln: A New Detection of the 19th Century's Most Famous Crime* (Beverly Hills, Calif.: New Millennium Press, 2004); John Chandler Griffin, *Abraham Lincoln's Execution* (Gretna, La.: Pelican, 2006).

2. Statement of Everton Conger, NARA, RG 94, M-619, reel 455, frames 0691–0703.

3. For a list of exhibits, see Edward Steers Jr., ed., *The Trial: The Assassination of President Lincoln and the Trial of the Conspirators* (Lexington: Univ. Press of Kentucky, 2003), CI–CIII.

4. Testimony of Lafayette C. Baker, *Impeachment Investigation: Testimony Taken before the Judiciary Committee of the House of Representatives in the Investigation of the Charges against Andrew Johnson,* 39th Cong., 2nd Sess., and 40th Cong., 1st Sess., 1867 (Washington, D.C.: Government Printing Office, 1867), 458.

5. Testimony of E. J. Conger, *Impeachment Investigation: Testimony Taken before the Judiciary Committee of the House of Representatives in the Investigation of the Charges against Andrew Johnson,* 39th Cong., 2nd Sess., and 40th Cong., 1st Sess., 1867 (Washington, D.C.: Government Printing Office, 1867), 323–24.

6. Otto Eisenschiml, *Why Was Lincoln Murdered?* (Boston: Little, Brown, 1937).

7. Booth's diary, along with many other artifacts associated with Lincoln's assassination, is on display at Ford's Theatre in Washington, D.C.

8. Eisenschiml, *Why Was Lincoln Murdered?,* 139.

9. Richard E. Sloan, telephone interview with the author, April 4, 2006.

10. Ibid., and in Richard Sloan, "The Case of the Missing Pages," *Journal of the Lincoln Assassination* 9, no. 3 (December 1995): 38–44. The *Journal of the Lincoln Assassination* is a privately printed newsletter edited by Frederick Hatch and published by Autograph Press, P.O. Box 2616, Waldorf, MD, 20604.

11. Sloan reported the story in *The Lincoln Log,* beginning with the No-

vember–December 1976 issue (vol. 1, no. 11) and continuing through the October–November 1977 issue (vol. 2, no. 6).

12. Richard D. Mudd, telephone interview with the author, January 3, 1998. In the same telephone conversation Richard Mudd told the author he received $1,500 to serve as a consultant to Sunn Classic Pictures.

13. David Balsiger and Charles E. Sellier Jr., *The Lincoln Conspiracy* (Los Angeles: Schick Sunn Classic Books, 1977).

14. Robert Fowler, "Was Stanton behind Lincoln's Murder?" *Civil War Times* 3, no. 5 (August 1961): 6–23.

15. Balsiger and Sellier, *The Lincoln Conspiracy*, 8.

16. William C. Davis, "Behind the Lines," *Civil War Times Illustrated* 21, no. 7 (November 1981): 26.

17. Among the many items obtained by Neff is a collection of documents known as the "Chaffey Papers." Included is an original (holograph) letterbook of James and John Chaffey whose contents date from 1831 to 1838 and have nothing to do with the Civil War or Lincoln's assassination. The remaining papers are typescript copies.

18. William C. Davis, "Behind the Lines: Caveat Emptor," *Civil War Times Illustrated* (August 1977): 33–37; William C. Davis, "Behind the Lines: 'The Lincoln Conspiracy'—Hoax?," *Civil War Times Illustrated* (November 1977): 47–49; William C. Davis, "Behind the Lines," *Civil War Times Illustrated* 21, no. 7 (November 1981): 26–28.

19. Davis, "Behind the Lines," 26.

20. Davis, "Behind the Lines: Caveat Emptor," 37.

21. Sloan, "The Case of the Missing Pages," 39.

22. Ibid., 40.

23. Davis, "Behind the Lines," 26.

24. Sloan, "The Case of the Missing Pages," 43.

25. The two specimens of Booth's writing supplied by the National Archives are the "To whom it may concern" letter dated 1864 and the "Dearest Beloved Mother" letter to Mary Ann Holmes Booth dated 1864. The two letters were discovered by James O. Hall in 1977 in the files of the Justice Department in the National Archives. For the complete text of these letters, see John Rhodehamel and Louise Taper, eds., *"Right or Wrong, God Judge Me": The Writings of John Wilkes Booth* (Urbana: Univ. of Illinois Press, 1997), 124–27, 130–31.

26. J. Dunning, "Examination of John Wilkes Booth's Diary," Report of the FBI Laboratory, No. 95-216208, Washington, D.C., October 3, 1977.

27. Ibid.

28. Sloan, "The Case of the Missing Pages," 40.

29. The entire transcript of the missing pages was first published in the *Surratt Courier* 19, no. 10 (October 1994): 3–9.

30. Laurie Verge, ed., "Those Missing Pages from the 'Diary' of John Wilkes Booth," *Surratt Courier*, 19, no. 10 (October 1994): 3–9.

31. Rhodehamel and Taper, eds., *"Right or Wrong, God Judge Me,"* 111.

32. Ibid., 114.

33. Junius Brutus Booth Jr., diary, 1864, Folger Shakespeare Library, Washington, D.C. Joe Simonds was Booth's close friend and business partner in Booth's oil venture.

34. Rhodehamel and Taper, eds., *"Right or Wrong, God Judge Me,"* 45.

35. Ibid., 83.

36. Ibid., 86.

37. There is no record that Baker employed or used Indian scouts in any of his operations.

38. Guttridge and Neff, *Dark Union,* 175.

39. The version in *Dark Union* differs slightly from the version in the Neff-Guttridge Collection, in which Conness is quoted as saying, "Oh my God, Oh my God."

40. Guttridge and Neff, *Dark Union,* 175–76.

41. The alleged excerpt from Julian's diary currently resides in the Neff-Guttridge Collection in the Special Collections Department of the Cunningham Memorial Library, Indiana State University, Terre Haute, Indiana. The collection consists of materials collected over the years by Ray Neff, the consultant to Sunn Classic Pictures who provided the documents used to make *The Lincoln Conspiracy.*

42. Grace Julian Clarke to Claude Bowers, July 22, 1926, Manuscript Department, Lilly Library, Indiana University, Bloomington, Indiana.

43. Appendix 4, "George Julian's Diary," Neff-Guttridge Collection. See also *Dark Union,* "Sources on Notes," chapter 13, page 258: "Claude Bowers, preparing his book, *The Tragic Era,* borrowed the 1865 diary and photographed its pages without Grace Clark's [*sic*] knowledge."

44. Appendix 4, "George Julian's Diary," Neff-Guttridge Collection.

45. Ibid. Although the explanatory document refers to both Guttridge and Neff being present, Guttridge stated in a telephone conversation with the author on October 15, 2003, that he was not present during the Smith interview or during the transcription of the alleged Smith copy.

46. "George W. Julian's Journal—The Assassination of Lincoln," *Indiana Magazine of History* 11, no. 4 (December 1915): 324–37.

47. Appendix 4, "George Julian's Diary," Neff-Guttridge Collection.

48. In addition to the research librarians' search of the Julian and Bowers papers, the curator in charge of the Claude Bowers papers wrote the following: "We keep very complete-use files and we have no record of Mr. Neff making use of our materials, either in person or through correspondence" (Saundra Taylor to James O. Hall, May 26, 1977, Manuscript Collection, Lilly Library, Indiana University, Bloomington, Indiana).

49. Mabel M. Herbert to Charles Cooney, September 12, 1977, original in possession of William C. Davis, photocopy in author's files.

50. Statement of Richard Stuart, NARA, RG 153, M-599, reel 6, frame 0209.

51. The two notes were introduced as evidence at the time of Andrew Johnson's impeachment hearing. They subsequently disappeared and were never seen again.

52. Statement of William Garrett, NARA, RG 94, M-619, reel 457, frames 0499–0525.

53. Statement of Luther B. Baker, aboard the *Montauk,* April 26, 1865, NARA RG 94, M-619, reel 455, frames 0665–0686.

54. Testimony of Luther B. Baker, *Impeachment Investigation: Testimony Taken before the Judiciary Committee of the House of Representatives in the Investigation of the Charges against Andrew Johnson,* 39th Cong., 2nd Sess., and 40th Cong., 1st Sess., 1867 (Washington, D.C.: Government Printing Office, 1867), 478–90.

CHAPTER THIRTEEN. Peanut John

1. Quoted in Timothy S. Good, *We Saw Lincoln Shot: One Hundred Eyewitness Accounts* (Jackson: Univ. Press of Mississippi, 1995), 102.

2. Gary R. Planck, *The Lincoln Assassination's Forgotten Investigator: A. C. Richards* (Harrogate, Tenn.: Lincoln Memorial Univ. Press, 1993), 18–19.

3. Ben: Perley Poore, ed., *The Conspiracy Trial for the Murder of the President, and the Attempt to Overthrow the Government by the Assassination of its Principal Officers,* 3 vols. (1865; reprint, New York: Arno Press, 1972), 1:225–35.

4. The spelling of Burroughs's name varies depending on the source. It appears as "Burroughs," "Borroughs," and "Borrows." The spelling in this chapter is the spelling used in the trial transcript.

5. It was at this time that Booth made preparations to brace the door of the box from the inside, preventing anyone from entering behind him. He cut a notch in the plaster wall and left the upright part of a music stand in the corner of the vestibule, where no one would notice it.

6. Poore, *The Conspiracy Trial,* 1:227–28.

7. Roy Z. Chamlee Jr., *Lincoln's Assassins* (Jefferson, N.C.: McFarland, 1990), 276.

8. William C. Kashatus, "Booth Aided in Escape by County Man," *Chester County Living,* Sunday, October 27, 2002, 3. There is no mention of Nathan Simms in the evidence file or trial record (microcopy M-599) in the National Archives and Records Administration.

9. Ibid.

10. Ibid.

11. Catharine Quillman, "Helping, Then Hindering Lincoln's Assassin," *Philadelphia Inquirer,* February 19, 2001, B 02.

12. Mary Arthur, a cousin of Giuseppe, states that the family spelling of the surname is "Ratti."

13. R. Gerald McMurtry, ed., "Did 'Coughdrop Joey' Ratto Hold Booth's Horse?" *Lincoln Lore,* no. 1571 (January 1969): 2–3.

CHAPTER FOURTEEN. The Man Who Never Was

Part of the material used for this chapter appeared in an article by Edward Steers Jr. and Joan C. Chaconas, "*Dark Union*: Bad History," *North & South* 7, no. 1 (January 2004): 12–30.

1. The Confederates' ill-fated submarine, CSS *Hunley*, successfully attached a torpedo to the hull of the Union ship USS *Housatonic* on the night of February 17, 1864. The *Housatonic* was part of the naval blockade of Charleston, South Carolina, at the time. The subsequent explosion resulted in the *Housatonic*'s sinking. The *Hunley*, however, never returned to its berth, sinking with its entire crew. It was not recovered until August 8, 2000.

2. James L. Swanson, *Manhunt: The 12-Day Chase for Lincoln's Killer* (New York: HarperCollins, 2006), 283.

3. Otto Eisenschiml, *Why Was Lincoln Murdered?* (Boston: Little, Brown, 1937), and Otto Eisenschiml, *In the Shadow of Lincoln's Death* (New York: Wilfred Funk, 1940).

4. "The Colburn Volume," Neff-Guttridge Collection, Special Collections Department, Cunningham Memorial Library, Indiana State University, Terre Haute, Indiana; Robert H. Fowler, ed., "Was Stanton behind Lincoln's Murder?" *Civil War Times* 3, no. 5 (August 1961): 5–23.

5. According to David Balsiger and Charles Sellier, "numerous Potter brothers, half brothers and cousins were members of Baker's secret police" (David Balsiger and Charles E. Sellier Jr., *The Lincoln Conspiracy* [Los Angeles: Schick Sunn Classic Books, 1977], 17).

6. Balsiger and Sellier, *The Lincoln Conspiracy*. 6.

7. Ibid. The book and movie of the same title were released simultaneously.

8. Ibid., 10.

9. Ibid., 247.

10. Ibid.

11. Ibid., 249.

12. Baker is believed to have died of typhoid fever, but Neff believes he died of arsenic poisoning (Robert H. Fowler, "Was Stanton behind Lincoln's Murder?" *Civil War Times* 3, no. 5 [August 1961]: 9).

13. Leonard F. Guttridge and Ray A. Neff, *Dark Union: The Secret Web of Profiteers, Politicians, and Booth Conspirators That Led to Lincoln's Death* (Hoboken, N.J.: John Wiley and Sons, 2003), 195.

14. Ibid.

15. Ibid.

16. Lew Wallace to Ulysses S. Grant, February 7, 1877, Neff-Guttridge Collection, Special Collections Department, Cunningham Memorial Library, Indiana State University, Terre Haute, Indiana. This letter is a typescript copy of an alleged original now in the Neff-Guttridge Collection.

17. Queries to Professor John Y. Simon, editor of the Ulysses S. Grant Papers, Ulysses S. Grant Association, Morris Library, Southern Illinois University, Carbondale, Illinois, concerning correspondence between Grant and Wallace that might corroborate Wallace's alleged role in heading up a private investigation ordered by Grant proved negative. Dr. Simon wrote: "Wallace wrote to Grant three times in 1872 about a diplomatic appointment to Bolivia. He wrote again on August 13, 1873, to send Grant a copy of his novel, *The Fair God,* and he wrote in January 1875 about a judicial appointment. Finally, in December 1876, he was in Florida observing the contested election and telegraphed Grant about the vote count. Following this alleged 1877 letter, he did not write to Grant for years. In other words, there is nothing that Wallace wrote in this period that even vaguely supports the unusual item you faxed to me."

18. Undated typed statement of Ray A. Neff entitled "The Potter Papers" in the Neff-Guttridge Collection, Special Collections Department, Cunningham Memorial Library, Indiana State University, Terre Haute, Indiana.

19. Ray A. Neff, *Valley of the Shadow* (Terre Haute, Ind.: RANA Publications, 1989), 220; author's personal conversation with Ray A. Neff, August 12, 2003.

20. Guttridge and Neff, *Dark Union,* 209.

21. Neff took on an established writer, Leonard Guttridge, as a coauthor and magnanimously named his collection the "Neff-Guttridge Collection."

22. Guttridge and Neff, *Dark Union,* 295.

23. Personal conversation with James O. Hall, 1995. In 1974, Hall conducted a series of interviews with Perry W. Browning, Browning family historian and direct descendant of Peregrine W. Browning. Browning informed Hall that William A. Browning was a bachelor.

24. Photocopy in the James O. Hall Research Center, Surratt House Museum, Clinton, Maryland.

25. Betty J. Ownsbey, *Alias "Paine"* (Jefferson, N.C.: McFarland, 1993).

26. The author is indebted to Michael Musick, Subject Area Expert, U.S. Civil War, NARA, for his expert assistance in these searches.

27. In 1863, Andrew Potter was allegedly sent to Indiana to investigate contraband activity in that state. The authors of *Dark Union* claim that Stanton persuaded Indiana governor Oliver P. Morton to confer a commission on Andrew Potter in the Indiana militia to protect him if captured by Confederates; no military record of Potter can be found in the Civil War records in the National Archives or in the military records of the Indiana State Archives.

28. The author is indebted to Dr. Alan January, Indiana State Archives, for conducting this search.

29. Andrew Potter, untitled autobiography, undated, Neff-Guttridge Collection, Special Collections Department, Cunningham Memorial Library, Indiana State University, Terre Haute, Indiana.

254 Notes to Page 230

30. Appendix 4, "James W. Boyd," Neff-Guttridge Collection, undated.

31. Most notorious during this period was a man named Charles A. Dunham, who used the aliases of Sandford Conover and James Watson Wallace. Dunham became the Federal government's chief witness against Jefferson Davis in the Lincoln conspiracy trial. It was later shown that he committed perjury, and eventually he was sent to jail. Conover was a master fabricator whose forgeries continued to fool people as late as 1996. See Stewart Evans and Paul Gainey, *Jack the Ripper: First American Serial Killer* (New York: Kodansha International, 1998).

INDEX

Abe Lincoln in Illinois (movie), 30
Abell, Elizabeth and Bennett, 136
"Abraham Lincoln–Jefferson Davis
  cabin," 4–5, 9, *12*
Abraham Lincoln Quarterly, 8
Across the Busy Years (Butler), 98–99
"American Charter, The," 91–92
Andrew, John A., 94
Andrews, Mary Raymond Shipman,
  102–6, 108–9, 114
Angle, Paul M., 43, 44–45, 46–48
Ankrum, Freeman, 71–72
Army Board for the Correction of
  Military Records (ABCMR),
  156–57, 159
Arnold, Samuel, 196
Ashe, James, 46
assassination, of Lincoln. *See* Lincoln
  assassination
Atlantic Monthly: Wilma Frances Minor
  hoax, 34–50
Atzerodt, George A., 172, 173, 174, 193
*Autograph Leaves of Our Country's
  Authors,* 117
autopens, 122–23

Baden, Joseph, 216
Bailey, F. Lee, 158
Baker, Jean, 126–27
Baker, Lafayette C.: in alleged Booth
  diary (Lynch pages), 191, 193; National
  Detective Police and, 178, 191, 214,
  215, 216–17; in Ray Neff's theory of
  Lincoln's murder, 185, 218; pursuit and
  capture of Booth, 178, 216; testimony
  on Booth's diary, 181
Baker, Luther B., 201, 216
Balsiger, David, 185, 186, 187, 197, 218
Bancroft, George, 117
Banks, Nathaniel Preston, 81

baptism: in the Baptist Church, 64; of
  Sarah Bush Johnston Lincoln, 70; of
  Thomas Lincoln, 70; Lincoln's alleged
  baptism, 66–79
Baptist Alley, *205, 207*
Baptist Church, 64–65
Barnum, Phineas T., 93
Barrett, Oliver R., 44
Barton, William E.: research on the
  Lincoln paternity controversy, 18–20,
  21, 26–27; Wilma Minor Frances hoax
  and, 35, 37, 44
Basler, Roy P., xvi–xvii, 90
Bates, Finis, 217
Bedell, Grace, 115
Bell, Isaac, 191
Benjamin, Judah P., 171, 189, 191
Berry, Richard, 27
Beveridge, Albert, 37
Biesecker, F. W., 110
Bigham, James W., 4–5, 8, 9, 12–13
Billheimer, Isaac, 72
Bingham, John A., 226
birthplace cabin: authenticity issues,
  3–13; "Davenport," *11;* Lincoln on, 2–3;
  Robert Todd Lincoln on, 7; memorial
  building, 1, 7, *8;* National Park Service
  and, 2, 3, 13; significance of, 1–2, 13
Bixby, Arthur Edward, 97
Bixby, Charles N., 97
Bixby, George A., 97
Bixby, Henry C., 97
Bixby, Lydia, 93, 94, 95–96, 97
Bixby, Oliver Cromwell, 97
Bixby letter, 93–101
Blair, Montgomery, 192
Bliss, Alexander, 117
Bloomington Pantograph (newspaper), 92
bodyguards, 143
Boetcker, William J. H., 91–92

255